Eclipse 4 Application Development

Eclipse RCP based on Eclipse 4.2 and e4

Lars Vogel

vogella

Because knowledge feels like **magic**

Eclipse 4 Application Development : Eclipse RCP based on Eclipse 4.2 and e4

Lars Vogel

Version 7.4

Publication date 25.05.2012

Dedication

For Jennifer, Kiran, Liam and Mira

Table of Contents

Foreword

The Eclipse platform is one of the world's most successful open source software projects. Millions of developers use Eclipse every day as their tooling platform. Millions of users every day use applications built on top of the Eclipse Rich Client Platform. The primary motivation of our community's newest major release - Eclipse 4 - is to make Eclipse an even better platform, particularly a better application platform. The Eclipse team has been working on this major revision for over four years, and Eclipse 4.2 will be the underlying platform for the Eclipse Juno simultaneous release in June of 2012. We are all excited to see this major new innovation launching into the mainstream of enterprise development.

One of the keys to Eclipse's success is the commitment of the development team to platform stability, and release-to-release compatibility. This requires remarkable effort and discipline on their part, but has made Eclipse a stable foundation on which to build. Eclipse 4 will make it even easier for Java developers to build and deploy great-looking and portable desktop applications, by bringing a simpler, yet more powerful, set of APIs for application developers to use.

Eclipse projects are driven by great developers, and the Eclipse 4 project has had many important contributors. I would like to recognize the contributions of just a few: the present Eclipse platform leader Mike Wilson, and project leaders Dani Megert, John Arthorne, all from IBM and Boris Bokowski, originally with IBM but now with Google. I would also like to recognize the special contributions to Eclipse 4 of Brian de Alwis, Oleg Besedin, Danail Branekov, Eric Moffatt, Bogdan Gheorghe, Paul Webster, Thomas Schindl, Remy Suen, Kai Tödter, and, of course, your author Lars Vogel. Finally, it bears mentioning that the Eclipse 4 platform would not exist without the continuing investment and resource commitments of IBM, BestSolution.at, and SAP.

Mike Milinkovich
Executive Director, Eclipse Foundation

Preface

1. Welcome

This book gives a detailed introduction into the Eclipse 4 platform and covers all relevant aspects of Eclipse 4 development. It assumes no previous experience with Eclipse plug-in or Eclipse RCP development.

If you come to this book after having read other books from the *Wizard's Wand* series, thanks for sticking with the series!

If you come to this book having learned about Eclipse 4 on my website vogella.com, then I like to thank you for getting the extended off-line version.

I tried very hard to put together consistent and comprehensive material so that you can perform your work as developer as efficient as possible. I sincerely hope that this book will augment your knowledge of Eclipse RCP and help you to get the most of out the Eclipse Platform.

2. How this book is organized

This book covers all relevant concepts of Eclipse 4 RCP development and contains exercises and tutorials to practice these concepts. The migration of existing Eclipse 3.x based RCP applications is also briefly covered.

After a short introduction into the Eclipse platform, you perform a full development cycle of an Eclipse 4 application, from creation to deployment.

After this first full development cycle, the book guides you through all aspects of Eclipse 4 development using an extended example which you continue to extend in the exercises.

You will learn about the new programming concepts of Eclipse 4, e.g. the application model, Dependency Injection, CSS styling, the Renderer Framework, the Event system and much more.

Proven Eclipse technologies like SWT, JFace Viewers, OSGi modularity and services, Databinding, Internationalization, etc. are also covered in detail.

The book was reviewed by well-known Eclipse experts and committers.

This book requires a working knowledge of Java and of using the Eclipse IDE but it assumes no previous knowledge of Eclipse plug-in and Eclipse RCP development.

3. Prerequisites

This book assumes that you have experience in Java development and in the usage of the Eclipse IDE. In other words you should have:

- Java 1.6 or higher installed
- Experience in developing Java applications in Eclipse

In case you picked this book to learn about Java and development with Eclipse, you should start with a different reference first.

4. Errata

Every book has errors to a certain degree. You can find a list of the known bugs on the errata page of the vogella.com webpage. The URL to this page is http://www.vogella.com/book/eclipse4book/errata.html

In case you find errors which are not yet reported please let me know by sending an email to: erratabooks@vogella.com.

Errors might be one of the following:

- Typographical errors
- Examples that do not work as described in the book
- Factual errors that cannot be open to interpretation

5. Tutorials, Exercises and Examples

In this book you find chapters labeled with *Tutorial*, *Exercise* or *Example*.

Tutorials will show you how to achieve the implementation of a certain task from start to end. Exercises will ask you to find a solution for a task by yourself.

Examples are included to demonstrate certain API's and serve as reference material.

Exercises are included to help the reader to check if he can apply the knowledge of the previous chapter and should be performed. If you face issues finding the solution for an exercise, you can checkout the source code of the examples.

6. Long lines

Sometimes the code example did not fit into one line. In this case I use *[CONTINUE...]* to break the lines. If you see such a line, the next line must continue at the position of *[CONTINUE...]*.

7. Source Code

The source code examples shown in this book are available for download from a GitHub repository. The URL for this repository is https://github.com/vogella/eclipse4book.

All source code of this book is licensed under the *Eclipse Public License* .

The appendix of this book contains a short description how you can use *EGit* to checkout this repository. Please note that a proxy or a firewall in your network might prevent you from checking out this repository.

To demonstrate certain chapter isolated, branches have been created. The repository contains in its master branch a `readme.txt` which explains the structure of the repository.

8. About the Author

Lars Vogel is the founder and CEO of the *vogella GmbH* and works as Eclipse and Android consultant, trainer and book author. He is a regular speaker at international conferences, as for example EclipseCon, Devoxx, Droidcon and

O'Reilly's Android Open and has presented at the Google Headquarters in Mountain View.

With more than one million visitors per month his website vogella.com is one of the central sources for Eclipse and Android programming information.

Lars is Committer in the Eclipse 4 project and received in 2010 the *Eclipse Top Contributor Award* and in 2012 the *Eclipse Top Newcomer Evangelist Award.*

9. Acknowledgment

The creation of this book did not follow the typical book creation process. It is based on tutorials available on my webpage.

I got many suggestions and corrections from countless readers of my website and I would like to express my deepest gratitude for their contributions.

I would like to thank Remy Suen, Paul Webster, Brian de Alwis, Tom Schindl, Eric Moffat, Kai Tödter and Boris Bokowski from the e4 development team for their shared efforts and their support in answering my questions over the last years. I'm very much impressed by their friendliness and knowledge.

A special thank you goes to Eric Moffat, Rabea Gransberger, Paul Webster, Remy Suen, Sopot Çela, Kai Tödter, Brian de Alwis, Matthew Hall, Phill Perryman, Marcel Bruch, Boris Bokowski, Daniel Stainhauser, Tom Schindel, Christoph Keimel and Holger Voormann for a detailed review of the material.

All remaining errors are my fault.

Part I. Overview of Eclipse 4

Table of Contents

1. Introduction into Eclipse

1.1. What is Eclipse?

Most people know Eclipse as an integrated development environment (IDE) for Java. Today it is the leading development environment for Java with a market share of approximately 65%.

Eclipse is created by an Open Source community and is used in several different areas, e.g. as a development environment for Java or Android applications. Eclipse's roots go back to 2001.

The Eclipse Open Source community has over 200 Open Source projects covering different aspects of software development.

The Eclipse projects are governed by the *Eclipse Foundation*. The *Eclipse Foundation* is a non-profit, member supported corporation that hosts the Eclipse Open Source projects and helps to cultivate both an Open Source community and an ecosystem of complementary products and services.

The Eclipse IDE can be extended with additional software components. Eclipse calls these software components *plug-ins*. Several Open Source projects and companies have extended the Eclipse IDE.

It is also possible to use Eclipse as a basis for creating general purpose applications. These applications are known as Eclipse Rich Client Platform (*Eclipse RCP*) applications.

1.2. Eclipse Public License

The *Eclipse Public License* (EPL) is an Open Source software license used by the *Eclipse Foundation* for its software. The EPL is designed to be business-friendly. EPL licensed programs can be used, modified, copied and distributed free of charge and receiver of EPL-licensed software can choose to use this software in closed source programs. Only modifications in the original EPL code must be released.

The *Eclipse Foundation* also validates that source code contributed to Eclipse projects is free of Intellectual property (IP) issues. This process is known as IP cleansing.

The permissive EPL and the IP cleansing effort of the *Eclipse Foundation* makes reusing the source code of Eclipse projects attractive.

1.3. What are Eclipse RCP applications?

Eclipse was originally started as a modular IDE application. In 2004 Eclipse version 3.0 was released. Eclipse 3.0 supported the re-use of the Eclipse platform to build stand-alone applications based on the same technology as the Eclipse IDE.

At this point the term *Eclipse RCP* was coined. Eclipse RCP is short for *Eclipse Rich Client Platform* and indicates that the Eclipse platform is used as a basis to create feature-rich stand-alone applications.

The Eclipse 4 platform simplifies and unifies the Eclipse programming model and extends the concept of building Eclipse based applications with new technologies, like dependency injection and declarative styling via CSS files.

1.4. Advantages of Eclipse based applications

The Eclipse platform forms the basis of the most successful Java IDE and therefore is very stable and broadly used. It uses native user interface components which are fast and reliable and with its strong modularity approach it allows to design component based systems.

Companies such as IBM and Google use the Eclipse framework for their products and therefore ensure that Eclipse is flexible, fast and continues to evolve.

The Eclipse platform also fosters a large community of individuals which provide support, information and extensions to the Eclipse framework. Tapping into this Ecosystem allows you to find required resources and information.

2. Eclipse 4

2.1. What is Eclipse 4?

Eclipse 4 introduces a new set of technologies which increase the flexibility of Eclipse plug-in development. The simultaneous release of Eclipse named *Juno* in June 2012 was based on Eclipse 4.2.

Eclipse 3.8 was released in parallel to Eclipse 4.2 but the Eclipse 3.x series will be discontinued after the Eclipse 3.8 release, i.e. there will not be an Eclipse 3.9 release. Eclipse 3.8 receives bug fixes for a year via service releases.

Eclipse 4 was an opportunity to rationalize the best parts of the Eclipse 3.x APIs and to fix pain points of Eclipse 3.x development. Eclipse 3.x changed from 3.0 to 3.8, and tough lessons were learned about the difficulties and flexibility of the APIs.

Eclipse 3.x developers will find that many of the concepts that know are carried across and found in Eclipse 4.

The major enhancements in Eclipse 4 compared to Eclipse 3.x are the following.

- The Eclipse application is described via a defined structure called the application model
- This application model can be modified at development and runtime
- This application model can be extended
- Eclipse 4 supports dependency injection
- Eclipse widgets can be styled via external CSS files, similar to webpages
- The application model is decoupled from its presentation, e.g. different user interface toolkits such as SWT or JavaFX, can be used to render the model

Eclipse 4 provides a compatibility layer which allows Eclipse 3.x plug-ins to run unmodified.

Eclipse 4 primarily contains enhancements for Eclipse based development. The user of the Eclipse IDE, e.g. a web developer or a Swing developer, will only indirectly benefit because tool development of Eclipse becomes easier. This allows Eclipse developers to create better tools for Eclipse users.

2.2. The Eclipse Platform project

The *Eclipse Platform* project provides the core frameworks and services upon which all Eclipse based applications are created. It also provides the runtime in which Eclipse components are loaded, integrated, and executed. The primary purpose of the Platform project is to enable other developers to easily build and deliver integrated tools and applications.

2.3. What is the Eclipse e4 project?

Eclipse e4 is the name used for the *Eclipse Platform's* incubator project. This incubator is used for exploratory projects relating to improving the Eclipse Platform. The new Eclipse 4 platform was originally developed within the incubator and the incubator name became synonymous with the new Eclipse Platform. Today the term *e4* it is only the name of the project.

The e4 project includes several technology evaluations. Some of these evaluations have been ported back to the core Eclipse framework. All functionality described in this document are part of the official Eclipse 4 release, except the *Eclipse e4 tooling* project.

The subproject *Eclipse e4 tooling* provides tools to develop Eclipse 4 applications. They are very useful, but have not been added to the Eclipse core because they are not as mature as the other components.

Projects such as XWT, TM or OpenSocial Gadgets, which are also part of the Eclipse e4 project, are not included in the standard Eclipse 4.2 core platform and are not described in this document.

2.4. Provisional API

Currently the Application Programming Interface (API) for Eclipse 4 is still marked as provisional, i.e. this means that the API might be changed in the future.

Eclipse 4.2 already runs the complete Eclipse IDE therefore it is unlikely that dramatic changes will occur in the future.

It is therefore relatively safe to start using the API now, but nevertheless you must be prepared that you might have to make some adjustments to your application.

3. Architecture of Eclipse

The following chapter gives an overview of the Eclipse architecture, explains how the Eclipse platform is created out of plug-ins and what extension points are.

3.1. Eclipse based applications

An Eclipse application consists of individual software components. The Eclipse IDE can be viewed as a special Eclipse application with the focus supporting software development.

The components of the Eclipse IDE are primarily the following. Please note that the graph should display the concept, the displayed relationship is not 100 % accurate.

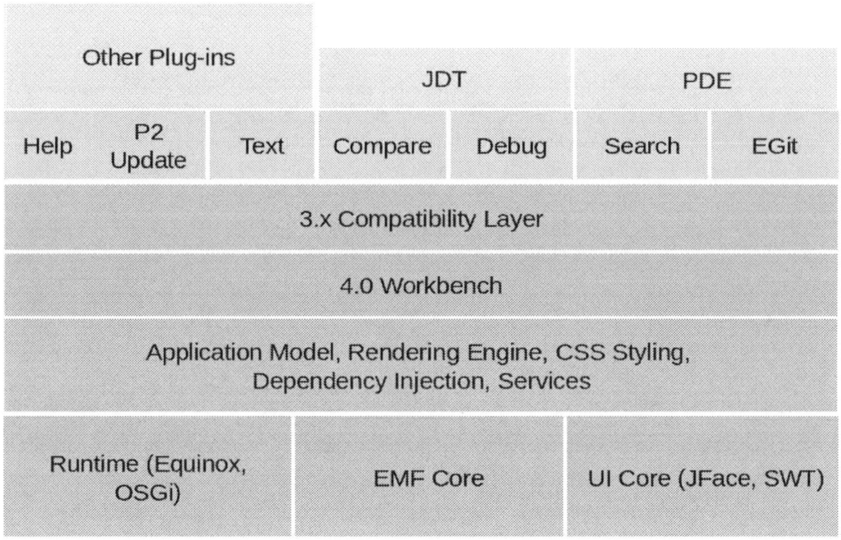

OSGi is a specification which describes a modular approach for Java application. Equinox is one implementation of OSGi and is used by the Eclipse platform. The Equinox runtime provides the necessary framework to run a modular Eclipse application.

SWT is the standard user interface component library used by Eclipse. JFace provides some convenient APIs on top of SWT. The workbench provides the framework for the application. The workbench is responsible for displaying all other UI components.

On top of these base components, the Eclipse IDE adds components which are important for an IDE application, for example the Java Development Tools (JDT) or version control support (EGit).

Eclipse 4 has a different programming model then Eclipse 3.x. Eclipse 4 provides the *3.x Compatibility Layer* component which maps the 3.x API to the 4.0 API. This allows Eclipse 3.x based components to run unmodified on Eclipse 4.

Eclipse based applications which are not primarily used as software development tools are called Eclipse RCP applications. An Eclipse 4 RCP application typically uses the base components of the Eclipse platform and adds additional application specific components.

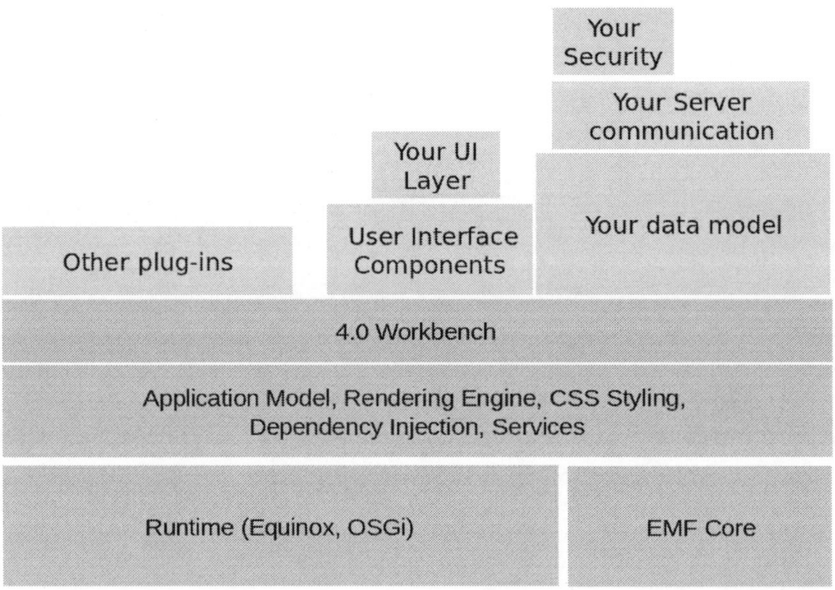

The programming model of OSGi (Equinox) allows you to define dynamic software components, i.e. OSGi services, which can also be part of an Eclipse based application.

3.2. Terminology

An Eclipse application consists of several Eclipse components. A software component in Eclipse is called a *plug-in*. A software component in OSGi is called a *bundle*. Both terms can be used interchangeably.

This book uses the terms *Eclipse based applications* , *Eclipse application*, *Eclipse 4 application* and *Eclipse RCP application* interchangeably for referring to an application which is based on the Eclipse 4 framework.

If a certain concept refers to Eclipse 3.x, then it is explicitly stated.

3.3. Important configuration files

An Eclipse plug-in has the following main configuration files.

- MANIFEST.MF - Contains the OSGi configuration information.
- plugin.xml - Contains information about Eclipse specific extension mechanisms

An Eclipse plug-in defines its API via the `MANIFEST.MF` file, e.g. the Java packages which can be used by other plug-ins and its dependencies, e.g. the packages or plug-ins which are required by the plug-in.

The `plugin.xml` file provides the possibility to define *extension points* and *extensions*. *Extension-points* define interfaces for other plug-ins to contribute functionality. *Extensions* contribute functionality to these interfaces. Functionality can be code and non-code based.

In Eclipse 4 the usage of extension points and extensions is very limited. They are mostly used to define pointers to other Eclipse 4 configuration files.

4. Important user interface components

This chapter gives an overview of the most important user interface components of an Eclipse 4 application.

4.1. Windows

Eclipse applications consist of one or more *Windows*. Typically an application has only one *Window* but you are not limited to that, e.g. if you want to support multiple displays for two connected monitors.

4.2. Parts

Parts are user interface components which allow you to navigate and modify data. *Parts* are typically divided into *Views* and *Editors*.

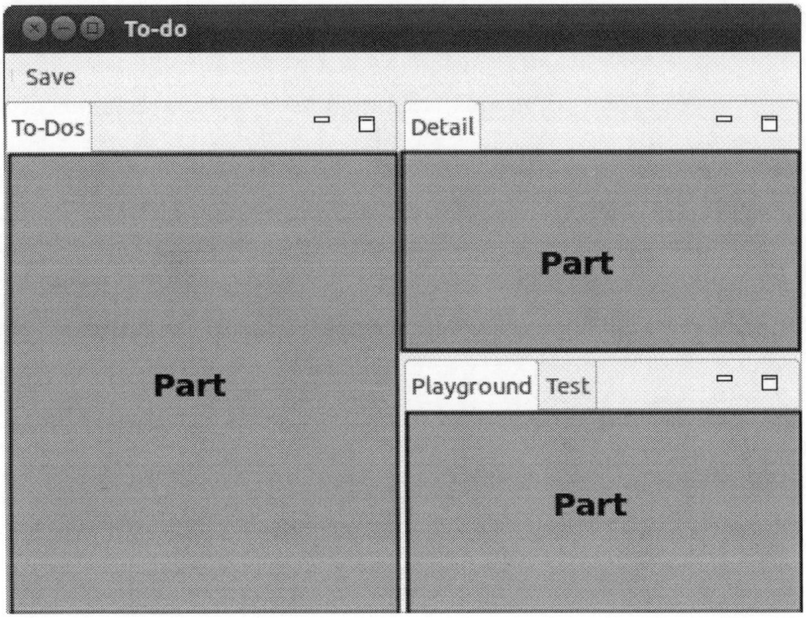

The distinction into *Views* and *Editors* is primarily not based on technical differences, but on a different concept of using and arranging these *Parts*.

A *View* is typically used to work on a set of data, which might be a hierarchical structure. If data is changed via the *View*, this change is typically directly applied to the underlying data structure. A *View* sometimes allows us to open an *Editor* for a selected set of the data.

An example for a *View* is the *Java Package Explorer*, which allow you browse the files of Eclipse Projects. If you choose to change data in the Package Explorer, e.g. if you rename a file, the file name is directly changed on the file system.

Editors are typically used to modify a single data element, e.g. a file or a data object. To apply the changes made in an editor to the data structure, the user has to explicitly save the editor content.

Editors were traditionally placed in a certain area, called the *editor area*. Until Eclipse 4 this was a hard limitation, it was not possible to move an *Editor* out of this area; Eclipse 4 allows the user to place *Editors* at any position in a *Perspective* or even outside a *Perspective*.

For example the Java Editor is used to modify Java source files. Changes to the source file are applied once the user selects the *Save* command.

4.3. Perspective

A *Perspective* is a visual container for a set of *Parts*. The Eclipse IDE uses *Perspectives* to arrange *Parts* for different development tasks.

You can change the layout and content within a *Perspective* by opening or closing *Parts* and by re-arranging them.

As of Eclipse 4 *Perspectives* are optional elements for Eclipse applications.

4.4. PartStacks and PartSashContainers

Parts can be directly assigned to a *Window* or a *Perspective*. If you want to group and arrange *Parts* you can use *PartStacks* and *PartSashContainers*.

PartStacks contain a stack of *Parts* of which only one is visible at the same time and can be selected via tabs. A *PartSashContainer* displays all its children at the same time either horizontally or vertically.

The following shows a simple Eclipse application layout using two *PartSashContainers* and a few *PartStacks*.

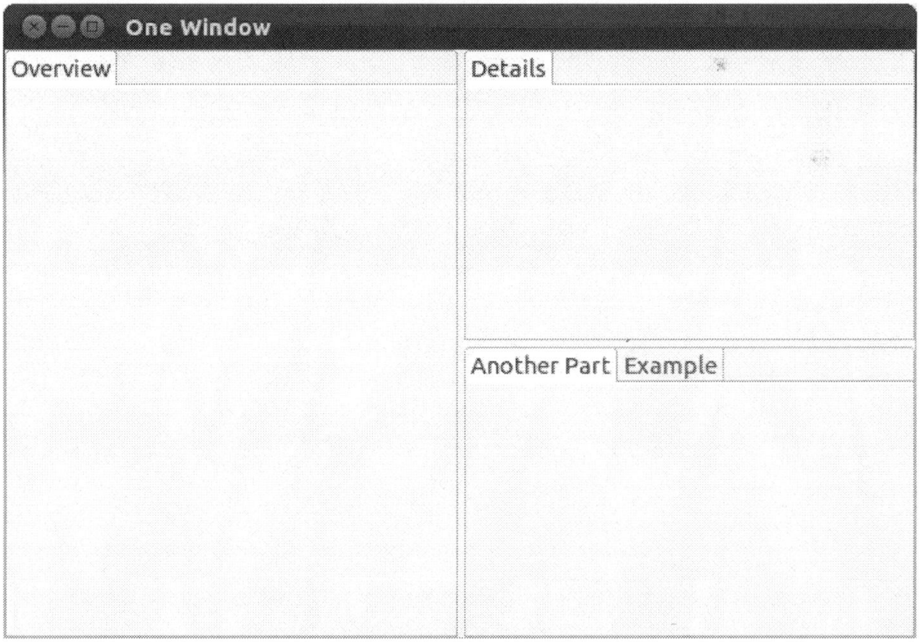

On the top of this layout there is a horizontal *PartSashContainer* which contains another *PartSashContainer* and some *PartStacks*. The hierarchy is depicted in the following graphic.

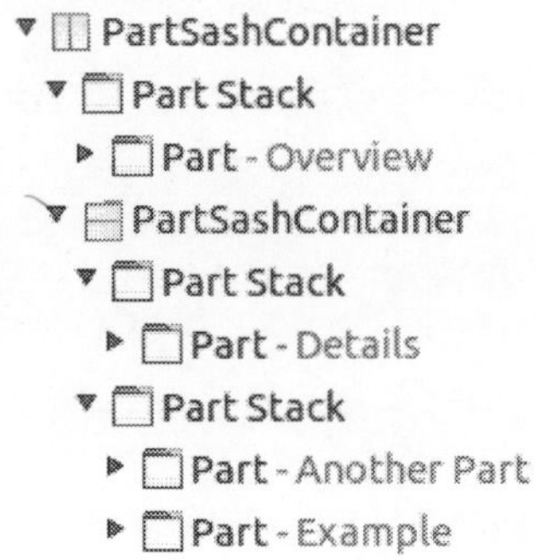

5. Eclipse 4.2 bugs

Eclipse 4.2 is a major design of the Eclipse platform. As every Eclipse release, the Eclipse 4.2 release contains a few bugs and has a few missing features.

The author of this book keeps a list of relevant bugs online under the following URL: http://www.vogella.com/articles/Eclipse4Bugs/article.html

In case you face issues with Eclipse 4 and this book, please also check the list of bugs in this online resource.

Part II. Getting started with Eclipse 4

Table of Contents

6. Tutorial: Installation of Eclipse 4.2

The following tutorial will explain how to install the Eclipse 4 IDE.

6.1. Prerequisites

The following assumes that you have Java installed in at least version 1.6.

6.2. Download and Install Eclipse 4.2

This book is based on the Eclipse 4.2 release. Download the *Eclipse for RCP and RAP Developers* package from the following URL.

```
http://www.eclipse.org/downloads/
```

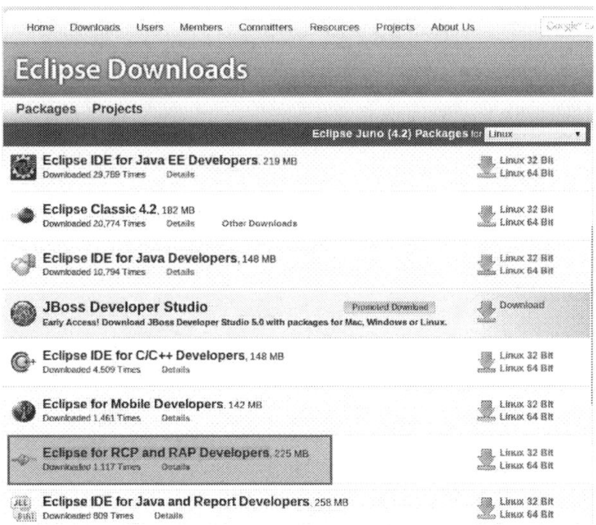

The download is a zip file, which is a compressed archive of multiple files. Most operating systems can extract zip files in their file browser. For example if you are using Windows7 as the operating system, right mouse click on the file in the explorer and select the *Extract all...* menu entry. If in doubt about how to unzip, search via Google for *How to unzip a file on ...* , replacing "..." with your operating system.

Do not extract Eclipse to a directory with a path which contains spaces as this might lead to problems in the usage of Eclipse.

After you extracted the zip file, double-click the `eclipse.exe` (Windows) or the `eclipse` file (Linux) (or the launcher icon specific to your platform) to start Eclipse.

To avoid any collision with existing work select an empty directory as the workspace for this book.

6.3. Install the Eclipse 4 tooling

The Eclipse SDK download does not include the Eclipse e4 tooling, which makes creating Eclipse 4 applications easier. These tools provide wizards to create Eclipse 4 artifacts and the specialized model editor for the application model.

The update site of the *Eclipse e4 tooling* for the Eclipse 4.2 release is the following.

`http://download.eclipse.org/e4/updates/0.12`

From this update site, install only the *E4 CSS Spy* and the *Eclipse e4 Tools*.

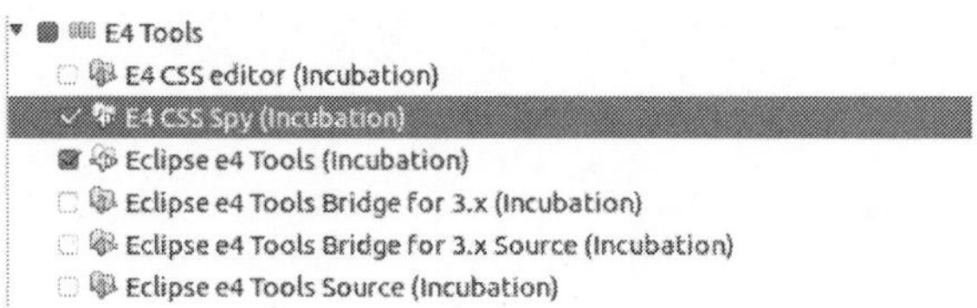

7. Tutorial: Eclipse IDE Configuration

7.1. Include all plug-ins into the Eclipse search

By default the Eclipse Java tools only consider Java components, e.g. classes or interfaces, from the standard Java libraries and from the the projects and their dependencies in the workspace as relevant for search operations.

For example the **Ctrl+Shift+T** (Open Type) shortcut will not find the `ISources` interface if it is not referred to in the current workspace.

You can add all classes from the current target platform, e.g. default is the Eclipse IDE, to be relevant for the Eclipse search via the following setting: Window → Preferences → Plug-in Development → Include all plug-ins from target into Java Search

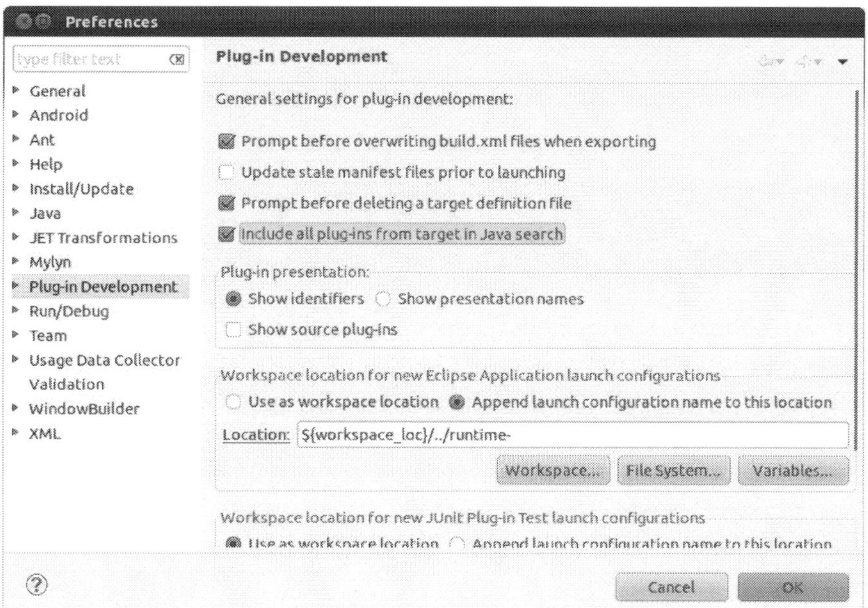

7.2. Remove warnings for provisional API access

The following part of the tutorial is optional.

The Eclipse 4 API has not yet been released. By default Eclipse will create warnings in your coding, if you use a provisional API.

You can turn off these warnings for your workspace via Window → Preferences → Java → Compiler → Errors/Warnings and by setting the *Discouraged Access* flag to *Ignore*.

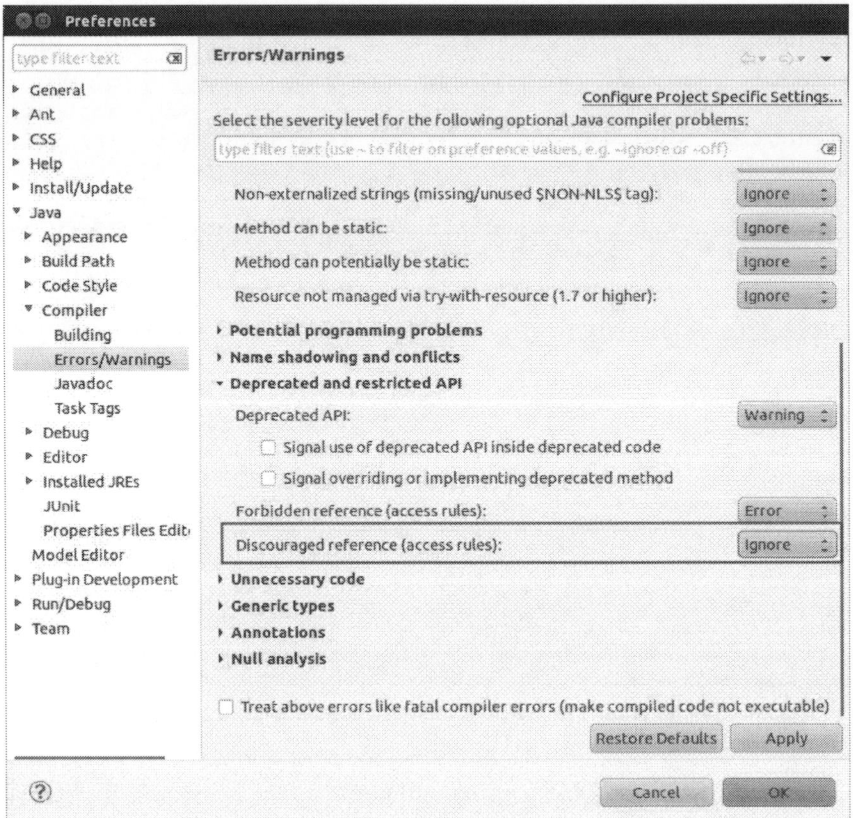

Alternatively you can turn off these warnings on a per project basis, via right-click on the project Properties → Java Compiler and afterwards use the same path as for accessing the global settings. You might have to activate the *Enable project specific settings* checkbox.

8. Tutorial: Eclipse 4 application using the wizard

The following tutorial demonstrates how to uses the project creation wizard provided by the *Eclipse e4 tooling* project to create an Eclipse 4 application. It also shows how to start the application via the Eclipse IDE.

8.1. Overview

The Eclipse 4 tooling project provides a project generation wizard which allows you to create a working Eclipse 4 based RCP application.

8.2. Create project

Select File → New → Others → Eclipse 4 → Eclipse 4 Application Project .

Create a project called `de.vogella.e4.rcp.wizard` using the default settings. This should be similar to the following screenshots.

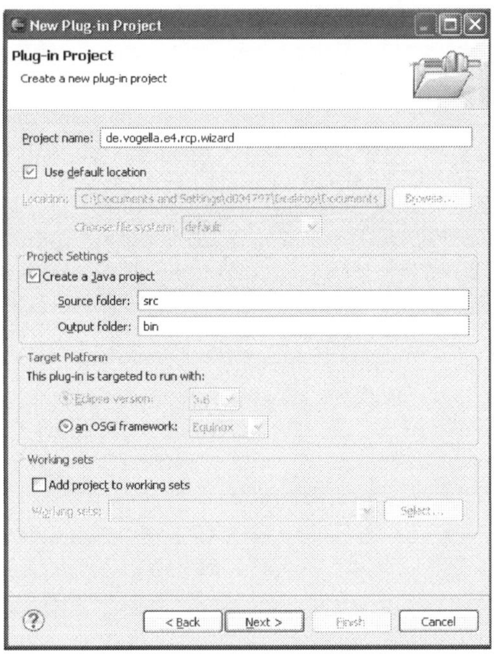

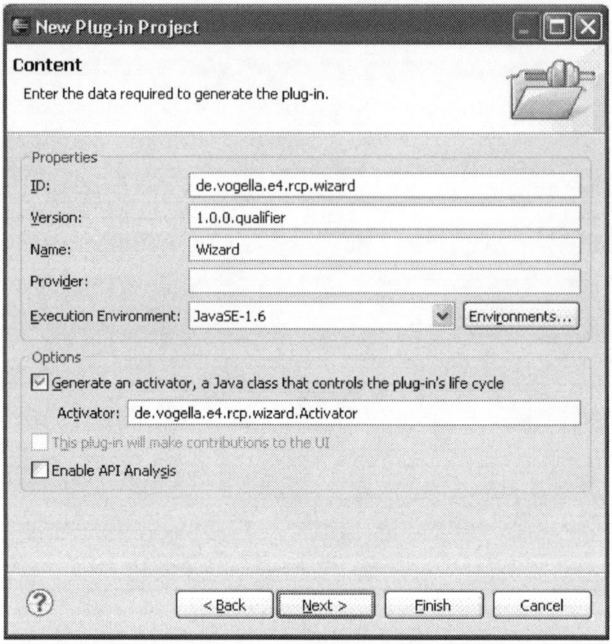
New Plug-in Project
Content
Enter the data required to generate the plug-in.
Properties
ID: de.vogella.e4.rcp.wizard
Version: 1.0.0.qualifier
Name: Wizard
Provider:
Execution Environment: JavaSE-1.6
Environments...
Options
Generate an activator, a Java class that controls the plug-in's life cycle
Activator: de.vogella.e4.rcp.wizard.Activator
This plug-in will make contributions to the UI
Enable API Analysis
< Back
Next >
Finish
Cancel

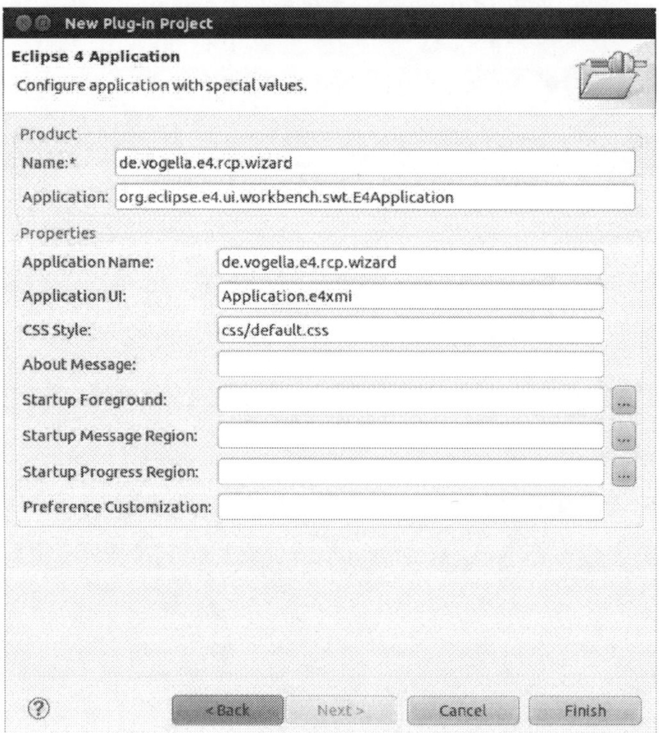
New Plug-in Project
Eclipse 4 Application
Configure application with special values.
Product
Name:* de.vogella.e4.rcp.wizard
Application: org.eclipse.e4.ui.workbench.swt.E4Application
Properties
Application Name: de.vogella.e4.rcp.wizard
Application UI: Application.e4xmi
CSS Style: css/default.css
About Message:
Startup Foreground:
Startup Message Region:
Startup Progress Region:
Preference Customization:
< Back
Next >
Cancel
Finish

This wizard creates all the necessary files to start your application. The central file for starting your application is the `.product` file, created in your project folder.

8.3. Launch

Open your `de.vogella.e4.rcp.wizard.product` product configuration file. Switch to the *Overview* tab and launch your product by pressing the *Launch an Eclipse application* hyperlink. This should start the generated Eclipse application.

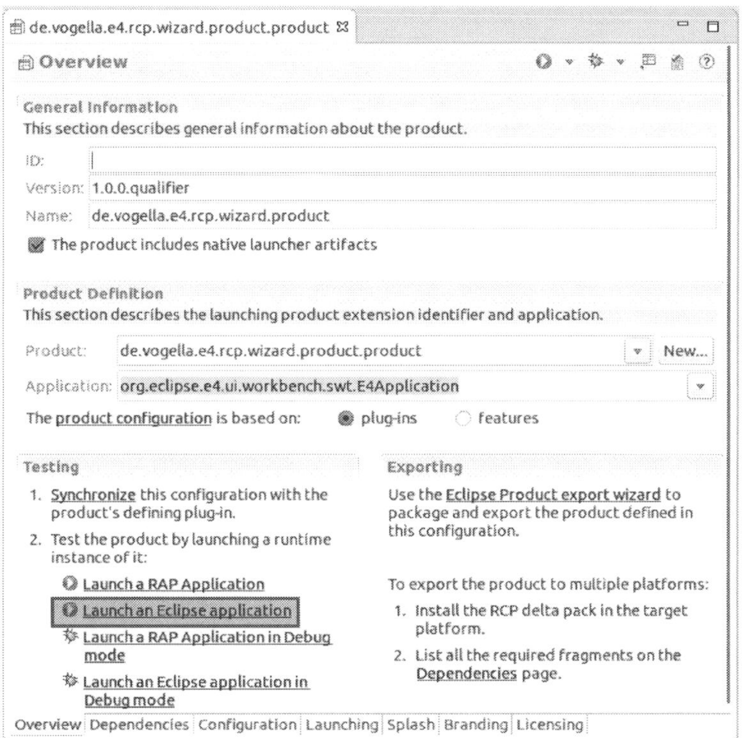

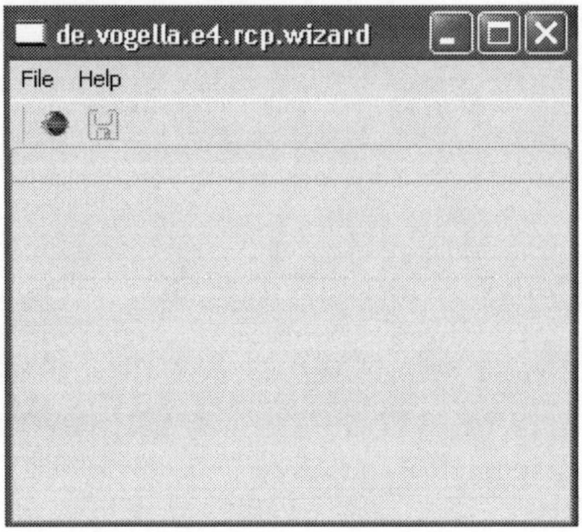
de.vogella.e4.rcp.wizard
File Help

9. Run Configurations

This chapter describes what a *run configuration* is, how to configure it, lists useful launch parameters and typical problems which are related to run configurations.

9.1. Overview

A *run configuration* in Eclipse defines the environment where a generic launch will be executed from within. For example it defines arguments to the Java virtual machine (VM), plug-in (classpath) dependencies etc. Sometimes a *run configuration* is called *launch configuration*.

If you start your Eclipse application, using the link in the product file, the run configuration will be automatically created.

You can use the created run configuration directly for starting the application again. Changes in the product configuration file will not be considered.

You can update the run configuration by starting the application from the product definition again.

To see and edit your run configuration select your product configuration file, right-click on it and select Run As → Run Configurations... .

On the *Main* tab in the field *location* you specify where the Eclipse IDE will create the files necessary to start your Eclipse based application.

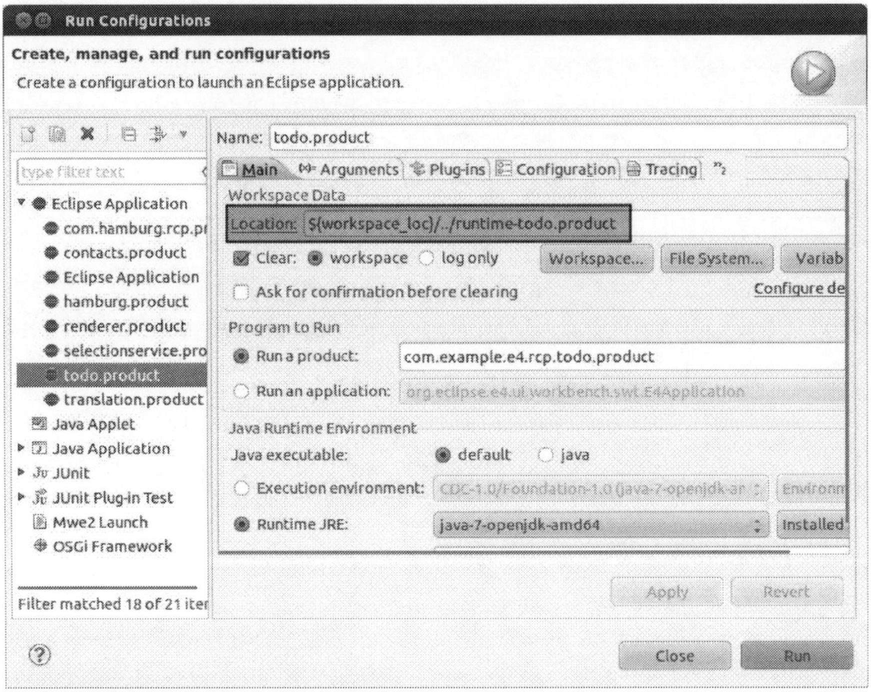

9.2. Launch parameters

The run configuration allows you to add additional parameters for your application on the *Arguments* tab. By default the `-consoleLog` parameter is included. This will write error messages of the running Eclipse application instance to the Eclipse IDE *Console* `View`.

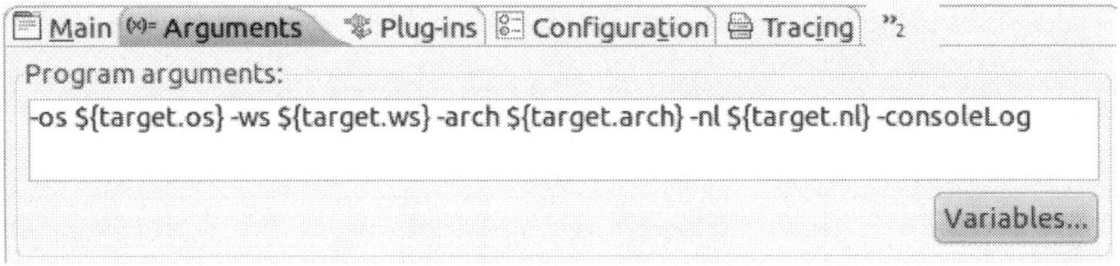

The following table lists useful launch parameters.

Table 9.1. Launch parameters

Parameter	Description
`consoleLog`	Error messages of the running Eclipse application are written to the Eclipse IDE *Console* `View` started this application.
`nl`	Specifies the runtime language for your application. For example `-nl en` will start your application based on the English language. Useful for testing translations.
`console`	Provides access to an OSGi console where you can check the status of your application.
`noExit`	Keeps the OSGi console open even if the application crashes.
`clearPersistedState`	Deletes runtime changes of the Eclipse 4 application model.

9.3. Common run configuration problems

Run configurations are frequently the source of problems.

The most common problem is that some required plug-ins are missing. Eclipse can check this automatically for you before every start. On the *Plug-ins* Tab select the *Validate plug-ins prior to launching* option. This will check if you have all the required plug-ins in your run configuration.

If this check reports that some plug-ins are missing, try clicking the *Add Required Plug-Ins* button. Also make sure you add all dependent plug-ins in your product.

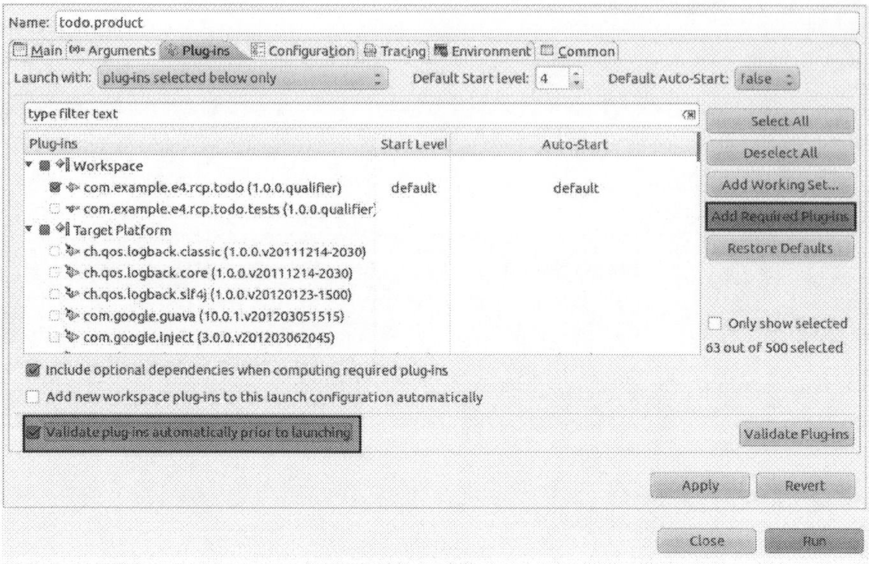

The following table lists potential problems and solutions.

Table 9.2. Run Configuration problems

Problem	Investigate
During start you get error messages such as "One or more bundles are not resolved because the following root constraints are not resolved" or "java.lang.RuntimeException: No application id has been found."	Check that all required plug-ins are included in your run configuration. Make sure that your product defines dependencies to all required plug-ins or features. Bundles may also require a certain version of the Java virtual machine, e.g. a bundle may require Java 1.6 and will therefore not load in a Java 1.5 VM. Check the `MANIFEST.MF` file on the *Overview* tab in the *Execution Environments* section which Java version is required.
Strange behavior but no error message.	Check if your run configuration includes the *`-consoleLog`* parameter. This option allows you to see errors from Eclipse based application in the console view of the Eclipse IDE.
Runtime configuration is frequently missing required plug-ins	Make sure that your product includes all required dependencies.

Problem	Investigate
A change in the product dependencies, e.g. a new plug-in is added but is not included in the run configuration.	A product updates an existing run configuration if you start the product directly from the product definition file. If you select the run configuration directly it will not be updated.
Application model changes are not reflected in the Eclipse 4 application.	Eclipse 4 persists user changes in the application model. During development this might lead to situations where model changes are not correctly applied to the runtime model, e.g. you define a new menu entry and this entry is not display in your application. Either set the *Clear* flag on the *Main* tab in your Run configuration or add the `-clearPersistedState` parameter for your product configuration file or Run configuration.
Services, e.g. key bindings or the selection service, are not working in an Eclipse 4 application.	Ensure that every *Part* correctly implements `@Focus`. Eclipse requires that one control get the focus assigned.

10. Features and product configuration files

This chapter describes the usage of feature projects and of product configuration files.

10.1. Feature project

An Eclipse feature project contains *features*. A feature has a name, version number, a software license and contains a list of plug-ins and other features which can be understood as a logical unit.

A feature is described via a `feature.xml` file in the Eclipse feature project.

Features are used by the Eclipse update manager, the build process and optionally for the definition of Eclipse products. Features can also be used as the basis for a launch configuration.

Eclipse provides several predefined features, e.g. `org.eclipse.rcp` for Eclipse 3.x based RCP applications or `org.eclipse.e4.rcp` for Eclipse 4 based RCP applications.

You can create a new feature project via the following menu path: File → New → Other → Plug-in Development → Feature Project.

If you open the `feature.xml` file you can change the feature properties via a special editor.

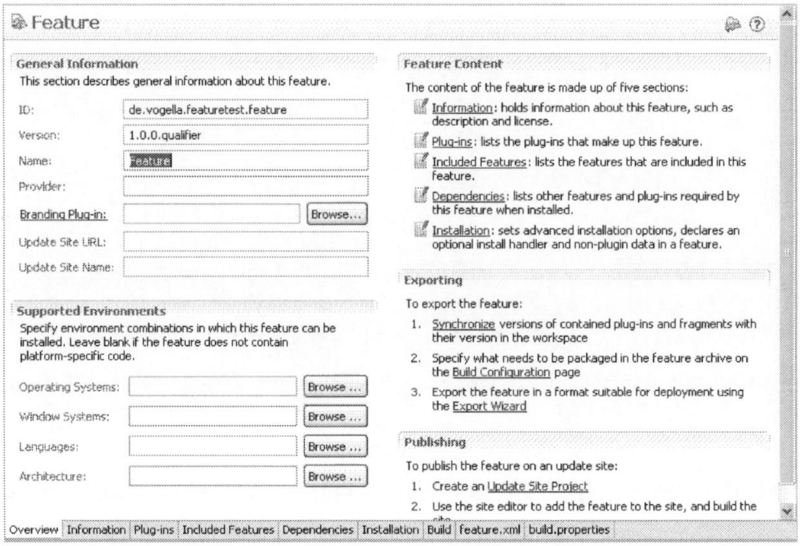

The *Plug-ins* tab allows you to change the included plug-ins in the feature.

The `feature.xml` file is a simple text file. For example the file might look like the following in a text editor.

```
<?xml version="1.0" encoding="UTF-8"?>
<feature
      id="de.vogella.featuretest.feature"
      label="Feature"
      version="1.0.0.qualifier">

   <description url="http://www.example.com/description">
      [Enter Feature Description here.]
   </description>

   <copyright url="http://www.example.com/copyright">
      [Enter Copyright Description here.]
   </copyright>

   <license url="http://www.example.com/license">
      [Enter License Description here.]
   </license>
```

```
    <plugin
          id="de.vogella.featuretest.testplugin"
          download-size="0"
          install-size="0"
          version="0.0.0"
          unpack="false"/>

</feature>
```

10.2. Product and application

A *product configuration file* (short: product) defines all the resources that go with your Eclipse application, e.g. icons, splash screen, external jars, other plug-ins, etc.

The product is a development artifact which describes the content of your application and is not required at runtime.

A product always points to one `Application` class. This `Application` class must implement the `IApplication` interface.

You define your product configuration via a `.product` file. A product configuration file can be created via a right-click on your project and by selecting New → Product Configuration.

This configuration file contains all the information about required plug-ins, configuration files, resources etc. The product configuration file is used for building your product.

It is recommended to leave the product ID blank, because the product export may have issues if the product ID is the same as a plug-in ID.

On the *Overview* tab of your product you can start the product and select the *Synchronize* link. This selection will write the relevant product configuration information into the `plugin.xml` file.

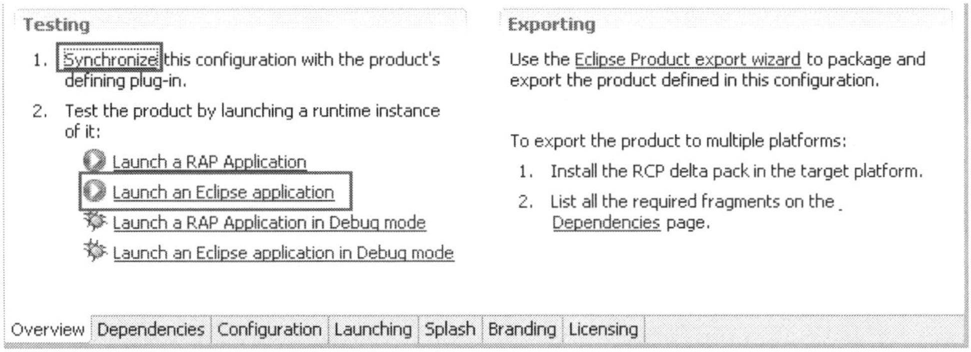

10.3. Dependencies

A product configuration file can either be based on plug-ins or features. This setting is done on the *Overview* tab of the product configuration file.

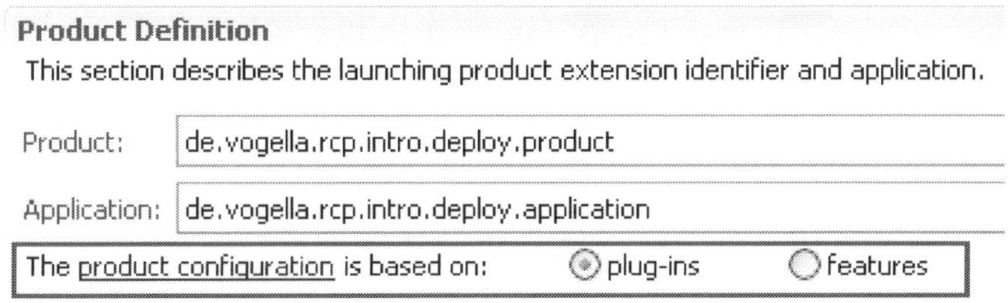

On the *Dependency* tab you maintain the plug-ins or features your products consists of. A product does not perform automatic dependency resolution. If you add a plug-in to your product and want to add its dependencies, press the *Add required* button.

10.4. Splash Screen, Launcher and Start Parameter

The *Splash* tab allows you to specify the plug-in which contains the splash screen. You need to put the `splash.bmp` file into the project main directory. This name and directory is predefined in Eclipse, but can be changed via the *`osgi.splashPath`* parameter.

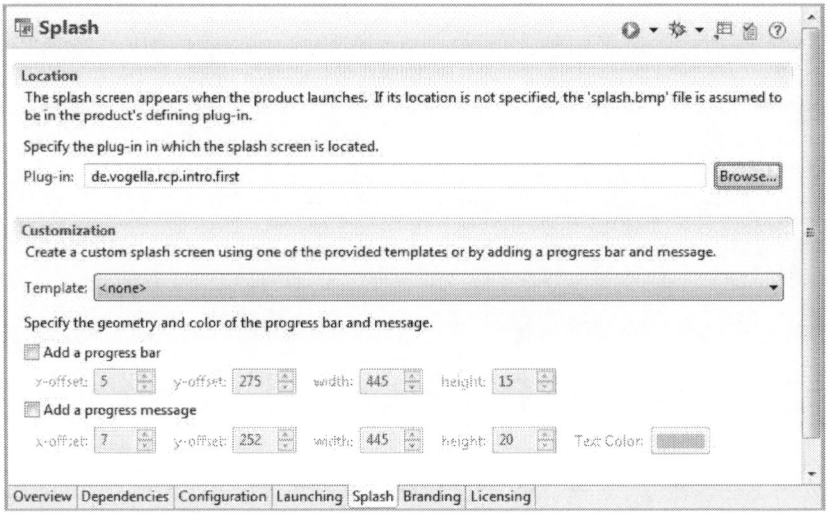

You can configure the launcher name and icon for your exported product. The launcher is the executable program that is created during the deployment of the product. A launcher is platform specific. For example `eclipse.exe` on the Windows platform. This launcher has also an icon associated with it. To change the name and the icon, select the *Launcher* tab of your product configuration.

Here you can specify the file name of the launcher and the icon which should be used. Make sure the format of the icons is correct, otherwise Eclipse will not use them.

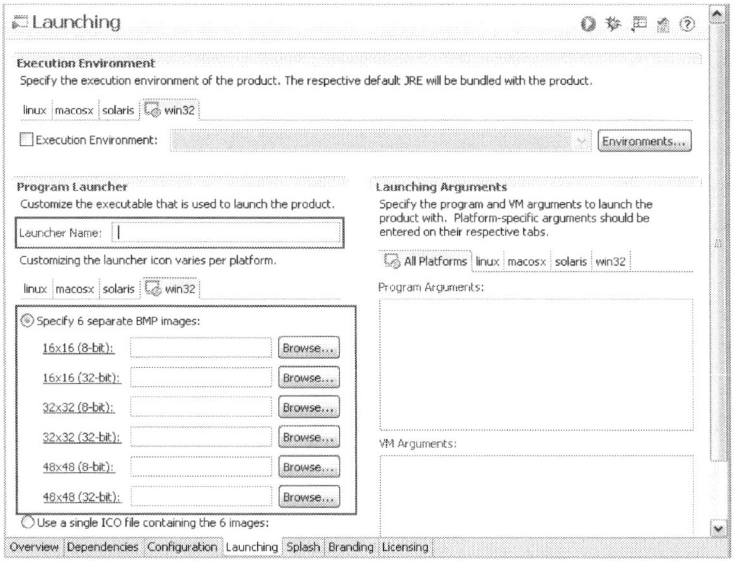

In the *launcher* section you can also specify parameters for your Eclipse application or arguments to the Java runtime environment.

10.5. Eclipse 4 product configuration limitations

Currently the splash handlers, which can be registered via the *Customizing* part of the *Splash* tab are not supported by the Eclipse 4 standard. Also the configuration which can be done in the *About Dialog* and the *Welcome Page* on the *Branding* tab are not supported in Eclipse 4.

11. Product Export

This chapter describes how to export an Eclipse application so that you can start it outside of the Eclipse IDE. It also gives a list with commonly encountered problems during product export.

11.1. Overview

Your product configuration file can be used to export your application to run outside of Eclipse.

Exporting your product will create a directory or a zipped file which contains all artifacts required to run your application. It will also contain a native launcher specific to the platforms, e.g. Windows or Linux, you have exported it for. The resulting directory can be shared with others.

11.2. Which artifacts are included in the export?

The included artifacts are defined by the `build.properties` file.

Eclipse will by default add the compiled Java classes. You have to add other files manually, e.g. icons or splash screen images.

Make sure the `META-INF` directory, the `plugin.xml` file and all other static files, e.g. icons, splash.bmp and in the case of an Eclipse 4 application the `Application.e4xmi` file and potentially CSS files, are flagged to be included in the exported product.

An Eclipse application started from the Eclipse IDE will have access to resources which are not contained in the `build.properties` file, but these files will not be contained in the exported application. Your exported application will therefore fail to find the files. Therefore it is a good rule to directly include new resources in the configuration.

11.3. Exporting the product

To export the product switch to your product configuration file, select the *Overview* tab and click on the *Eclipse Product export wizard* link. On the second page of the wizard you can specify the `destination` directory and the `root` directory for the exported application.

This `root` directory will be a sub-folder in the `destination` directory and will contain the complete application.

The following screenshots show the export wizard in action.

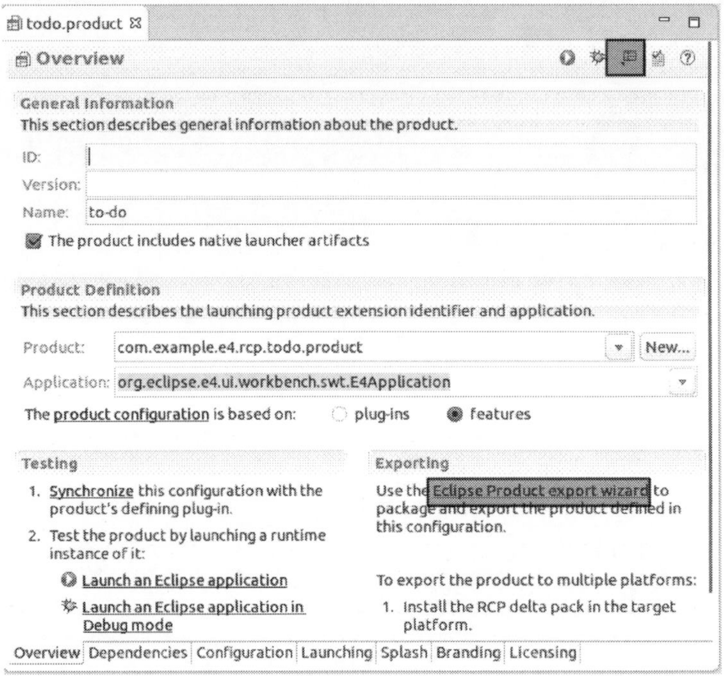

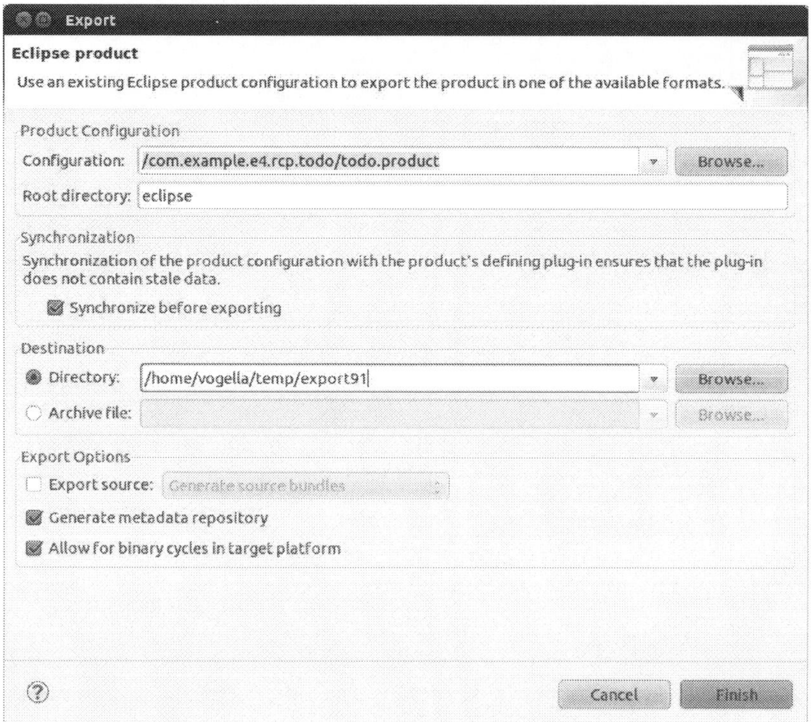

After the export check the `root` folder in the `destination` folder. A double-click on the native launcher should start your application.

If you transfer the content of this directory to another machine (with the same architecture, e.g. Linux 64 bit) your application should run on this machine. The machine only needs to have Java installed. The export dialog allows you to create an archive file directly, which makes it easier to transfer all files to another machine.

11.4. Export for multiple platforms via the deltapack

11.4.1. Deltapack

The *deltapack* contains the platform specific features and plug-ins which are required for building and exporting Eclipse application for multiple platforms. It also includes binary launchers for all platforms in the `org.eclipse.equinox.executable` feature.

The *deltapack* can be found on the Eclipse download page on the following URL:

```
http://download.eclipse.org/eclipse/downloads/
```

Click on the release for are interested in, e.g. 4.2 and search on the resulting page for the *Delta* word.

Download it and extract it to a new directory.

11.4.2. Target Platform

To make the *deltapack* available to the Eclipse IDE, add it to your target platform under Windows → Preferences → Preferences → Plug-in Development → Target Platform

Add the directory in which the *deltapack* is located to the target platform.

Afterwards you can export your Eclipse application for multiple platforms.

11.5. Including the required JRE into the export

You can also deploy your own RCP application bundled with a JRE to make sure that a certain JRE is used. An Eclipse application first searches in the installation directory for a folder called `jre` and for a contained Java-VM. If it finds one, then this JRE is used to start the Eclipse application.

To include the JRE from your running environment, select the *Bundle JRE for this environment with the product* flag on the *Launching* tab of your product configuration file.

11.6. Common product export problems

If the export encounters a problem please have a look into the following table for a solution:

Table 11.1. Problems with the product export

Problem	Possible cause
Export fails	Try using an empty target directory, sometimes the export cannot delete the existing files and therefore fails.
No .exe file after the export	Check the flag "The product includes native launcher artifacts" in your .product file on the *Overview* tab.

Problem	Possible cause
Product could not be found	Validate that all dependencies are included in the product. Delete an existing launch configuration and restart the product from the IDE to see if everything is configured correctly.
Splash Screen or other icons are missing	Check the `build.properties` file to see if all required images and icons are included in the export.
Splash Screen is missing	Ensure that you have entered the defining plug-in in the "Splash" tab on the product configuration file. Not defining it works, if you start the plug-in from Eclipse, but not if you start the exported product.
Issues during startup	Check the log file in the workspace folder of your export product to see the error messages during startup. Alternatively add the "-consoleLog" parameter to the ".ini" file in folder of the export product.
applicationXMI argument is missing	Check the `build.properties` file to see if the `Application.e4xmi` and the `plugin.xml` files are included in the export.
Service could not be found or injected	Make sure that the service start level is set to "auto" so that the bundle which defines the OSGi service is started. Also make sure that the `org.eclipse.equinox.ds` bundle is started before your bundle which define a service via declarative services.
Application ID could not be found	If you are using declarative services and have defines a start level for the ds plug-in them, set a lower start-level for the `org.eclipse.core.runtime` plug-in. This should not be necessary but may help to start your application.
Translations not available in the exported product	Check the `build.properties` file of the plug-in which provides the property files, if the property files are included in the export.

12. Exercise: Export your product

Use the `.product` file of your `de.vogella.e4.rcp.wizard` project to export your Eclipse application.

Make sure that you can start the application outside Eclipse.

Add a splash screen to your application. For this create a `splash.bmp` bitmap file and add this file to the main directory of your application. On the *Splash* tab of your product configuration file define that your application plug-in contains the splash screen.

Verify that the splash is displayed if you start your application from Eclipse. Export your product again and start it.

If you face issues during the product export, check the list of common export problems from the previous chapter and try to solve the problem.

Part III. Eclipse 4 Core Development

Table of Contents

13. Eclipse 4 application model

13.1. What is the application model?

The visual part of an Eclipse application consists of *Perspectives*, *Parts* (Views and Editors), Menus, Toolbars, etc. An Eclipse application also includes non-visual components, e.g. *Handlers*, *Commands* and *Key bindings*.

Eclipse 4 uses an abstract description, called the *application model*, to describe the structure of an application. This application model contains the visual elements as well as some non-visual elements of the Eclipse 4 application.

Each model element has attributes which describe its current state, e.g. the size and the position for a *Window*. Model elements might be in a hierarchical order, for example *Parts* might be grouped below a *Perspective*.

The application model defines the structure of the application; it does not describe the content of the individual user interface components.

For example the application model describes which *Parts* are available. It also describes the *Parts* properties, e.g. if a *Part* is closable, its label, ID, etc.

But it does not describe the content of the *Part*, e.g. the labels, text fields and button it consists of. The content of the *Part* is still defined by your source code.

If the application model was be a house, it would describe the available rooms (*Parts*) and their arrangement (*Perspectives*, *PastStacks*, *PartSashContainer*) but not the furniture of the rooms. This is illustrated by the following image.

13.2. Where is the application model defined?

The application model is extensible. The basis of this model is typically defined as a static file. The default name for this file is `Application.e4xmi` and the default location is the main directory of your application plug-in.

You can change the default name and location via the `org.eclipse.core.runtime.products` extension point. Via the `applicationXMI` parameter you specify the local and name of the model file. See the appendix for a detailed description of this procedure.

The XMI file is read at application startup and the initial application model is constructed from this file.

13.3. How is the model connected to my Java classes?

Application model elements can contain references to Java classes via an Uniform Resource Identifier (URI).

The URI describes the location of the Java class. The first part of this URI is the plug-in, the second one the package and the last one the class.

For example a model description for a *Part* contains attributes such as labels, tooltips and icon URIs. It also contains a class URI which points to a Java class for this element. This class provides the behavior of the *Part* — using the house/rooms metaphor from earlier, the class is responsible for defining the furnishings and the layout of the room, and how the interactive objects behave.

If the model elements get activated this class will get instantiated.

The objects created based on the application model are called *model objects*.

13.4. URI in the Model

URIs follow one of two patterns, one for identifying *resources* and another one for identifying *classes*. The following table describes these two patterns. The example assumes that the bundle is called *test*.

Table 13.1. URI pattern

Pattern	Description
bundleclass://Bundle-SymbolicName/ package.classname Example: bundleclass://test/test.parts.MySavePart	Used to identify Java classes. It consists of the following parts: "bundleclass://" is a fixed schema, Bundle-SymbolicName as defined in the `MANIFEST.MF` file, and the fully qualified classname.
platform:/plugin/Bundle-SymbolicName/ path/filename.extension Example: platform:/plugin/test/icons/save_edit.gif	Identifier for a resource in the plug-in. "platform:/plugin/" is a fixed schema, followed by the Bundle-SymbolicName of the `MANIFEST.MF` file, followed by the path to the file and the filename.

13.5. Application model editor

The Eclipse tooling project provides an editor which makes it easier to work on an application model.

To open the model editor double-click on your `Application.e4xmi` file (or right click on it and select Open With → Eclipse 4 model editor .

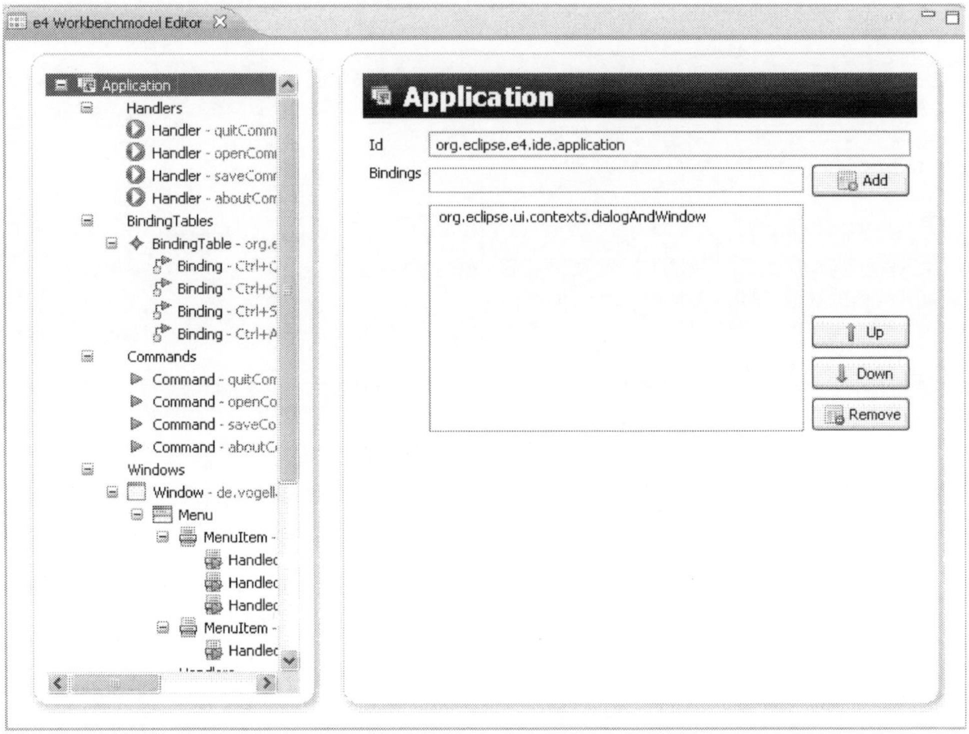

The model editor has several preference settings which can be reached via Window → Preferences → Model Editor. The following screenshot shows the preference page.

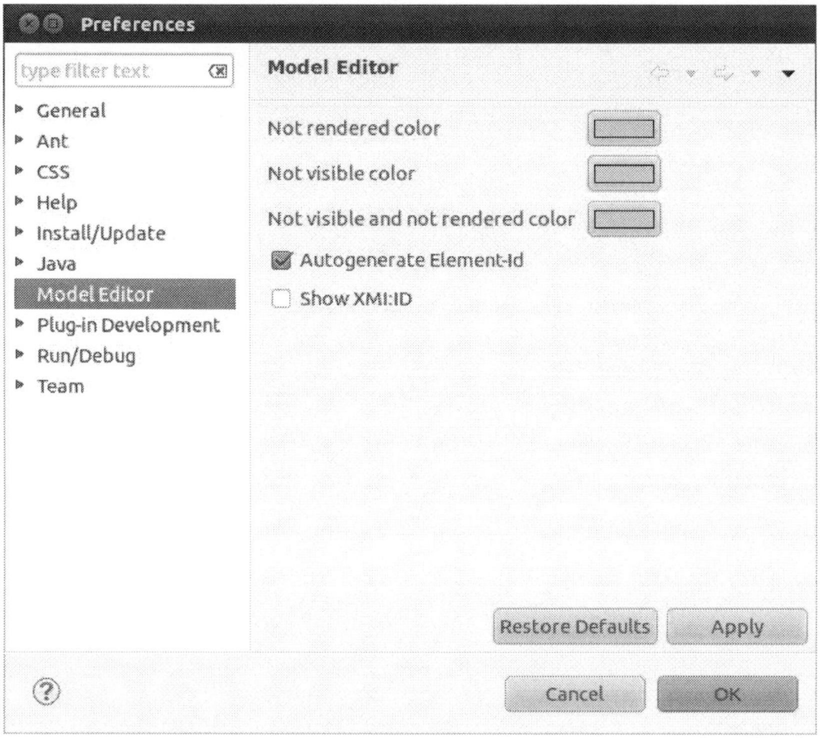

13.6. Model access at runtime

The application model is also available at runtime. The application can access the model and change it via a defined API.

Add the `org.eclipse.e4.tools.emf.liveeditor` plug-in and its dependencies to your launch configuration to make the model editor available in your application.

Afterwards you can open the model editor for your running application via the **Alt+Shift+F9** shortcut. This also works for the Eclipse 4 IDE itself.

Opening the live editor in your Eclipse 4 application requires that your application has keybindings configured.

You can change your application model directly at runtime by using the model editor. Most changes are directly applied, e.g. if you change the orientation of a `PartSashContainer` your user interface will update itself automatically. If you modifying the Eclipse IDE model you should be careful as this might put the running Eclipse IDE into a bad state.

In the live model editor, you can select the *Part* element, right click on it and select *Show Control* to get the *Part* highlighted.

13.7. Meta-model of the application model

The possible structure of the application model is defined by an meta-model created with the Eclipse Modeling Framework (EMF). A meta-model describes the structure of a data model, e.g. it defines which properties a Part has.

EMF is a popular general purpose modeling framework and is the basis for lots of Eclipse based projects. EMF allows to generate Java classes from a meta-model.

Eclipse EMF uses an `.ecore` file to define the meta-model.

The meta-model of the Eclipse 4 applications is stored in the `org.eclipse.e4.ui.model.workbench` plug-in in `model` folder. The base model definition can be found in the `UIElements.ecore` file. The Eclipse 4 model classes have been generated based on this model.

If you want to investigate this model, you could install the EMF tooling via the Eclipse update manager and import the defining plug-in into your workspace. To import a plug-in from your current Target Platform (default is the Eclipse IDE) into your workspace, use the *Plug-ins* `View`, right click on a plug-in and select Import As → Source Project.

The `Application.e4xmi` file, which describes the Eclipse application model, is a persisted version of an EMF model.

13.8. Creation of the Application model

During startup the Eclipse runtime creates the application model based on the `Application.e4xmi` and instantiates the referred classes in the model if required.

The life cycle of every model object is therefore controlled by the Eclipse runtime. The Eclipse runtime instantiates and destroys the model objects.

13.9. Overview of available Model elements

Model elements have Java classes associated with them. As the model is interactive you can use these model elements to change its attributes or children.

The following is a table of important model elements based on their Java classes. These model elements can also get injected.

Table 13.2. Eclipse 4 model element

Model element	Description
MApplication	Describes the application object. Can be used for example to add new windows to your application
MWindow	Represents a Window in your application.
MTrimmedWindow	Represents a Window in your application. The underlying SWT shell has been created with the SWT.SHELL_TRIM attribute which means, it has a tile, a minimize, maximize and resize button.
MPerspective	Object for the perspective model element.
MPart	Represents the model element part, e.g. a View or a Editor.
MDirtyable	Property of MPart which can be injected. If set to true, this property informs the Eclipse platform that this Part contains unsaved data (is dirty). In a Handler you can query this property to trigger a save.
MPartDescriptor	MPartDescriptor is a template for new Parts. You define in your application model a PartDescriptor. A new Part based on this PartDescriptor can be created via the EPartService and shown its `showPart()` method.
Snippets	Snippets can be used to pre-configure model parts which you want to create via your program. You can use `EcoreUtil.copy` to copy a Snippet and assign it to another model element, e.g. on a `MSash` you can add a newly copied `MStack` called *copy*, via `getChildren().add(copy)`. Also the model service has some methods to create and clone a snippet.

13.10. Model Addons

13.10.1. Overview

Eclipse 4 tries to keep the core framework as minimal as possible. `Addons` model object can be registered globally on the application model and can enhance the application with additional functionality. `Addons` are normal Java objects.

`Addons` use the `bundleclass://` URI convention in the application model to refer to the Java objects.

Having these Addons registered allows them to be enhanced or replaced by the Eclipse platform team or by a customer specific implementation in case the need arises.

13.10.2. Framework Addons

Currently the following standard Addons are useful for Eclipse applications. Their class names give an indication of their provided functionality. Check their Javadoc to get a short description of their purpose.

- CommandServiceAddon
- ContextServiceAddon
- BindingServiceAddon
- CommandProcessingAddon
- ContextProcessingAddon
- BindingProcessingAddon

Additional Addons are available, e.g. to support drag-and-drop of *Parts* in your application.

To support drag-and-drop for *Parts* you need to add the `org.eclipse.e4.ui.workbench.addons.swt` plug-in to your product configuration file. Then you can use the `DnDAddon` and the `CleanupAddon` from this bundle as Addons in your application model.

13.10.3. Relationship to other services

`Addons` are created before the rendering engine renders the model and after the EventAdmin Service has been created.

This allows `Addons` to alter the user interface that is produced by the rendering engine. For example, the min/max `Addon` changes the tab folders created for `MPartStacks` to have min/max buttons in the corner.

The `EventAdmin` services provides the notifications about Eclipse events, e.g. if a *Part* is activated. As the `EventAdmin` services is created before `Addons` are created , the `Addons` can to subscribe to events from the Eclipse platform.

14. Model identifier and naming conventions

14.1. Identifiers for model elements

Every model element allows you to define an ID. This ID is used by the Eclipse framework to identify this model element. Make sure you always maintain an ID for every model elements and ensure that these IDs are unique.

Therefore make sure that all your model elements have an ID assigned to them.

14.2. Best practices for naming conventions

The following suggest best practice for naming conventions, which are also used in this book.

Table 14.1. Naming conventions

Object	Description
Project Names	The plug-in project name is the same as the top-level package name.
Packages	For plug-in containing lots of user interface components use sub-packages based on the primary purpose of the components. For example the `com.example` package may have the `com.example.parts` and `com.example.handler` sub-package.
Class names for model elements	Use the primary purpose of the model element as a suffix in the class name. For example a class which represents a Part which displays `Todo` objects, might be called `TodoOverviewPart`.
IDs	Define clear rules for naming IDs in plugin.xml. IDs should always start with the top-level package. If appropriate use the sub-package of the implementing class also. The remainder of the ID should be descriptive for the purpose of the component. For example: "com.example.parts.todolist". ID should be only lower cases (some Eclipse projects also use camelCase for the last part of the ID).

15. Tutorial: Create an Eclipse plug-in

In the following tutorial you create a standard Eclipse plug-in called *com.example.e4.rcp.todo*.

15.1. Create a plug-in project

In Eclipse select File → New Project → Plug-in Development → Plug-in Project.

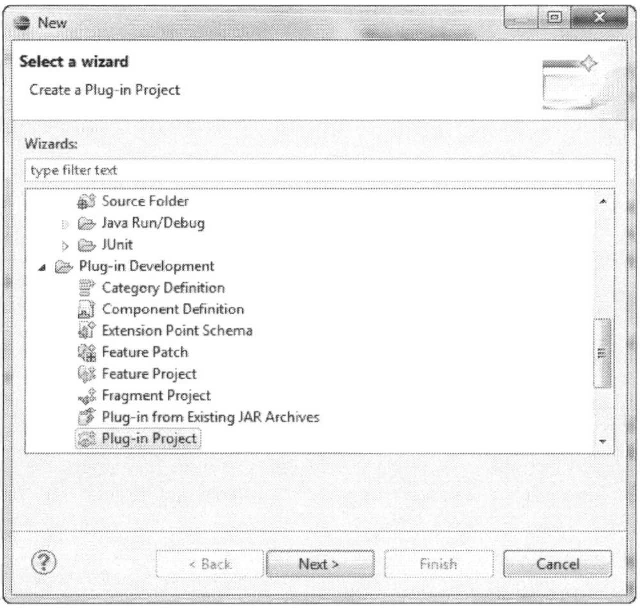

Give your plug-in the name *com.example.e4.rcp.todo*.

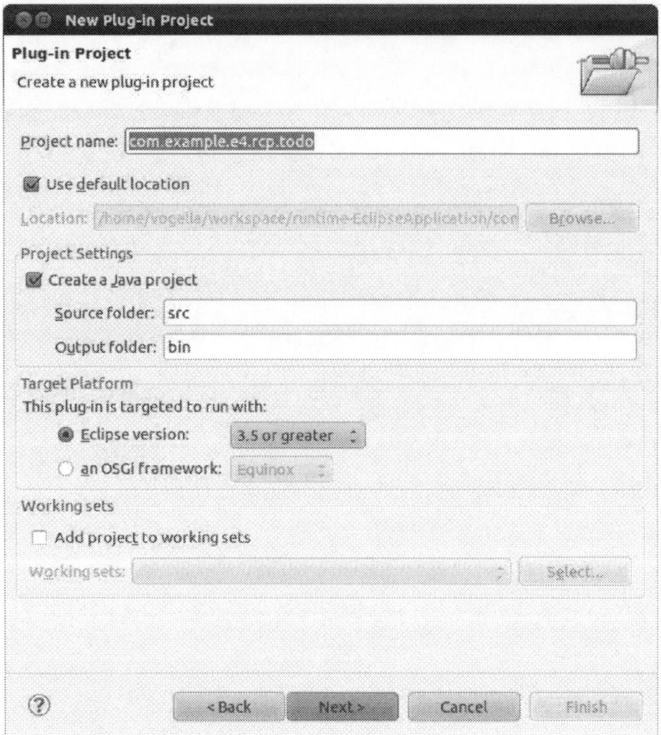

Press *Next* and make the following settings. Select *No* at the question *Would you like to create a rich client application* and uncheck *This plug-in will make contributions to the UI* . Uncheck the *Generate an activator, a Java class that controls the plug-ins life-cycle* option.

Press the *Finish* button; we will not use a template.

15.2. Validate the result

Open the project and check if any Java classes were created. You should have no classes in the source folder.

Open the `MANIFEST.MF` file and switch to the *Extensions* tab. Validate that the list of Extensions is currently empty.

16. Tutorial: From plug-in to Eclipse 4 application

In this chapter we convert the Eclipse plug-in into an Eclipse 4 application.

16.1. Create Product configuration

Right click on your project and select New → Product Configuration. Create a `todo.product` product configuration file.

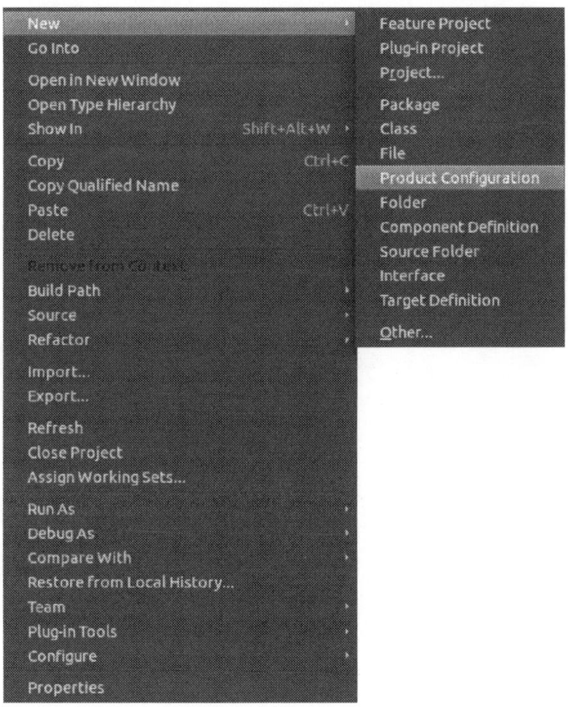

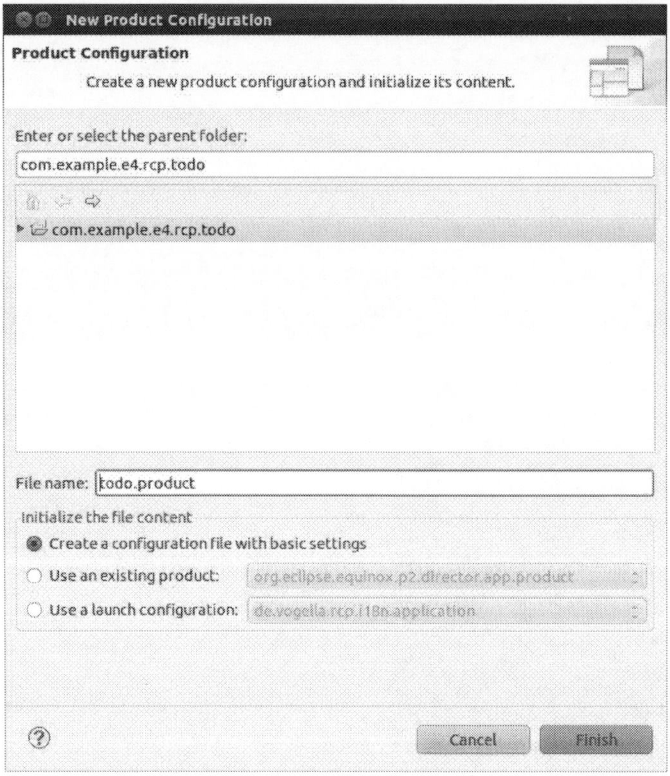

Press the *New* button on the *Overview* tab of the product editor.

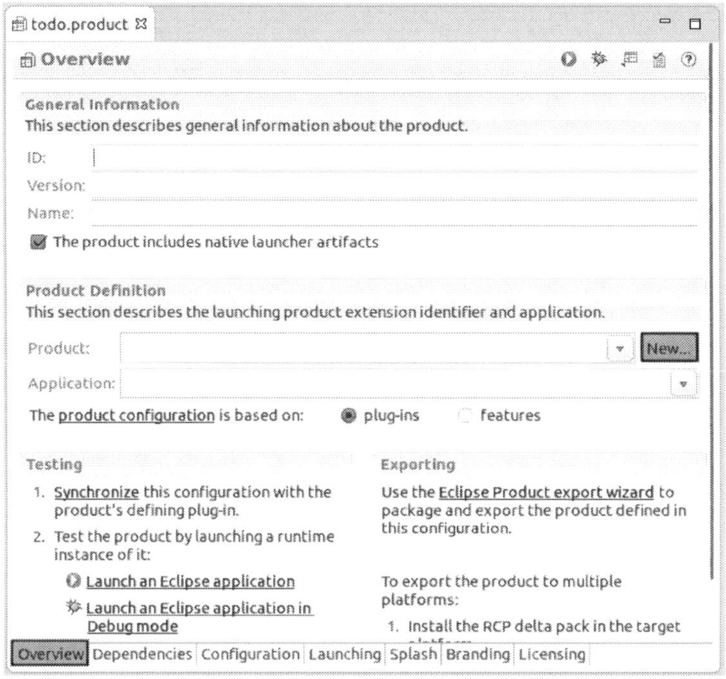

Enter *to-do* as the name, the defining plug-in is your plug-in and use the name *product* as the ID. Select as *Application* the `E4Application` application class.

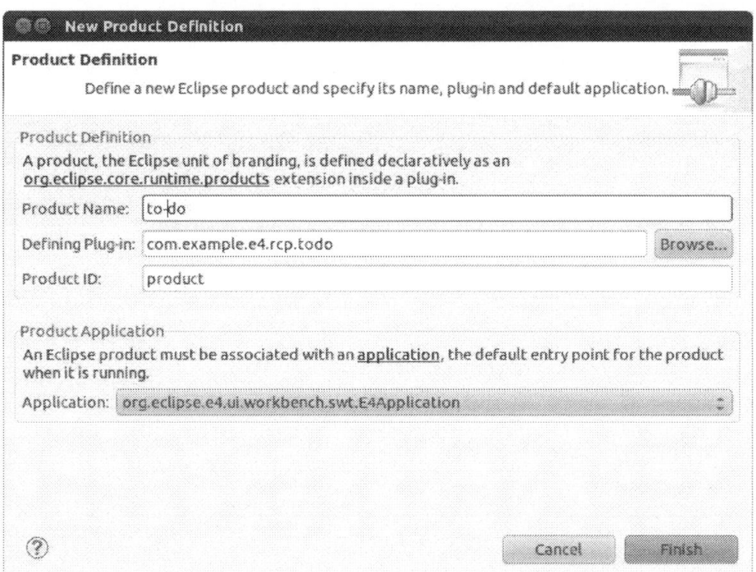

16.2. Create a feature project

Create a new feature project called *com.example.e4.rcp.todo.feature*.

Include the `com.example.e4.rcp.todo` plug-in into this feature.

16.3. Enter feature dependencies in product

Change your product configuration file to use features. To do this open your product configuration file and select the *Feature* option on the *Overview* tab of the product editor.

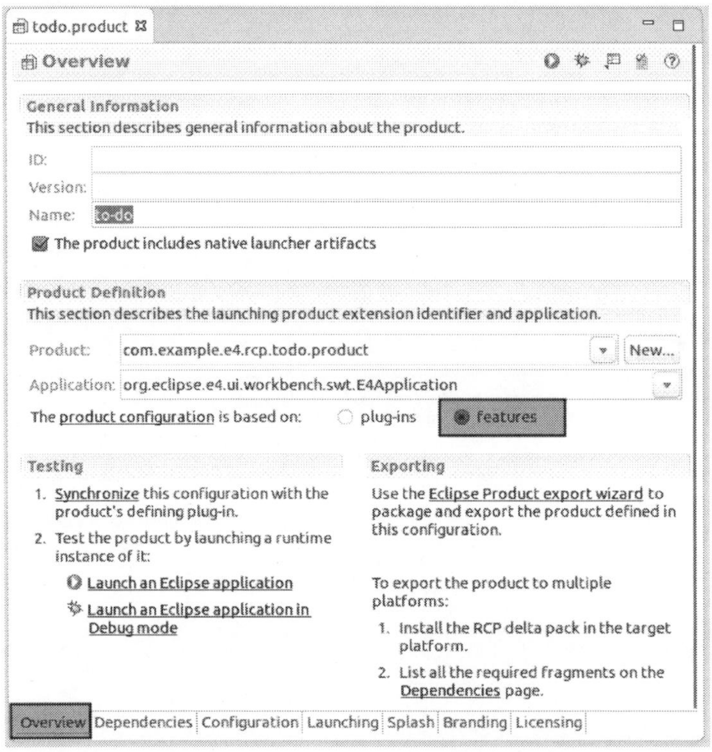

Select the *Dependencies* tab and add the `org.eclipse.e4.rcp` and the `com.example.e4.rcp.todo.feature` features as dependencies via the *Add* button.

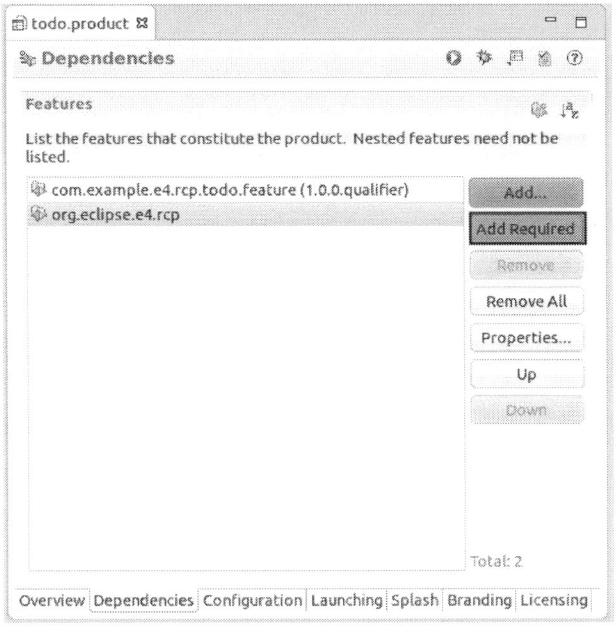

Press the *Add Required* button. This will add the `org.eclipse.emf.common` and `org.eclipse.emf.ecore` features to the dependencies.

16.4. Create Application model

Select File → New → Other → Eclipse 4 → Model → New Application Model to open a wizard. Use the project as the container and the filename suggested by the wizard.

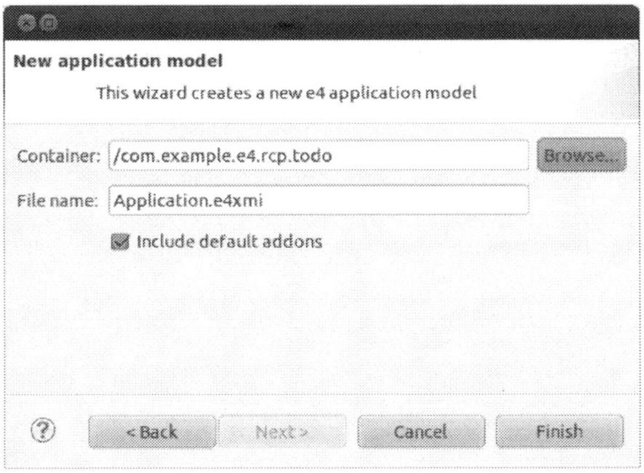

This will create the `Application.e4xmi` file and open this file with the application model editor.

16.5. Add model elements to the application model

Add one `Window` to your application model so you have a visual component.

Select the *Windows* node and press the *Add* Button for a `TrimmedWindow`.

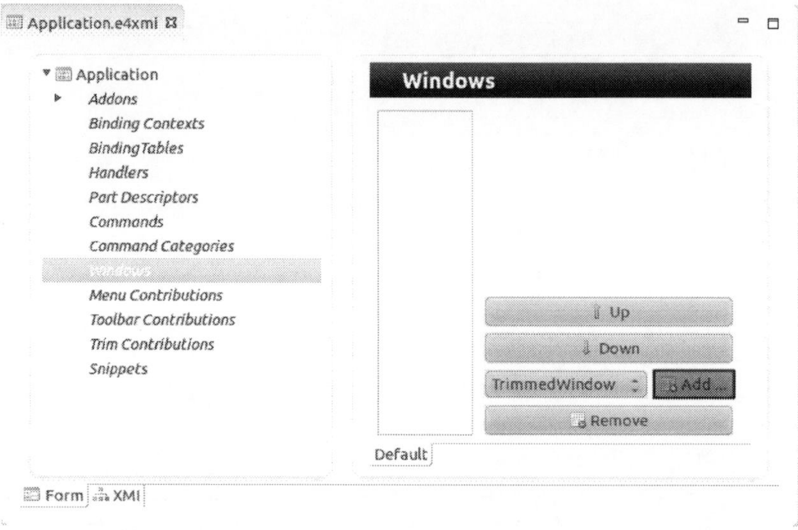

Enter an ID, the position and size of the window and a label as shown in the screenshot below.

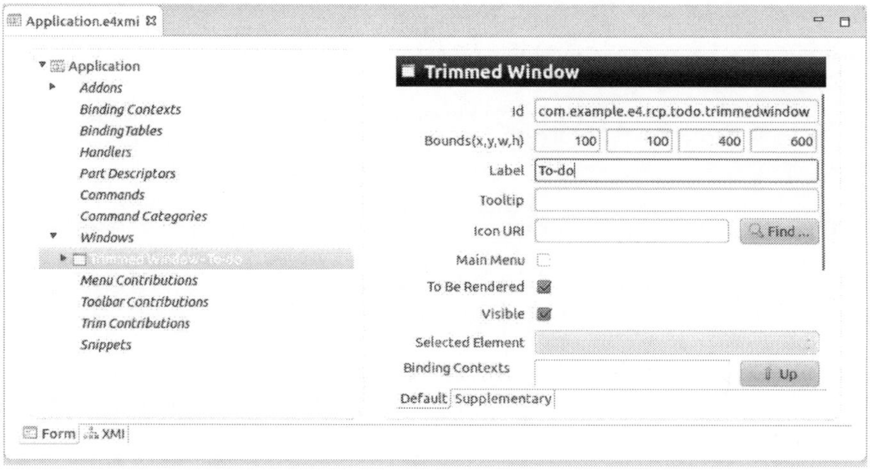

16.6. Start application

Open the product file and select the *Overview* tab. Press the *Launch an Eclipse application* hyperlink in the *Testing Section.*

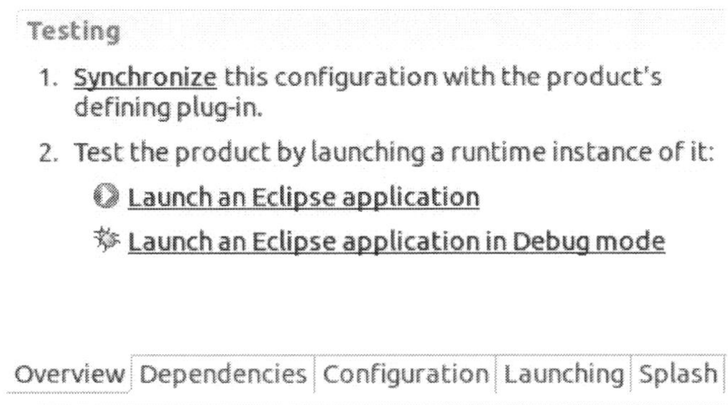

Validate that your application starts. It should be an empty application, which can be moved and closed.

16.7. Add plug-in dependencies

In the upcoming exercises you will use the functionality from other Eclipse plug-ins. This requires that you define a dependency to these plug-ins in your application. The exact details of applying this modular approach will be covered in a later chapter.

Open your `META-INF/MANIFEST.MF` file and select the *Dependencies* tab. Use the *Add* button in the *Required Plug-ins* section to add the following plug-ins as dependency.

- org.eclipse.swt
- javax.inject
- org.eclipse.e4.core.di
- org.eclipse.e4.ui.workbench
- org.eclipse.e4.ui.di

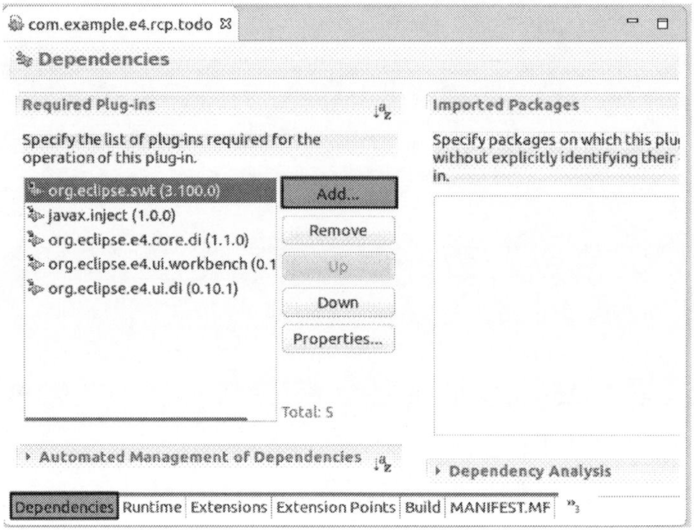
com.example.e4.rcp.todo
Dependencies
Required Plug-ins
Specify the list of plug-ins required for the operation of this plug-in.
org.eclipse.swt (3.100.0)
javax.inject (1.0.0)
org.eclipse.e4.core.di (1.1.0)
org.eclipse.e4.ui.workbench (0.1
org.eclipse.e4.ui.di (0.10.1)
Add...
Remove
Up
Down
Properties...
Total: 5
Imported Packages
Automated Management of Dependencies
Dependency Analysis
Dependencies
Runtime
Extensions
Extension Points
Build
MANIFEST.MF

17. Tutorial: Modeling a user interface

17.1. Overview

In this chapter you will extend the user interface of your Eclipse 4 application.

You will add a *Perspective* to the Window. This *Perspective* will contain a *PartSashContainer*. This container will divide its children horizontally.

The *PartSashContainer* will contain a *PartStack* and another *PartSashContainer*. This second *PartSashContainer* will contain two *PartStacks* and divide them vertically.

Each *PartStacks* will contain one *Part*.

After these changes, your user interface should look like the following screenshot.

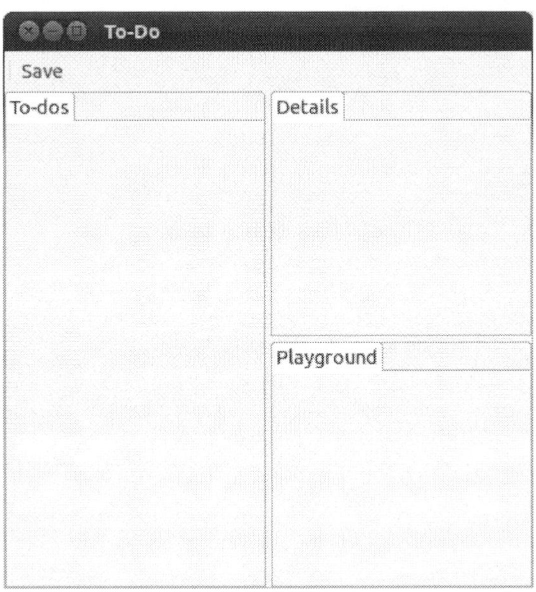

17.2. Adding model elements

Open the `Application.e4xmi` file. Go to your *To-do* Window and select the *Controls* node. Add a *PerspectiveStack*. Press the *Add* button to create a *Perspective* entry.

Enter the value *To-Do* in the *Label* field and the value *com.example.e4.rcp.todo.perspective* in the *Id* field.

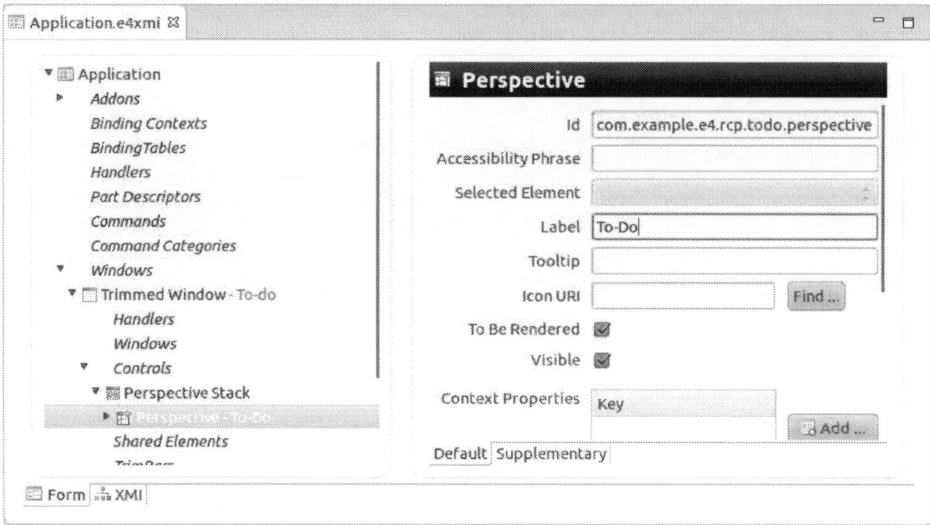

Select *Controls* below the newly created *Perspective* and add a *PartSashContainer*. Change its *Orientation* attribute to *Horizontal*.

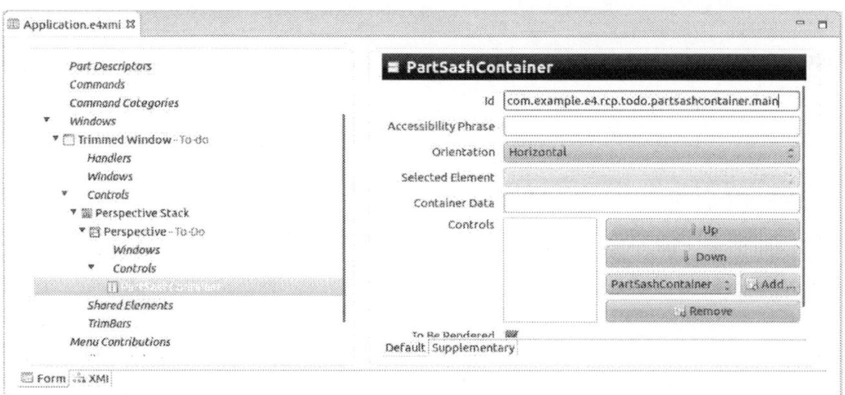

In the drop-down list of the *PartSashContainer* select *PartStack* and press the *Add* button.

Re-select the parent *PartSashContainer* and add another *PartSashContainer*. Now add two *PartStacks* to the second *PartSashContainer*. This should result in a tree in your application model similar to the following screenshot.

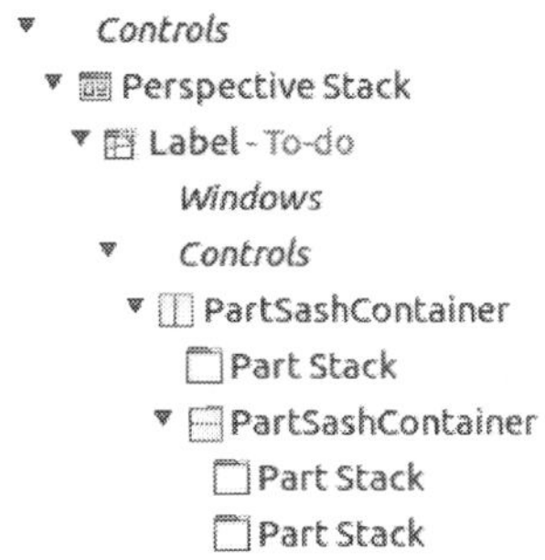

Add a *Part* to each *PartStack*. As ID for the *Parts* use the prefix `com.example.e4.rcp.todo.part` and the suffix from the following table.

Table 17.1. Label and ID from the Parts

ID Suffix	Label
*.todooverview	To-Dos
*.tododetails	Details
*.playground	Playground

The following screenshot shows the data for one *Part*.

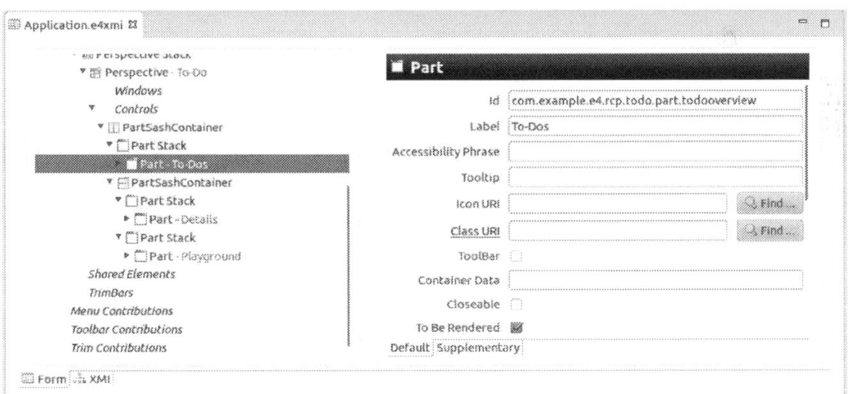

Start your product and validate that the user interface looks as planned. Reassign your *Parts* to other *PartStacks*, if required. The model editor supports drag-and drop for reassignment.

Please note that you have not yet created a Java class for your application.

17.3. Create Java classes and connect to the model

You will now create Java objects and connect them to the application model.

Create the `com.example.e4.rcp.todo.ui.parts` package.

Create three Java classes called *TodoOverviewPart* *TodoDetailsPart* and *PlaygroundPart* in this package. These classes do not extend another class, nor do they implement any interface.

The following code shows the `TodoOverviewPart` class.

```
package com.example.e4.rcp.todo.ui.parts;

public class TodoDetailsPart {

}
```

Open the `Application.e4xmi` file and connect the class with the correct model object. You can do this via the *Class URI* property of the *Part* model element.

The following table gives an overview of which elements should be connected.

Table 17.2. Connecting Java classes with Model Element

Class	Part ID suffix
TodoOverviewPart	*.todooverview
TodoDetailsPart	*.tododetail
PlaygroundPart	*.playground

The Eclipse 4 model editor allows you to search for an existing class via the *Find...* button. The initial list is empty, start typing the class name to see the results.

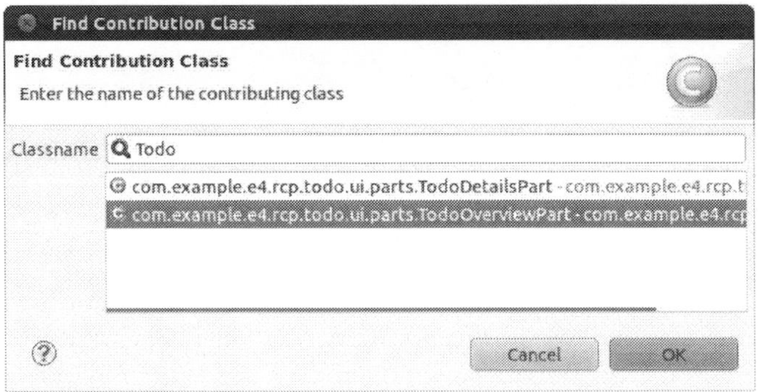

17.4. Test

Run your application. It should start, but you should see no difference in your user interface.

To validate that the model objects are created by the Eclipse runtime, create a no-argument constructor, e.g. with no parameters, for one of the classes and add a `System.out.println()` statement. Afterwards verify that the constructor is called, once you start your application.

17.5. Tutorial: Configure the deletion of persisted model data

Eclipse 4 persists certain user changes in your application. During development this might lead to situations where changes are not correctly applied and displayed, e.g. you define a new menu entry and this entry is not displayed in your application.

Either set the *Clear* flag on the *Main* tab in your Run configuration or add the `clearPersistedState` parameter for your product configuration file or Run configuration.

The following screenshot shows this setting in the product configuration file.

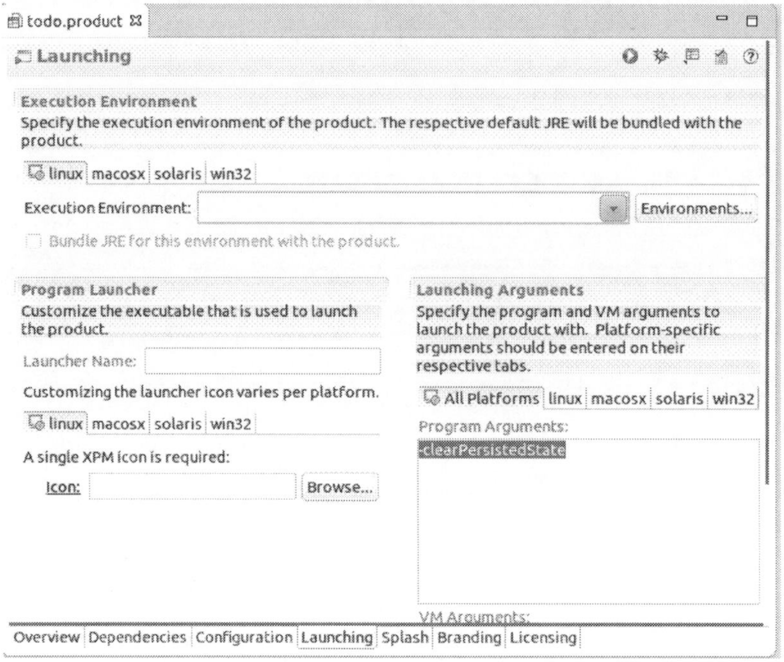

It is recommended that you set this during your development phase to avoid unexpected behavior. Please note that parameters must be specified via the - sign, e.g. `-clearPersistedState`.

18. Dependency injection and annotations

18.1. What is Dependency Injection?

The general concept behind dependency injection is called *Inversion of Control*. A class should not configure its dependencies but should be configured from outside.

Dependency injection is a concept which is not limited to Java. But we will look at dependency injection from a Java point of view.

A Java class has a dependency on another class if it uses this class as a variable. For example a class which accesses a logger service has a dependency on this service class.

Ideally Java classes should be as independent as possible from other Java classes. This increases the possibility of reusing these classes and to be able to test them independently from other classes, for example for unit testing.

If the Java class directly creates an instance of another class via the `new` operator, it cannot be used and tested independently from this class.

To decouple Java classes its dependencies should be fulfilled from the outside. A Java class would simply define its requirements like in the following example:

```
public class MyPart {

 @Inject private Logger logger;
 // DatabaseAccessClass would talk to the DB
 @Inject private DatabaseAccessClass dao;

 @Inject
 public void init(Composite parent) {
  logger.info("UI will start to build");
  Label label = new Label(parent, SWT.NONE);
  label.setText("Eclipse 4");
  Text text = new Text(parent, SWT.NONE);
  text.setText(dao.getNumber());
 }

}
```

Another class could read these dependencies and create an instance of the class, injecting objects into the defined dependency. This can be done via the Java reflection functionality. This class is usually called the dependency container and is a framework class.

This way the Java class has no hard dependencies, i.e. it does not rely on an instance of a certain class. For example if you want to test a class which uses another object which directly uses a database, you could inject a *mock* object.

Mock objects are objects which act as if they are the real object but only simulate their behavior. Mock is an old English word meaning to mimic or imitate.

If dependency injection is used, a Java class can be tested in isolation, which is good.

Dependency injection can happen on:

- the constructor of the class (construction injection)
- a method (method injection)
- a field (field injection)

Dependency injection can happen on static as well as on non-static fields and methods.

18.2. Define dependencies in Eclipse

Eclipse 4 supports constructor, method and field injection. It uses the standard Java `@Inject` and `@Named` annotations, which were defined in the Java Specification Request 330 (JSR330). In addition to these standard annotations, it declares the `@Optional` and `@Preference` annotations.

The following table gives an overview of the dependency injection (DI) annotations.

Table 18.1. Annotations for Dependency Injection

Annotation	Description
@javax.inject.Inject	Marks a field, a constructor or a method. The Eclipse framework tries to inject the parameter.
@javax.inject.Named	Defines the name of the key for the value which should be injected. By default the fully qualified class name is used as key. Several default values are defined as constants in the `IServiceConstants` interface.

Annotation	Description
@Optional	Marks an injected value to be optional. If it can not be resolved, `null` is injected. Without @Optional the framework would throw an Exception. The specific behavior depends where @Optional is used: • for parameters: a `null` value will be injected; • for methods: the method calls will be skipped • for fields: the values will not be injected.
@Preference	Eclipse can store key/values pairs as so-called preferences. The @Preference annotation defines that the annotated value should be filled from the preference store.

The `org.eclipse.e4.core.di.annotations` package contains the `@Optional` annotation and the `@Preference` annotation is included in the `org.eclipse.e4.core.di.extensions` package. Both are part of the `org.eclipse.e4.core.di` plug-in.

18.3. Dependency injection in Eclipse 4

The Eclipse 4 runtime creates objects for the Java classes referred by the application model. During this instantiation the Eclipse runtime scans the class definition for annotations.

Based on these annotations the Eclipse framework performs the injection. First the constructor injection is performed and afterwards the field and method injections.

Constructors are called before the fields are injected. Accessing an injected field in the constructor will result in an Exception thrown by the Framework.

The Eclipse framework also tracks the injected values and if they change, it can re-inject the new values. This means applications can be freed from having to install (and remove) listeners.

For example you can define that you want to get the current selection injected. If the selection changes, the Eclipse framework will inject the new value.

19. Scope of injection

19.1. What can be injected?

We covered how dependency injection works and which annotations can be used to define the behavior of the Java classes. But we have not yet covered what the scope of injection is, i.e. what you can inject into your model classes.

The Eclipse runtime creates a context in which the possible values for injection can be stored. This context can be modified, e.g. the application and the framework can add elements to the context.

The Eclipse context contains:

- all objects associated with the application model
- all other objects which have explicitly been added to the context
- all Preferences - key/value pairs which typically used to configure the application
- OSGi services - software components which can be dynamically consumed

Applications can define their own injection suppliers too.

For the purpose of this book, all elements of the context will be called *context elements*.

19.2. Key/values pairs and Context Variables

Objects can be places in the context via the Class name or via a String. If the key is a String, this key/value pair is called a *Context variable*.

Key/value pairs or *Context variables* can be present at different levels in the context hierarchy.

Context variables and key/value pairs in the context allow to separate the interesting state from the source of the state. For example in the Eclipse IDE a lot of components use the active editor to drive their views, but it means their views are coupled to the active editor; the editor could instead set a context variable to their state and the views react to that variable change instead.

The Eclipse platform places several key/value pairs and *Context variables* into the context. Several *Context variables* keys are defined in the `IServiceConstants` interface.

19.3. How are objects searched?

All possible values for dependency injection can be accessed via the context.

The context contains Java objects which can be accessed by keys. Keys can manifest themselves in two forms: Strings and Class objects.

If a String is used as a key, the corresponding key/value pair is called a *Context Variable*.

Access to the context works in a similar way to accessing a Java `Map` data structure.

The context is not a flat structure like a `Map`. It is hierarchical and can also dynamically compute values for requested keys.

A context can be local to an object and can have a parent context.

Model elements which implements the `MContext` interface have a local context. These are currently `MApplication`, `MWindow`, `MPerspective`, `MPart` and `MPopupMenu`.

The main context is created by the Eclipse Framework and all context objects of the model elements are hierarchically connected to the main context object.

Model objects that implement the `MContext` interface have their own local context. This is for example the case for `MWindow` and `MPart`. Each context for a model element contains a reference to the Model object itself.

If for example a *Part* requests an object by a certain key from the context, Eclipse will first search for this object in the local context of the part. If it does not find the key in the local context it will search the parent context. This process continues until the main context has been reached. At this point the framework would check for fitting OSGi services in the OSGi registry.

The following picture visualizes this context hierarchy.

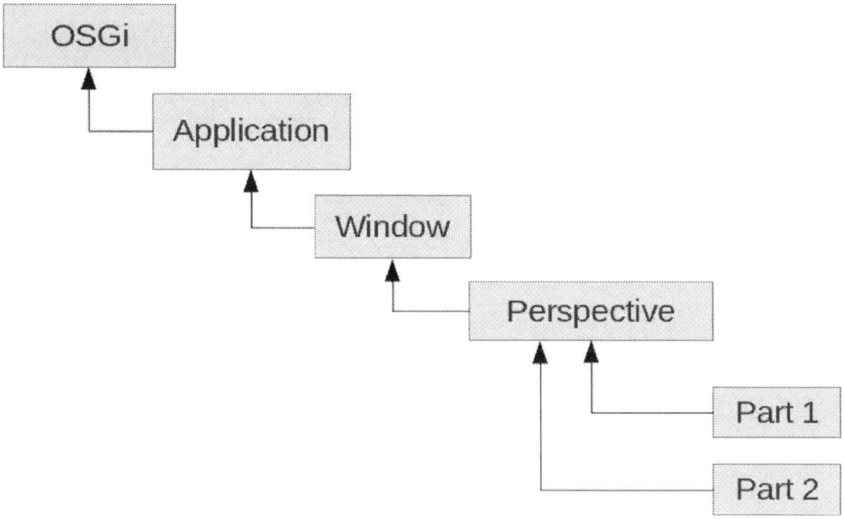

The context is hierarchical to avoid collisions in injected values and to increase the isolation of the classes in terms of what they need. For example a *Part* needs a unique `Composite` objects to create its user interfaces. Since *Parts* have different local contexts, their `@Inject` gets the needed implementation from the actual context.

The search happens transparently for the caller of the injection.

19.4. What are the relevant classes and interfaces

The interface for the context object is the `IEclipseContext` interface.

The Eclipse platform uses the `OSGiContextStrategy` class to search for OSGi services if the Eclipse framework does not find the requested key in the hierarchy of `IEclipseContext` objects.

19.5. Who creates the context for model elements?

Eclipse 4 has a flexible renderer framework. For each model element the framework determines a renderer class which is responsible for creating the Java object associated with the model element. This renderer class creates, if required, the local context for the model element via the `EclipseContextFactory` class and connects this local context to the context hierarchy.

For example the `ContributedPartRenderer` class is responsible for creating the Java objects for *Parts* in the model. The interface for *Parts* is `MPart`.

`ContributedPartRenderer` creates a `Composite` for every *Part* and injects this `Composite` into the local context of the *Part*.

Another example is the `WBWRenderer` class which is responsible for creating a *Window*. This class puts an instance of the `IWindowCloseHandler` and the `ISaveHandler` interface into the context of the *Window*. The first is responsible for the behavior of a *Window* during close, the other one for saving. For example the default `IWindowCloseHandler` would prompt you if you want to save *Parts* which indicate that they have saveable content via the `MDirtyable` model attribute. You can change this default `IWindowCloseHandler` implementation via the `MWindow` model object. The following example shows this.

```
@Execute
public void execute(final Shell shell, EModelService service,
 MWindow window) {
 IWindowCloseHandler handler = new IWindowCloseHandler() {
  @Override
  public boolean close(MWindow window) {
   return MessageDialog.openConfirm(shell,
   "Close",
   "You will loose data. Really close?");
  }
 };
window.getContext().set(IWindowCloseHandler.class, handler);
}
```

20. Behavior annotations

20.1. API definition via inheritance

In general, every framework defines an application programming interface (API).

If you use a framework you need to have a convention for which methods are called at which point of the execution of your program. For example if a Java class is responsible for handling a toolbar button click, the framework needs to know which method of this class it should call.

The "traditional" way of defining an API is via inheritance. This approach requires that your classes extend or implement framework classes and interfaces. This is how Eclipse 3.x defined its API.

The framework defines via an abstract class which methods must be implemented. In this example the method might be called `execute()` and the framework knows that this method must be called once the toolbar button is clicked.

For example in Eclipse 3.x a `View` class would extend the abstract `ViewPart` class. This class defines the `createPartControl()` method.

The Eclipse 3.x framework knows that `createPartControl()` is responsible for creating the user interface and calls this method once the `View` becomes visible.

API definition via inheritance is a simple way to define an API, but it also couples the classes tightly to the framework. For example testing the class without the framework is difficult. It also makes extending or updating the framework difficult.

20.2. API definition via annotations

Eclipse 4 does not require that classes extend framework classes. To be precise Eclipse 4 does not provide any such classes.

Eclipse 4 uses annotations to indicate that a certain behavior is expected from the framework.

I will call these annotations *behavior annotations*.

Behavior annotations are used to indicate that certain methods should be called at certain events. The following tables list the available behavior annotations.

Table 20.1. Eclipse lifecycle annotations for Parts

Annotation	Description
@PostConstruct	Is called after the class is constructed and the field and method injection has been performed.
@PreDestroy	Is called before the class is destroyed. Can be used to clean up resources.
@Focus	Indicates that this method should be called, once the Part gets the focus. It is *required* to set the focus on one user interface control otherwise certain workbench functionality does not work.
@Persist	Is called if a save request on the Part is triggered. Can be used to save the data of the Part.
@PersistState	Is called before the model object is disposed, so that the Part can save its state.

Table 20.2. Other Eclipse Behavior Annotations

Annotation	Description
@Execute	Marks a method in a handler class to be executed
@CanExecute	Marks a method to be visited by the Command-Framework to check if a handler is enabled
@GroupUpdates	Indicates that updates for this @Inject should be batched. If you change such objects in the `IEclipseContext` the update will be triggered by the `processWaiting()` method on `IEclipseContext`.
@EventTopic and @UIEventTopic	Allows you to subscribe to events send by the EventAdmin service.

All these annotations will also trigger dependency injections. Therefore you do not need to add the `@Inject` annotation if you use these annotations.

The `@PostConstruct`, `@PreDestroy` annotations are included in the `javax.inject` package.

The `org.eclipse.e4.core.di.annotations` package contains the `@Execute`, `@CanExecute` annotations.

`@Persists`, `@PersistState` and `@Focus` are part of the `org.eclipse.e4.ui.di` package.

20.3. Lifecycle Hooks

Typically some functionality should be triggered if an application is started or stopped. Eclipse 4 allows you to register a class to predefined events of this lifecycle. For example you can use these lifecycle hooks to create a login screen before the actual application is started.

The `org.eclipse.core.runtime.product` extension point allows you to define this lifecycle class with a property with the `lifeCycleURI` key.

This property points to a class via the `bundleclass://` schema.

In the lifecycle class you can use the following annotations. The annotated methods will be called by the framework depending on the life cycle of your application.

Table 20.3. Life Cycle Annotations

Annotation	Description
@PostContextCreate	Is called after the Application's `IEclipseContext` is created, can be used to add objects, services, etc. to the context. This context is created for the `MApplication` class.
@ProcessAdditions	Is called directly before the model is passed to the renderer, can be used to add additional elements to the model.
@ProcessRemovals	Same as @ProcessAdditions but for removals.
@PreSave	Is called before the application model is saved. You can modify the model before it is persisted.

The following example shows how to register a lifecycle class in your `plugin.xml` file.

```
<?xml version="1.0" encoding="UTF-8"?>
<plugin>

   <extension
         id="product"
         point="org.eclipse.core.runtime.products">
      <product
        name="testing"
        application="org.eclipse.e4.ui.workbench.swt.E4Application">
         <property
```

```
            name="appName"
            value="testing">
         </property>
         <property
           name="applicationXMI"
           value="testing/Application.e4xmi">
         </property>
         <property
           name="applicationCSS"
           value="platform:/plugin/testing/css/default.css">
         </property>
         <property
           name="lifeCycleURI"
           value="bundleclass://testing/testing.LifeCycleManager">
         </property>
      </product>
   </extension>

</plugin>
```

The following coding for the lifecycle class will display a shell.

```
package testing;

import org.eclipse.e4.core.services.events.IEventBroker;
import org.eclipse.e4.ui.workbench.UIEvents;
import org.eclipse.e4.ui.workbench.lifecycle.PostContextCreate;
import org.eclipse.swt.SWT;
import org.eclipse.swt.widgets.Shell;
import org.osgi.service.event.Event;
import org.osgi.service.event.EventHandler;

public class LifeCycleManager {
 @PostContextCreate
 void postContextCreate() {
  final Shell shell = new Shell(SWT.TOOL | SWT.NO_TRIM);
  shell.open();
 }

}
```

21. Tutorial: Using dependency injection

21.1. Getting a Composite

In the following tutorial we extend our classes to use dependency injection.

Change the `TodoOverviewPart` class to the following:

```
package com.example.e4.rcp.todo.ui.parts;

import javax.inject.Inject;

import org.eclipse.swt.widgets.Composite;

public class TodoOverviewPart {

  @Inject
  public TodoOverviewPart(Composite parent) {

 // Assuming that dependency injection works
 // parent will never be null
 System.out.println("Woh! Got Composite via DI.");

 // Does it have a layou manager?
 System.out.println("Layout: " + parent.getLayout().getClass());
 }
  }
}
```

21.2. Validation

Run your application and check in the *Console View* of your Eclipse IDE to see if the *`Composite`* parameter was injected. Note down the layout class which the `Composite` has assigned to, if it is not `null`.

22. Tutorial: Define Part lifecycle

22.1. Overview

Although the user interface of a *Part* can be created in the constructor, it is recommended that the user interface should instead be created in a `@PostConstruct` method. When the constructor is fired, no marked fields or methods will have been injected, which can lead to subtle errors.

Realizing the user interface of a *Part* in a `@PostConstruct` requires that `@Inject` methods be aware that the user interface might not yet be created.

In the following tutorial we use the `@PostConstruct` and `@PreDestroy` annotations in our *Parts*.

22.2. Using @PostConstruct and @PreDestroy

Add the following method to your `TodoOverviewPart`, `TodoDetailsPart` and `PlaygroundPart` classes.

```
// Declare a field label, required for @Focus
Label label;

public void createControls(Composite parent) {
 label = new Label(parent,SWT.NONE);
}
```

Annotate the method with `@PostContruct`.

Create an empty `public void dispose()` method and annotate it with `@PreDestroy`.

Remove all constructors from your classes.

22.3. @Focus

Implement a `@Focus` method in each *Part*. Setting the focus to one of SWT controls is mandatory otherwise the Eclipse services do not work reliably.

```
@Focus
private void setFocus() {
 label.setFocus();
}
```

22.4. Validate

Run your application and validate that the `@PostContruct` method is called. Use either debugging or a `System.out.println()` statement. Every Part needs to assign focus to one of its controls, otherwise certain services will not work. Therefore we added a SWT label to be the focus control. Even though a label cannot take focus, it triggers the `SWT.ACTIVATE` event, which is sufficient for the Eclipse services to work correctly.

If you are familiar with SWT, add a few more controls to your user interface.

23. Commands, Handler, Menus and Toolbars

23.1. Overview

The Eclipse application model can contain commands and handlers.

A command in Eclipse is a declarative description of an abstract action which can be performed, for example *save*, *edit* or *copy*. A command is independent from its implementation details.

The behavior of a command is defined via a handler. A handler defines a class via the `contributionURI` attribute of the handler. This attribute is displayed as "Class URI" in the model editor. The handler can be global to the application, or scoped to a window or even a part.

This class uses the `@Execute` annotation to define which method is called once the handler is executed. The `@CanExecute` annotation defines the method which evaluates if the handler is currently active. If the handler can always execute, it does not need to supply a `@CanExecute` method.

`@CanExecute` is called by the framework if the `SWT.SHOW` event happens. This event is for example triggered if a new Part is displayed. Also if you add items to the toolbar, a timer is automatically registered by the Eclipse framework which, as of the time of this writing, executes every 400 Milliseconds. This timer will check the @CanExecute to enable or disable the related toolbar entry.

In the handler class you can determine the command ID if the command was triggered via the user interface. Determining the ID is not possible, if it was triggered via the command service (limitation). The following code snippet shows how to get the command ID.

```
@Execute
public void execute(MHandledItem item) {
  MCommand command = item.getCommand();
  // Prints out the commmand ID
  System.out.println(command.getElementId());
}
```

23.2. Default commands

If you know Eclipse 3.x you are probably searching for the predefined commands which you can re-use. The Eclipse 4 platform tries to be as lean as possible.

Eclipse 4 does not include standard commands anymore. You have to define all your commands.

23.3. Menus and Toolbar

You can add menus and toolbars to the application model for the Window and for Parts. Menu and toolbars items contain references to commands. If a command is select the runtime will determine the relevant handlers for the command.

For simple cases you can also use the "Direct MenuItem" or a "Direct ToolItem", which allows you to define a class to be executed directly. This is useful if you just want to respond to the user clicking on a menu item or tool item.

Using commands togehter with handlers gives you more flexibility, for example you can have different Handlers for different scopes (Applications or Views) and you can define key bindings for the handler's associated commands.

Toolbars in the application are encapsulated in the application model via the *trimbar* model element. A trimbar can be defined for Windows. Via its attribute you define if the trimbar should be placed on the top, left, right or bottom corner of the Window.

The related command is assigned to the menu and toolbar entry. Menus and toolbars support separators. Menus can have submenus.

23.4. View Menus

To show a menu for a `View` you have to add a tag to the corresponding entry in the `Application.e4xmi` file. This tag must be defined before the menu children are defined and looks like the following.

```
<tags>ViewMenu</tags>
```

Only one Menu in a Part should contain this tag.

To add such a View menu entry, select the entry *Menu* under our Part, select *ViewMenu* and press the *Add* button.

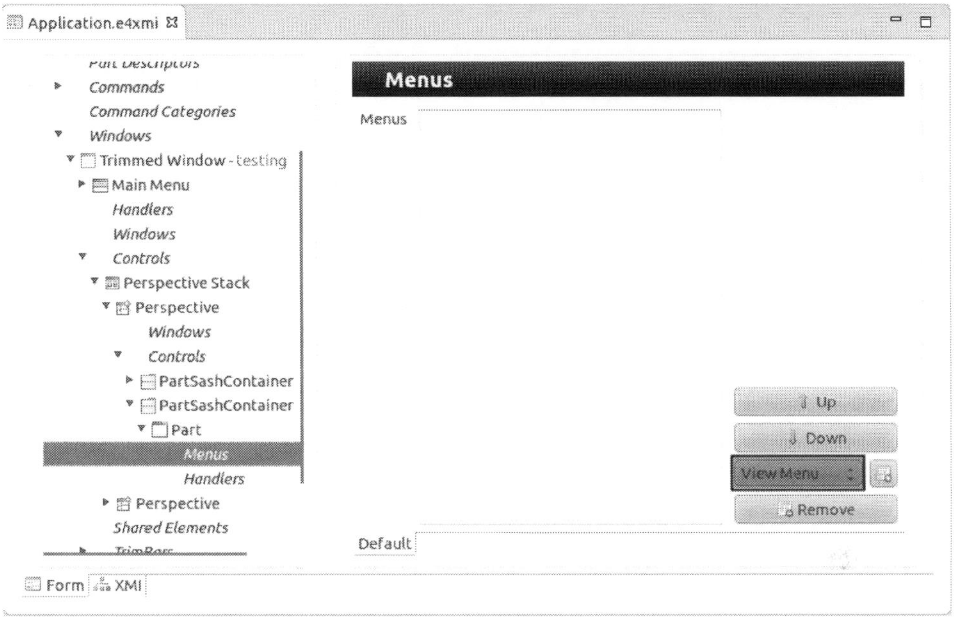

23.5. Popup Menu - Context Menu

You can also define a popup menu for *SWT* controls. For this you define a *Popup Menu* for your *Part* in the application model.

You can then assign it via the `EMenuService` class to a *SWT* control. The following coding shows an example.

```
package com.example.e4.rcp.todo.ui.parts;

import javax.annotation.PostConstruct;

import org.eclipse.e4.ui.workbench.swt.modeling.EMenuService;
import org.eclipse.swt.SWT;
import org.eclipse.swt.widgets.Composite;
import org.eclipse.swt.widgets.Text;

public class Detail {

 @PostConstruct
 public void createUi(Composite parent, EMenuService service) {
  final Text text = new Text(parent, SWT.BORDER);
  text.setText("Hello");
  // Popup Menu should have its elementId
  // set to "popuptest"
  service.registerContextMenu(text, "popuptest");
```

```
  }
}
```

If you want to implement this example you also need to add a dependency to the `org.eclipse.e4.ui.workbench.swt` plug-in in your application.

23.6. Scope of handlers

Each command can have only one valid handler for a given scope. The application model allows you to define a handler for the application, for a *Window* and for a *Part*.

If more than one handler is defined for a command, Eclipse will select the handler most specific to the model element.

For example if you define a handler for the "Copy" command for your Window and if you define another "Copy" handler for your Part, the runtime will select the handlers closest to model element.

Once the handler is selected, `@CanExecute` is called so the handler can determine if it is able to execute in the given context. If it returns false it will disable any menu and tool items that point to that command.

23.7. Several methods with @Execute

You can also annotate several methods with `@Execute`. The Eclipse runtime will pick the method with the highest number of parameters. A method can only be selected if its parameters can be found in the Eclipse Context.

This way you can prepare your class for different content in the Context.

23.8. Passing parameters to commands

You can also pass parameters to commands.

To define that a command accepts a parameter, select your command you press the *Add* button in the *Parameter* section.

The ID is the identifier which you can use to get the parameter via the `@Named` annotation.

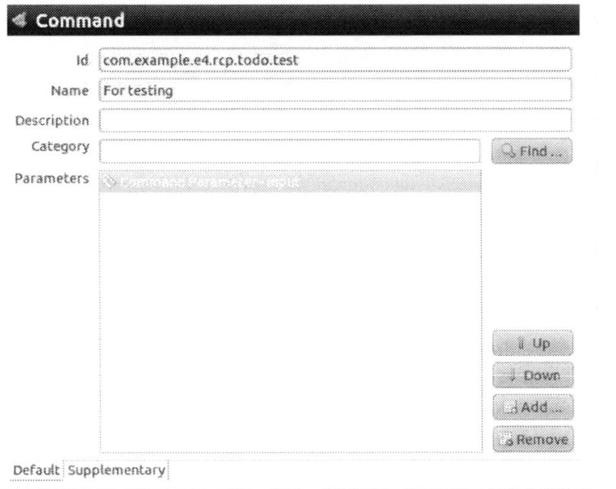

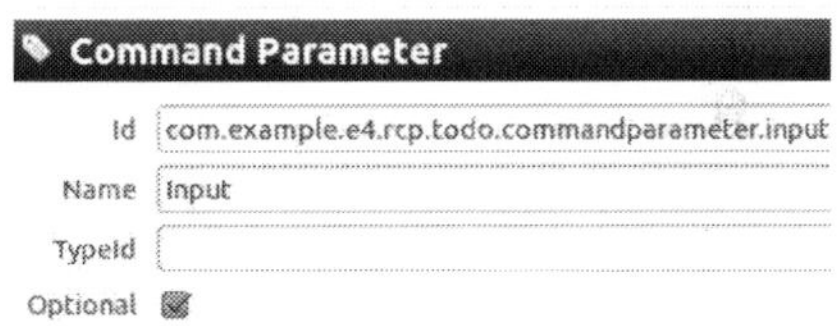

Getting the parameter via `@Named` annotation in your handler is demonstrated in the following code example.

```
package com.example.e4.rcp.todo.handlers;

import javax.inject.Named;

import org.eclipse.e4.core.di.annotations.CanExecute;
import org.eclipse.e4.core.di.annotations.Execute;

public class TestHandler {
 @Execute
 public void execute(@Named("com.example.e4.rcp.todo" +
   ".commandparameter.input") String param) {
  System.out.println(param);
 }


}
```

In your menu or toolbar entries you use the ID of the command in the *Name* field. The entry in the *Value* field is passed to the command.

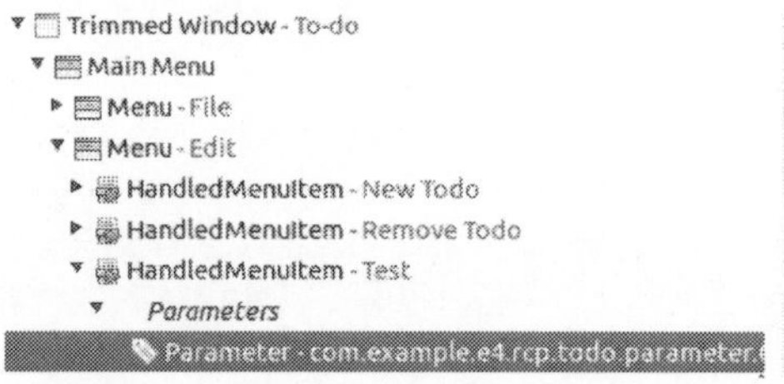

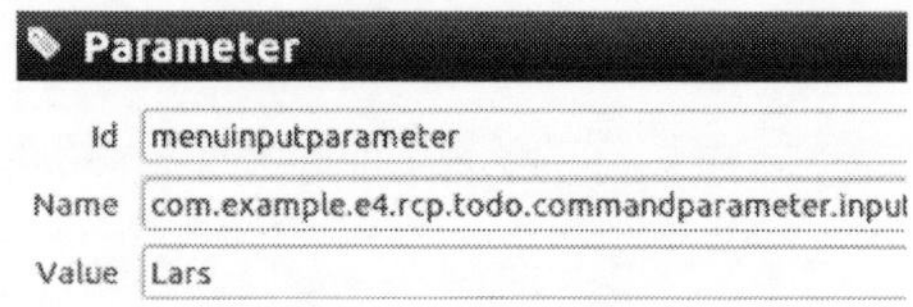

23.9. Core expressions

The visibility of menus, toolbars and their entries can be restricted via the *core expressions*. You add the corresponding attribute in the application model to the ID defined by the `org.eclipse.core.expressions.definitions` extension point in the `plugin.xml` file.

To add this extension point to your application, open the `plugin.xml` file and select the *Dependencies* tab in the editor. Add the `org.eclipse.core.expressions` plug-in in the *Required Plug-ins* section.

Afterwards select the *Extensions* tab, press the *Add* button and add the `org.eclipse.core.expressions.definitions` extension. You define an ID under which the core expression can be referred to in the application model.

Via right mouse click on the extension you can start building your expression.

You can assign this core expression to your menu entry in the application model. The following screenshot shows this for the *Test* menu entry.

The following example can be used to restrict the visibility of a menu entry based on the type of the current selection. You will later learn how to set the current selection. Please note that the variable for the selection is currently called `org.eclipse.ui.selection`. In Eclipse 3.x this variable is called `selection`.

```
<extension
      point="org.eclipse.core.expressions.definitions">
  <definition
            id="com.example.e4.rcp.todo.selectionset">
```

```
        <with variable="org.eclipse.ui.selection">
    <iterate ifEmpty="false" operator="or">
      <instanceof value="com.example.e4.rcp.todo.model.Todo">
      </instanceof>
    </iterate>
        </with>
  </definition>
</extension>
```

This expression can be used to restrict the visibility of model elements.

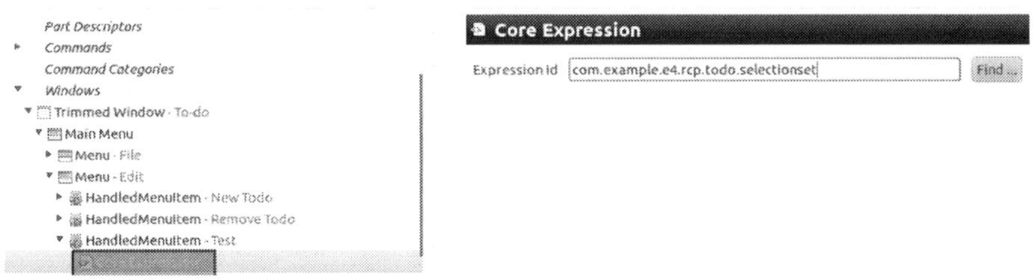

This approach is similar to the definition of core expressions in Eclipse 3.x.

The values available for Eclipse 3.x are documented in the Eclipse Wiki under the following link: Core Expressions [http://wiki.eclipse.org/Command_Core_Expressions] and contained in the `ISources` interface. Eclipse 4 does not always support the same variables, but the wiki might still be helpful.

23.10. Evaluate your own values in Core expressions

You can also place values in the `IEclipseContext` of your application and use these for your visible-when evaluation.

Later you will learn more about modifying the `IEclipseContext` but the following codes is an example `Handler` which places a value for the *myactivePartId* key in the context.

```
@Execute
public void execute(IEclipseContext context) {
// put an example value in the context
  context.set("myactivePartId",
  "com.example.e4.rcp.ui.parts.todooverview");
}
```

The following shows an example core expression which evaluates to `true` if an *myactivePartId* key with the value `com.example.e4.rcp.ui.parts.todooverview` is found in the context.

This core expression can get assigned to a menu entry and control the visibility.

```
<extension
        point="org.eclipse.core.expressions.definitions">
     <definition
           id="com.example.e4.rcp.todo.todooverviewselected">
        <with
              variable="myactivePartId">
           <equals
                 value="com.example.e4.rcp.ui.parts.todooverview">
           </equals>
        </with>
     </definition>
  </extension>
```

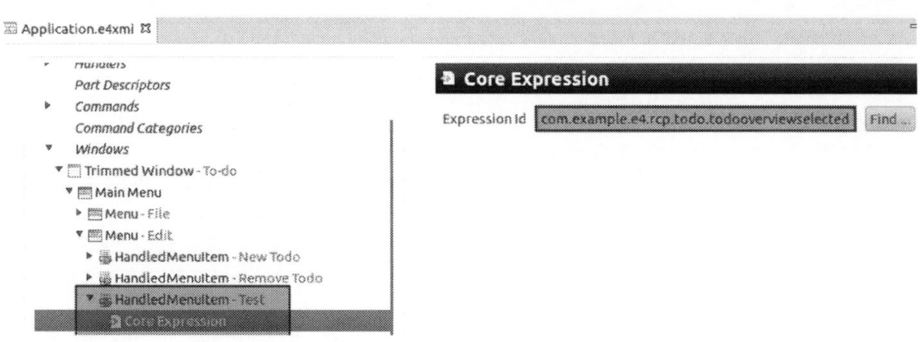

23.11. Naming schema for command and handler IDs

A good convention is to start IDs with the *top level package name* of your project and to use only lower case.

The IDs of commands and handler should reflect their relationship. For example if you implement a command with the `com.example.contacts.commands.show` ID, you should use `com.example.contacts.handler.show` as the ID for the handler. If you have more than one handler defined, add another suffix to it, describing its purpose, e.g. *com.example.contacts.handler.show.details*.

In case you implement commonly used functions, e.g. save, copy, you should use the existing platform IDs, as some Eclipse contributions expect these IDs. A more complete list of command IDs is available in `org.eclipse.ui.IWorkbenchCommandConstants`.

Table 23.1. Default IDs for commonly used commands

Command	ID
Save	org.eclipse.ui.file.save
Save All	org.eclipse.ui.file.saveAll
Undo	org.eclipse.ui.edit.undo
Redo	org.eclipse.ui.edit.redo
Cut	org.eclipse.ui.edit.cut
Copy	org.eclipse.ui.edit.copy
Paste	org.eclipse.ui.edit.paste
Delete	org.eclipse.ui.edit.delete
Import	org.eclipse.ui.file.import
Export	org.eclipse.ui.file.export
Select All	org.eclipse.ui.edit.selectAll
About	org.eclipse.ui.help.aboutAction
Preferences	org.eclipse.ui.window.preferences
Exit	org.eclipse.ui.file.exit

24. Tutorial: Defining and using Commands and Handlers

24.1. Overview

You will now define commands and handlers for your application. We will define our handlers for the whole application.

24.2. Defining Commands

Open the `Application.e4xmi` file and select *Commands*.

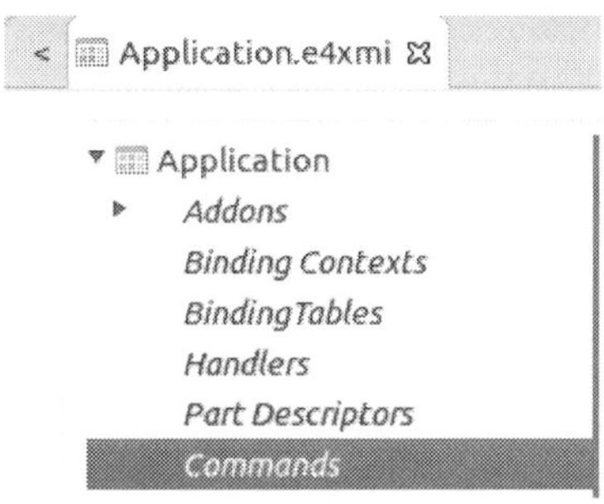

Via the *Add* button you can create new commands. The name and the ID are the important fields. Create the following commands.

Table 24.1. Commands

ID	Name
org.eclipse.ui.file.saveAll	Save
org.eclipse.ui.file.exit	Exit
com.example.e4.rcp.todo.new	New Todo
com.example.e4.rcp.todo.remove	Remove Todo
com.example.e4.rcp.todo.test	For testing

24.3. Defining Handler classes

Create the `com.example.e4.rcp.todo.handlers` package for your handler classes.

All handler classes will implement the `execute()` method.

```
package com.example.e4.rcp.todo.handlers;

import org.eclipse.e4.core.di.annotations.CanExecute;
import org.eclipse.e4.core.di.annotations.Execute;

public class SaveAllHandler {
 @Execute
 public void execute() {
   System.out.println("Called");
 }

 // Technically not needed
 // will default to true
 @CanExecute
 public boolean canExecute() {
  return true;
 }

}
```

Using this template for all classes, implement the following classes.

- SaveAllHandler
- ExitHandler
- NewTodoHandler
- RemoveTodoHandler
- TestHandler

24.4. Defining Handlers in your model

Select the entry *Handlers* in your application model and create the handlers from the following table for your commands. For the definition of handlers the ID, the command and the class is relevant information.

Use the *com.example.e4.rcp.todo.handlers* prefix for all handlers IDs.

Table 24.2. Handlers

Handler ID	Command - Class
*.save	Save - SaveAllHandler
*.exit	Exit - ExitHandler
*.new	New Todo - NewTodoHandler

Handler ID	Command - Class
*.remove	Remove Todo - RemoveTodoHandler
*.test	For testing - TestHandler

The application model editor shows both the name and the ID of the command. The class URI follows the `bundleclass://` schema, the table only defines the class name to make the table more readable. For example for the save handler this looks like the following:

```
bundleclass://com.example.e4.rcp.todo/[CONTINUE...]
com.example.e4.rcp.todo.handlers.SaveAllHandler
```

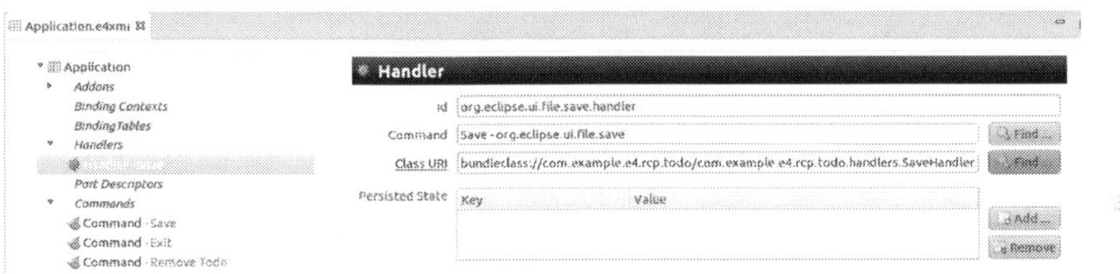

24.5. Adding a Menu

You will now add a Menu to your application model.

Select the `Application.e4xmi` file. To add a menu to a *Window* select your *TrimmedWindow* entry in the model and flag the *Main Menu* attribute.

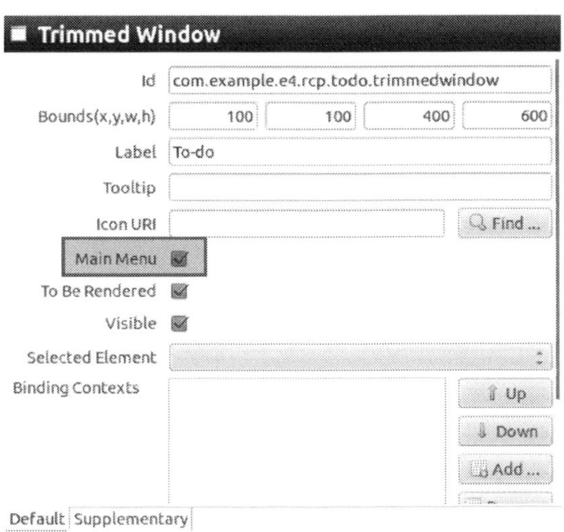

Assign the *org.eclipse.ui.main.menu* ID to your main menu.

Add two menus, one with the name *File* and the other one with the name *Edit* in the `Label` attribute.

Also set the *org.eclipse.ui.file.menu* ID for the *File* menu. Use *com.example.e4.rcp.todo.menu.edit* as ID for the *Edit* menu.

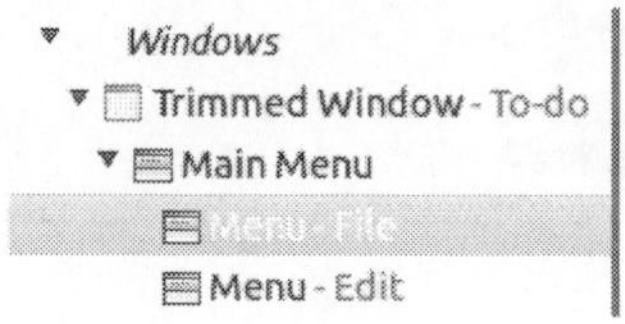

Add a *HandledMenuItem* to the *File* menu. This item should point to the *Save* command via the `Command` attribute.

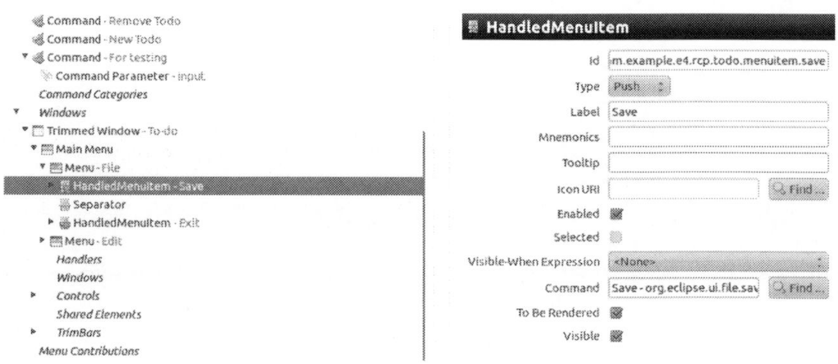

Add a *Separator* after the save menu item and add after that an entry for the exit command.

Add all other commmands to the *Edit* menu.

24.6. Adding a Toolbar

Select the *TrimBars* node under your *Window* entry and press the *Add* button. The `Side` attribute should be set to `Top`, so that all toolbars assigned to that *TrimBar* appear on the top of the application.

Add a *ToolBar* to your TrimBar. Add a *Handled ToolItem* to this ToolBar, which points to the `org.eclipse.ui.file.saveAll` command.

Set the label for this entry to `Save`.

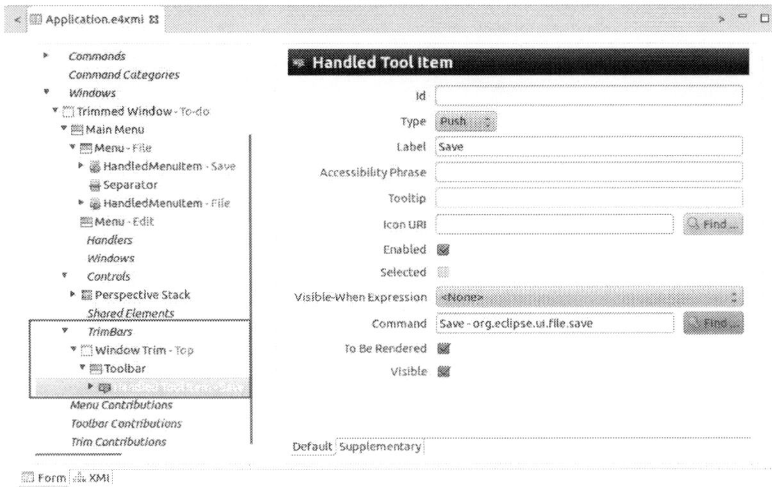

24.7. Closing the application

To test if your handler is working, change your `ExitHandler` class, so that it will close your application.

```
package de.vogella.e4.todo.handler;

import org.eclipse.e4.core.di.annotations.Execute;
import org.eclipse.e4.ui.workbench.IWorkbench;

public class ExitHandler {
 @Execute
 public void execute(IWorkbench workbench) {
  workbench.close();
 }
}
```

24.8. Simulate save

Change your `SaveAllHandler` class, so that `System.out.println` writes the following message to the console: "SaveAllHandler called.".

25. Key bindings

25.1. Overview

It is also possible to define key bindings (shortcuts) for your Eclipse application. This requires two steps, first you need to enter values for the *BindingContext* node of your application model.

Afterwards you need to enter the keybindings for the relevant *BindingContext* in the *BindingTable* node of your application model. There can only be one *BindingTable* for each *BindingContext*, and their IDs must match.

BindingContexts are defined in a hierarchical fashion, so that keybindings in child *BindingContexts* override the matching keybinding in the parent *BindingContext*.

25.2. BindingContext entries using by JFace

The `BindingContext` is defined via its ID. You can use any ID you like. `BindingContext` IDs can be assigned to a Window in the application model. This would define which `BindingContexts` are valid for this Window.

Eclipse JFace uses predefined BindingContext identifier which are based on the `org.eclipse.jface.contexts.IContextIds` class. JFace distinguishes between shortcuts for dialogs, windows or both.

The following gives an overview of the supported ID and the validity of keybindings defined with reference to this Context ID.

Table 25.1. Default BindingContext values

Context ID	Description
org.eclipse.ui.contexts.dialogAndWindow	Key bindings valid for Dialogs and Windows
org.eclipse.ui.contexts.dialog	Key bindings valid in Dialogs
org.eclipse.ui.contexts.window	Key bindings valid for Windows

As an example, **Ctrl+C** (Copy) would be defined in *dialogAndWindows* as it is valid everywhere, but **F5** (Refresh) might only be defined in windows.

25.3. Define Shortcuts

The *BindingTable* node in the application model allows you to define shortcuts for a specific *BindingContext*.

To define a shortcut you create a new node for *BindingTable* and define a reference for the Context ID.

In your keybinding you define the key *Sequence* and the command associated with this shortcut.

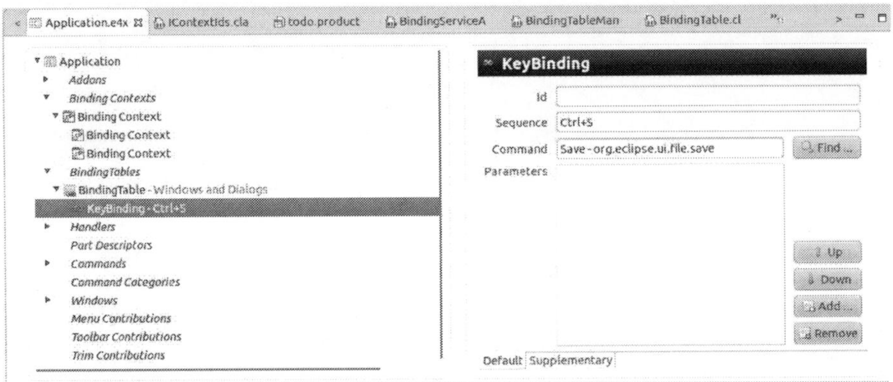

The control keys are different for the different platforms, e.g. on the Mac vs. a Linux system. For example you can use Ctrl but this would be hardcoded. It is better to use the M1 - M4 metakeys .

Table 25.2. Key Mapping

Control Key	Mapping for Windows and Linux	Mapping for Mac
M1	Ctrl	Command
M2	Shift	Shift
M3	Alt	Alt
M4	Undefined	Ctrl

These values are defined in the `SWTKeyLookup` class

25.4. Key Bindings for a Part

You can assign a specific *BindingContext* to be active while a Part is active.

25.5. Activating Bindings

If there are several valid key bindings defined the `ContextSet` class is responsible for selecting the default one. `ContextSet` uses the `BindingContext` hierarchy to determine the lookup order. A `BindingContext` is more specific depending on how many ancestors are between it and a root `BindingContext` (the number of levels it has). The most specific `BindingContext` are considered first, the root `BindingContext` are considered last.

You can also use the `EContextService` service which allows you to explicitly activate and deactivate a `BindingContext` via the `activateContext()` and `deactivateContext()` methods.

25.6. Issues with Keybinding

The keybinding implementation requires that all *Parts* correctly implement `@Focus`. Eclipse requires that one control get the focus assigned.

26. Exercise: Define key bindings

Add the JFace default *BindingContent* IDs to your application model. First define `org.eclipse.ui.contexts.dialogAndWindow`. Afterwards add `org.eclipse.ui.contexts.dialog` and `org.eclipse.ui.contexts.window` as subcontexts to it.

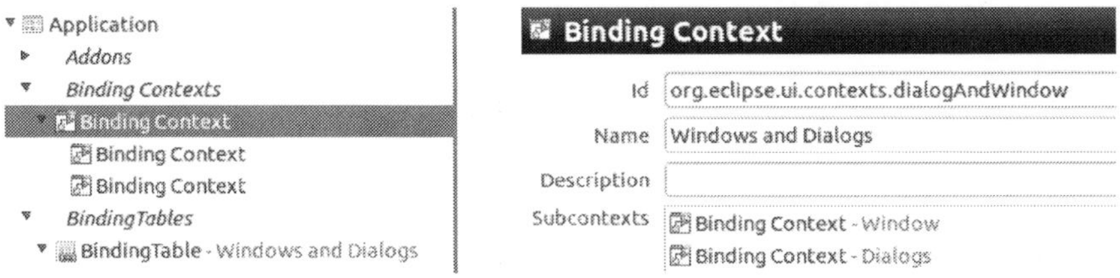

Create a keybinding for your Save command to the **M1+S** shortcut. Also a keybinding for your Exit command to **M1+X** shortcut.

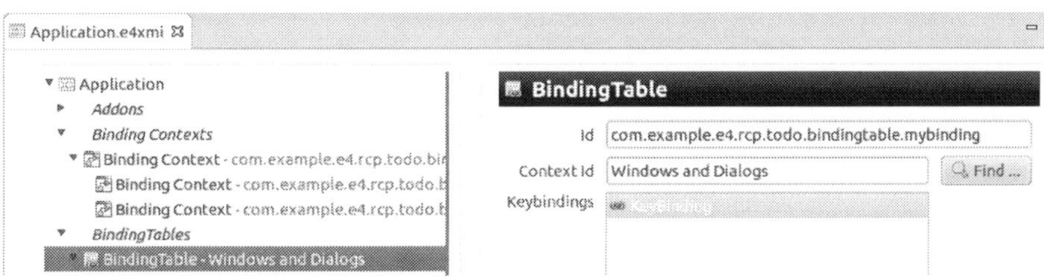

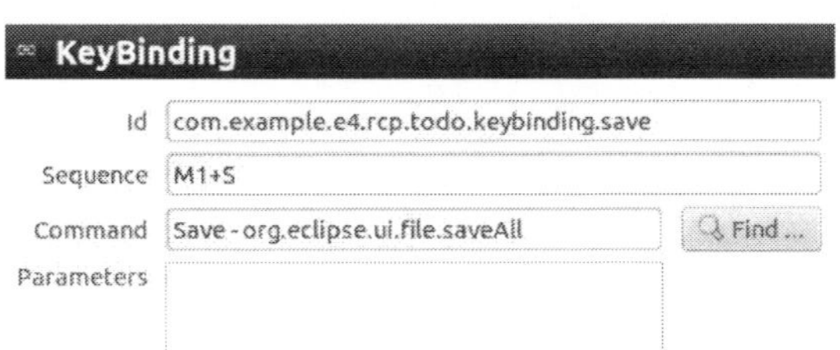

Run your program and test it.

27. Exercise: Integrating the live model editor

Integrate the live model editor and its dependencies into your Run Configuration for your product. The live editor is included in the `org.eclipse.e4.tools.emf.liveeditor` plug-in.

To integrate the live editor temporary into your application, add the plug-in and its dependencies to the *Run configuration* of your product. Afterwards press the *Run* button.

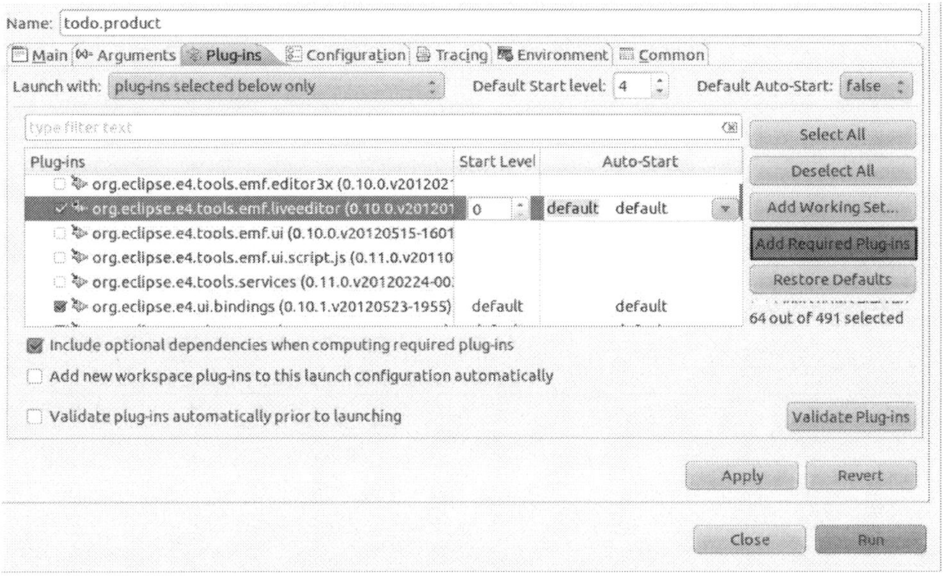

Start your application and use the **Shift+Alt+F9** shortcut to open the live editor for your application model.

Please note that the integration of the live editor into an Eclipse 4.2 application sometimes shows not issues which have been hard to reproduce. Therefore this exercise might not work for you.

Part IV. Eclipse Core Technologies

Table of Contents

28. Standard Widget Toolkit

28.1. Overview

The Standard Widget Toolkit (*SWT*) is the user interface library used by Eclipse. It provides widgets, e.g. buttons and text fields, as well as layout managers. Layout managers are used to arrange the widgets according to a certain rule set.

SWT supports several platforms, e.g. Windows, Linux and Mac OS X. The design target of *SWT* is to stay closely to the operating system (OS); therefore the *SWT* API (Application Programming Interface) is very close to the native API of the OS.

As the *SWT* API is very rudimentary, programmers typically also use *JFace*.

SWT uses the native widgets of the platform whenever possible. The native widgets of the OS are accessed by the *SWT* framework via the Java Native Interface framework. The Java Native Interface (JNI) is a programming framework that enables Java code running in a Java Virtual Machine (JVM) to call, and to be called by, native applications and libraries written in other languages such as C, C++ and assembler.

The approach of using native widgets can also be found in `AWT`, a standard user interface library available in Java. In comparison *SWT* provides more widgets than `AWT`, as `AWT` does not provide widgets if they are not natively available on all platforms. In case a widget is not available on one platform but on other, SWT will emulate this widget on the first and uses the native widget on the latter. For example `AWT` does not have table or tree widgets included, while *SWT* has.

28.2. Relationship to JFace

JFace is a set of APIs which builds on top of *SWT* and provides higher level abstraction APIs and commonly used functions. *JFace* does not hide the *SWT* API but extends it. Therefore it is important to have a solid understanding of *SWT*, even if JFace is used.

28.3. Display and Shell

The `Display` and `Shell` classes are key components of *SWT* applications.

A `org.eclipse.swt.widgets.Shell` class represents a window.

The `org.eclipse.swt.widgets.Display` class is responsible for managing event loops, for controlling the communication between the UI thread and other threads and for managing fonts and colors. `Display` is the basis for all *SWT* capabilities.

Every *SWT* application requires at least one `Display` and one or more `Shell` instances. The main `Shell` gets, as a default parameter, a `Display` as a constructor argument. Each `Shell` should be constructed with a `Display` as an input parameter.

28.4. Event loop

An event loop is needed to communicate user input events from the underlying native operating system widgets to the SWT event system.

SWT does not provide its own event loop. This means that the programmer has to explicitly start and check the event loop to update the user interface. The loop will execute the `readAndDispatch()` method which reads events from the native widgets and dispatches them to SWT event system. The loop is executed until the main shell is closed. If this loop is left out, the application would terminate immediately.

For example the following creates an *SWT* application and creates and executes the event loop.

```
Display display = new Display();
Shell shell = new Shell(display);
shell.open();
// Create and check the event loop
while (!shell.isDisposed()) {
 if (!display.readAndDispatch())
  display.sleep();
}
display.dispose();
```

If *SWT* is used in an Eclipse Plug-in or an Eclipse RCP application, this event loop is provided by the Eclipse framework.

28.5. Using SWT

It is possible to use *SWT* for standalone applications.

Eclipse applications typically use *SWT* for the user interface. But it is possible to use other user interface toolkits, e.g. JavaFX, as Eclipse 4 provides a flexible

Rendering Framework which allows you to specify the classes responsible for rendering.

If you develop Eclipse Plug-ins which extend the Eclipse IDE itself you have to use *SWT* as the Eclipse IDE Workbench uses an *SWT* renderer.

To use *SWT* you need to have the *SWT* library available. There are several ways of doing this. You can either download the *SWT* library or create an Eclipse plug-in project and define a dependency in this project.

28.6. Using SWT in a plug-in project

The Eclipse IDE ships with the *SWT* library and you can use this library in your project. The SWT library is packaged as an Eclipse component, i.e. plug-in.

Eclipse provides plug-in projects, which allows you to define dependencies to other plug-ins. Eclipse uses itself (or more specifically the Target Platform defined in the Eclipse Preference) to make the plug-ins available to your project based on your dependency definition. Eclipse automatically adds the corresponding `jar` file to your project class path.

This is a simple way of developing your *SWT* stand-alone application. If you export this application you need to add the *SWT* library to your export.

Dependencies for plug-ins are defined in the `MANIFEST.MF` file which is located in the `META-INF` folder. Eclipse provides a default editor for this file. You can add dependencies on the *Dependencies* tab of this editor.

Create an Eclipse plug-in and define a dependency to `org.eclipse.swt` in the `MANIFEST.MF` file.

```
Manifest-Version: 1.0
Bundle-ManifestVersion: 2
Bundle-Name: My SWT-based Plug-in
Bundle-SymbolicName: de.vogella.swt
Bundle-Version: 1.0.0.qualifier
Require-Bundle: org.eclipse.swt
Bundle-RequiredExecutionEnvironment: JavaSE-1.6
```

28.7. Manually adding the SWT library

If you do not want to use Eclipse plug-in capabilities you can download the SWT library from http://www.eclipse.org/swt/ [http://www.eclipse.org/swt/]. This zip file contains a `swt.jar` file which you need to add to the *classpath* of your SWT project.

28.8. SWT Widgets

28.8.1. Overview

SWT widgets are located in the packages `org.eclipse.swt.widgets` and `org.eclipse.swt.custom`. Widgets extend either the `Widget` or the `Control` class.

While *SWT* tries to use native widgets as much as possible it is not possible to fulfill all common requirements with the native widgets. Therefore some widgets extend the capabilities of the native platform. These are part of the `org.eclipse.swt.custom` package and usually start with the additional prefix `C` to indicate that they are custom widgets, e.g. `CCombo`.

Compared to the `Combo` class, the `CCombo` class provides the ability to set the height of the widget.

Another example is `StyledText`, a class which provides advanced features for displaying text, e.g. like drawing a background.

Widgets from the package `org.eclipse.swt.custom` are implemented in pure Java while widgets from `org.eclipse.swt.widgets` use native code. Custom widgets are not supposed to use the internal classes of *SWT* as these classes may be different on different platforms. Every custom widget must extend the `Composite` or `Canvas` class. API compliance is guaranteed only for these base classes.

If the new custom widget is supposed to contain other widgets, it should extend `Composite`. Otherwise it should extend the `Canvas` class.

28.8.2. Memory management

SWT widgets are not automatically garbage collected. If you release an *SWT* widget, you have to call its `dispose()` method. Fortunately a container, e.g. a `Shell` will call the `dispose()` method for all its children.

The automatic release does not work for `Fonts`, `Images` and `Color` objects. These SWT objects need to be manually disposed.

28.8.3. Constructing widgets

SWT widgets, except `Shell`, are always constructed with a parent widget which contains them. This is similar to AWT and different to Swing, where the `add()` method is used.

In the constructor of the widget *stylebits* are passed to the widget as a second parameter. Depending on the provided stylebits the widget adjusts its look and feel as well as its behavior. Each widget documents its supported stylebits in its Javadoc.

The possible stylebits are predefined in the *SWT* class. If no special style is required you can pass `SWT.NONE`.

For example the following creates a push button.

```
new Button(shell, SWT.PUSH);
```

And the following creates a checkbox button.

```
new Button(shell, SWT.CHECK);
```

28.8.4. Basic Containers

The `Composite` class is a container which is allowed to contain other widgets. The `Group` class is also a container which is allowed to contain other widget but it also draws a border around itself and allows you to set a header for the box.

28.9. Event Listener

On controls you can register listeners for specific events, e.g. a `ModifyListener` to listen to changes in a Text field or a `SelectionLister` for selection (click) events.

```
// Define PUSH Button
// For a checkbox button use SWT.CHECK stylebit

Button button =  new Button(shell, SWT.PUSH);
button.addSelectionListener(new SelectionAdapter() {
 @Override
 public void widgetSelected(SelectionEvent e) {
  // Handle the selection event
  System.out.println("Called!");
```

```
    }
  });
```

What kind of event listeners are available depends on the user interface component. `ModifyListener`, `FocusListener` and `SelectionListener` are examples for these listener interfaces.

Eclipse usually provides default implementations for these interfaces. They follow the naming convention: *`Name`* `Listener` → *`Name`* `Adapter` .

For example `SelectionListener` has the abstract class `SelectionAdapter` which pre-implements the methods of `SelectionListener`. This allows you to use `SelectionAdapter` as base for an anonymous class where only one of the two declared methods are needed.

If you want to add a listener to the whole application you can use the `Display` class. For example to add a global mouse listener use `addFilter(SWT.MouseMove, listener)`.

28.10. SWT Snippets, Examples and Nebula

The *SWT Snippets* give examples for stand-alone *SWT* applications using different kinds of SWT widgets. The SWT Snippet site is located at the following URL: http://www.eclipse.org/swt/snippets/.

You can copy these snippets and paste them directly into Eclipse on a Java package. Eclipse will automatically create the Java class for you.

If you do this on a project which has *SWT* already available, the snippet can be started immediately.

The *SWT Examples* page provides useful programs that are written in SWT. These are typically much larger and more comprehensive than SWT Snippets.The *SWT Examples* are located at the following URL: http://www.eclipse.org/swt/examples.php

In addition the Eclipse Nebula project provides additional widgets for SWT. The homepage can be found at the URL: http://eclipse.org/nebula/

Another source for SWT widgets is the Opal widget homepage: http://code.google.com/a/eclipselabs.org/p/opal/

29. SWT widget examples

The following lists a few SWT widget examples. These examples are included in this book to serve as reference material which can be quickly found if needed.

29.1. Example: Create SWT project

Create a new plug-in project `com.examle.swt.widgets` via File → New → Other → Plug-in Development → New Plug-in Project.

Enter the data in the wizard similar to the screenshot below. Make sure you de-select the *This plug-in will make contributions to the UI* and *Generate an activator, a Java class that controls the plug-in's life cycle* checkboxes.

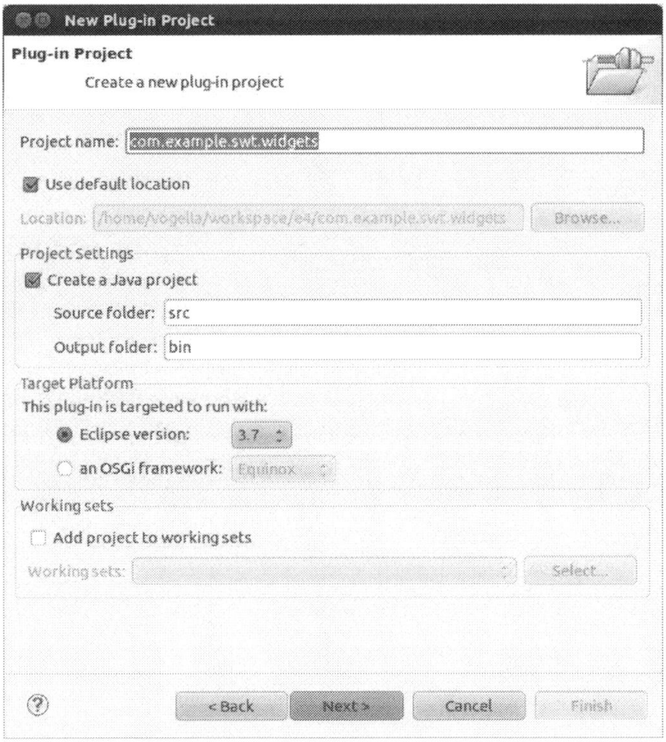

Press the *Finish* button on the second page of the wizard.

Open the `MANIFEST.MF` file in the `META-INF` folder and select the *Dependencies* tab.

Press the *Add* button in the *Required Plug-ins* part and enter `org.eclipse.swt` as dependency.

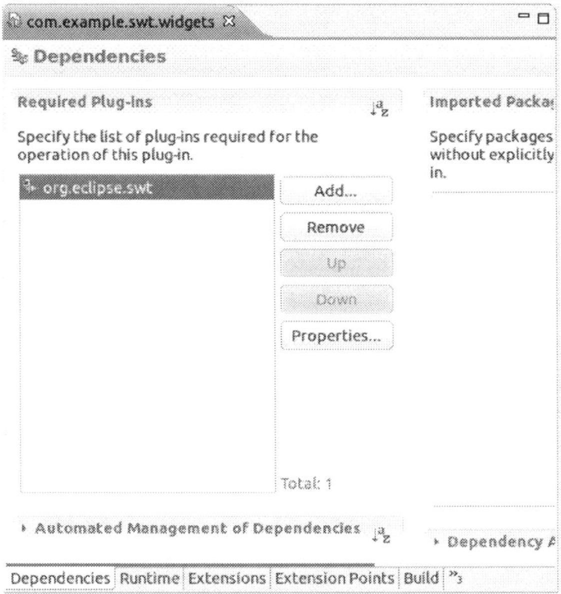

Create the following class for a simple *SWT* application.

```
package com.example.swt.widgets;

import org.eclipse.swt.widgets.Display;
import org.eclipse.swt.widgets.Shell;

public class FirstSWTApplication {

 public static void main(String[] args) {
  Display display = new Display();

  Shell shell = new Shell(display);
  //TODO Add contents of the Shell
  shell.open();
  while (!shell.isDisposed()) {
   if (!display.readAndDispatch())
    display.sleep();
  }
  display.dispose();
 }
}
```

To start your application, right click on your Java class, and select Run-As → Java Application. You will receive an empty window (`Shell`).

Change the TODO in the code to the following. Make sure you use `org.eclipse.swt` and not `java.awt` when adding the missing imports.

```
// Shell can be used as container
Label label = new Label(shell, SWT.BORDER);
label.setText("This is a label:");
label.setToolTipText("This is the tooltip of this label");
Text text = new Text(shell, SWT.NONE);
text.setText("This is the text in the label");
text.setBackground(display.getSystemColor(SWT.COLOR_BLACK));
text.setForeground(display.getSystemColor(SWT.COLOR_WHITE));

// If you do not use a layout manager
// set widgets size to their preferred size
text.pack();
label.pack();
```

If you now start the application you will get a `Shell` with two `Widgets` included.

29.2. DateTime widget

SWT provides `DateTime` widgets. Create the following class.

```
package de.vogella.swt.widgets;

import org.eclipse.swt.SWT;
import org.eclipse.swt.layout.GridLayout;
import org.eclipse.swt.layout.RowLayout;
import org.eclipse.swt.widgets.Composite;
import org.eclipse.swt.widgets.DateTime;
import org.eclipse.swt.widgets.Display;
import org.eclipse.swt.widgets.Shell;

public class DateTimeExample {

 public static void main(String[] args) {

   // setup the SWT window
   Display display = new Display();
   final Shell shell = new Shell(display);
   shell.setSize(520, 200);
   shell.setLayout(new RowLayout());

   // initialize a parent composite with a grid layout manager
```

```
    Composite parent = new Composite(shell, SWT.NONE);
    GridLayout gridLayout = new GridLayout();
    gridLayout.numColumns = 1;
    parent.setLayout(gridLayout);
    DateTime calender = new DateTime(parent, SWT.CALENDAR);
    DateTime date = new DateTime(parent, SWT.DATE);
    DateTime time = new DateTime(parent, SWT.TIME);
    // Date Selection as a drop-down
    DateTime dateD = new DateTime(parent, SWT.DATE | SWT.DROP_DOWN);
    // show the SWT window
    shell.open();
    while (!shell.isDisposed()) {
      if (!display.readAndDispatch())
        display.sleep();
    }
    // tear down the SWT window
    display.dispose();
  }
}
```

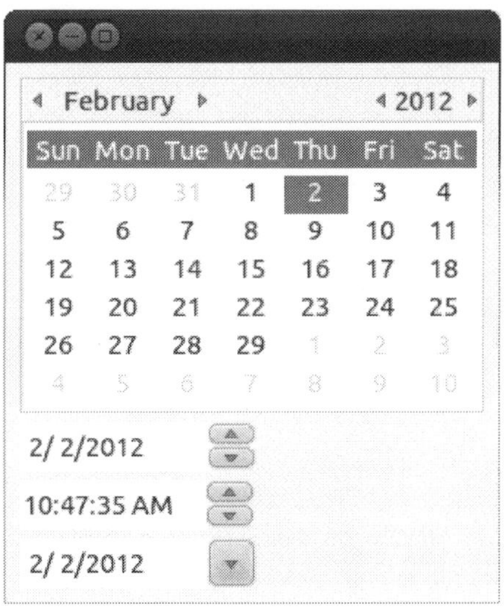

Please note that the SWT `DateTime` widget requires a selection, i.e. you cannot use this widget without a date selection.

29.3. Image

Images can be displayed via labels. The following class demonstrates that using some system images.

```
package de.vogella.swt.widgets;
```

```
import java.util.ArrayList;
import java.util.List;

import org.eclipse.swt.SWT;
import org.eclipse.swt.graphics.Image;
import org.eclipse.swt.layout.GridLayout;
import org.eclipse.swt.layout.RowLayout;
import org.eclipse.swt.widgets.Composite;
import org.eclipse.swt.widgets.Display;
import org.eclipse.swt.widgets.Label;
import org.eclipse.swt.widgets.Shell;

public class Photo {

 public static void main(String[] args) {

  // setup the SWT window
  Display display = new Display();
  final Shell shell = new Shell(display);
  shell.setLayout(new RowLayout());
  shell.setText("Photo Application");

  // initialize a parent composite with a grid layout manager
  // since the demo application uses 4x pictures the grid has exactly
  // 4x columns
  Composite parent = new Composite(shell, SWT.NONE);
  GridLayout gridLayout = new GridLayout();
  gridLayout.numColumns = 7;
  parent.setLayout(gridLayout);

  // Get the Display default icons
  List<Image> imageList = new ArrayList<Image>();

  imageList.
   add(Display.getDefault().getSystemImage(SWT.ICON_CANCEL));
  imageList.
   add(Display.getDefault().getSystemImage(SWT.ICON_WARNING));
  imageList.
   add(Display.getDefault().getSystemImage(SWT.ICON_WORKING));
  imageList.
   add(Display.getDefault().getSystemImage(SWT.ICON_QUESTION));
  imageList.
   add(Display.getDefault().getSystemImage(SWT.ICON_SEARCH));
  imageList
    .add(Display.getDefault().getSystemImage(SWT.ICON_INFORMATION));
  imageList.
   add(Display.getDefault().getSystemImage(SWT.ICON_ERROR));

  for (Image image : imageList) {
   Label label = new Label(parent, SWT.NONE);
   label.setImage(image);
  }
  // show the SWT window
```

```
    shell.pack();
    shell.open();

    while (!shell.isDisposed()) {
     if (!display.readAndDispatch())
      display.sleep();
    }
    // tear down the SWT window
    display.dispose();
    // if you do not use system images you would have to release them
    // not necessary in this example
    // for (Image image : imageList) {
    // if (image != null) {
    //  image.dispose();
    // }
    // }
  }
}
```

The result should look similar to the following.

29.4. CTabFolder

CTabFolder and CTabItem allow to create the folder experience with different tabs.

```
package de.vogella.swt.widgets;

import org.eclipse.swt.SWT;
import org.eclipse.swt.custom.CTabFolder;
import org.eclipse.swt.custom.CTabItem;
import org.eclipse.swt.layout.GridData;
import org.eclipse.swt.layout.GridLayout;
import org.eclipse.swt.widgets.Display;
import org.eclipse.swt.widgets.Shell;
import org.eclipse.swt.widgets.Text;

public class CTabFolderExample {
 public static void main(String[] args) {
  Display display = new Display();
  Shell shell = new Shell(display);
```

```
    shell.setLayout(new GridLayout());
    // SWT.BOTTOM to show at the bottom
    CTabFolder folder = new CTabFolder(shell, SWT.BOTTOM);
    GridData data = new GridData(GridData.FILL,
      GridData.FILL, true, true,
      2, 1);
    folder.setLayoutData(data);
    CTabItem cTabItem1 = new CTabItem(folder, SWT.NONE);
    cTabItem1.setText("Tab1");
    CTabItem cTabItem2 = new CTabItem(folder, SWT.NONE);
    cTabItem2.setText("Tab2");
    CTabItem cTabItem3 = new CTabItem(folder, SWT.NONE);
    cTabItem3.setText("Tab3");

    Text text = new Text(folder, SWT.BORDER);
    text.setText("Hello");
    cTabItem1.setControl(text);

    shell.pack();
    shell.open();
    while (!display.isDisposed()) {
     if (!display.readAndDispatch()) {
      display.sleep();
     }
    }
  }
}
```

If you run this application you will see several register cards with tabs on them. The `SWT.BOTTOM` stylebit on the folder widget, makes the tab appear at the bottom.

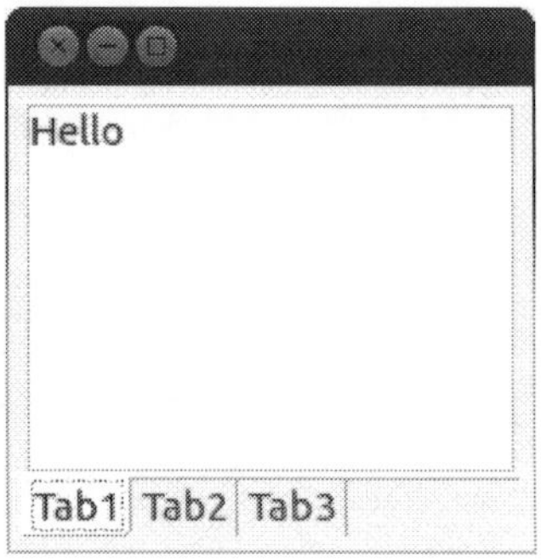

30. SWT layouts

30.1. Overview

A layout manager is responsible for arranging the UI components of a container (`Composite`) on the screen. *SWT* offers several standard layout managers.

Table 30.1. Layout Manager

Layout Manager	Description
AbsoluteLayout	Allows you to define the exact position and width and height of components. As user interfaces may be used on screens with different sizes this layout manager should be avoided.
FillLayout	Layout equal-sized widgets in a single row or column.
RowLayout	Layout widgets in a row or rows, with fill, wrap, and spacing options.
GridLayout	Layouts widgets in a grid.
FormLayout	Layouts widgets by creating attachments for each of the sides of its container.

30.2. Layout Data

Each *SWT* widget can get layout specific settings assigned to it via a specific class, e.g. `GridData` for a `GridLayout`.

For example you can specify that a certain widget should take two columns in a `GridLayout` via the following coding.

```
button = new Button(parent, SWT.NONE);
GridData gridData = new GridData();
gridData.horizontalSpan = 2;
button.setLayoutData(gridData);
```

Please note that the `LayoutData` must match that used by the layout manager, otherwise the runtime will throw an exception.

The layout will be automatically calculated when the container is displayed. You can tell a `Composite` to recalculate the layout with the `composite.layout()` method.

30.3. FillLayout

`FillLayout` divides the available space provided by the container equally to all widgets and can be set to arrange the widgets either horizontally(`SWT.HORIZONTAL`) or vertically (`SWT.VERTICAL`). It also allows you to set the space between the widgets (attribute `spacing`) and the margins of the widgets to the container via the `marginWidth` and `marginHeight` attributes.

30.4. RowLayout

`RowLayout` orders UI components in a row (`SWT.HORIZONTAL`) or in a column (`SWT.VERTICAL`). `RowLayout` supports wrapping of fields (field `wrap`) by default. You can define if widgets should have their preferred size (default) or if they should grab the available space via the field `pack`. You can also set margins at the top, bottom, left and right. If you set justify, the widgets will be spread through the available space.

Each element can define its height and width via a `RowData` element.

30.5. GridLayout

`GridLayout` allows you to arrange the user interface components in a Grid with a certain number of columns, with the option to define column and row spanning.

`GridData` objects should not be re-used as the `GridLayout` class expects that every user interface element has a unique `GridData` object.

You can use `new  GridData()` and assign properties to the new object. Alternatively you can use one of its richer constructors to define certain attributes during construction. For example via the following constructor.

```
new GridData(horizontalAlignment,
  verticalAlignment,
  grabExcessHorizontalSpace,
  grabExcessVerticalSpace,
  horizontalSpan,
  verticalSpan)
```

The most important attributes are defined as following:

Table 30.2. GridData

Parameter	Description
horizontalAlignment	how the control will be positioned horizontally within a cell, one of: `SWT.LEFT`, `SWT.CENTER`, `SWT.RIGHT`, or `SWT.FILL`
verticalAlignment	how the control will be positioned vertically within a cell, one of: `SWT.TOP`, `SWT.CENTER`, `SWT.END` (same as `SWT.BOTTOM`), or `SWT.FILL`
grabExcessHorizontalSpace	whether the cell will be made wide enough to take all the remaining horizontal space
grabExcessVerticalSpace	whether cell will grab any remaining vertical space
horizontalSpan	the number of column cells that the control will take up
verticalSpan	the number of row cells that the control will take up
heightHint	heightHint specifies the preferred height in pixels
widthHint	widthHint specifies the preferred width in pixels

If the widget has the `grabExcessHorizontalSpace` attribute set to true, it will grab available space in its container. `SWT.FILL` tells the widget to fill the available space. `grabExcessHorizontalSpace` and `SWT.FILL` are often used together.

30.6. Tab Order of elements

You can specify the tab order of controls via the `setTabList()` method of a `Composite`.

```
package de.vogella.swt.widgets;


import org.eclipse.swt.SWT;
import org.eclipse.swt.layout.RowLayout;
import org.eclipse.swt.widgets.Button;
import org.eclipse.swt.widgets.Control;
import org.eclipse.swt.widgets.Display;
import org.eclipse.swt.widgets.Shell;

public class TabExample {
 public static void main(String[] args) {
  Display display = Display.getDefault();
  Shell shell = new Shell(display);
  shell.setLayout(new RowLayout());
  Button b1 = new Button(shell, SWT.PUSH);
```

```
    b1.setText("Button1");
    Button b2 = new Button(shell, SWT.PUSH);
    b2.setText("Button2");
    Button b3 = new Button(shell, SWT.PUSH);
    b3.setText("Button3");

    Control[] controls = new Control[] { b2, b1, b3 };
    shell.setTabList(controls);
    shell.pack();
    shell.open();
    while (!display.isDisposed()) {
      if (!display.readAndDispatch()) {
        display.sleep();
      }
    }
  }
}
```

30.7. Example: Layouts in SWT

The following shows an example for the usage of the `GridLayout` class in the `com.example.swt.widgets` project.

```
package de.vogella.swt.layouts;

import org.eclipse.swt.SWT;
import org.eclipse.swt.layout.GridData;
import org.eclipse.swt.layout.GridLayout;
import org.eclipse.swt.layout.RowLayout;
import org.eclipse.swt.widgets.Button;
import org.eclipse.swt.widgets.Composite;
import org.eclipse.swt.widgets.Display;
import org.eclipse.swt.widgets.Group;
import org.eclipse.swt.widgets.Label;
import org.eclipse.swt.widgets.Shell;
import org.eclipse.swt.widgets.Spinner;
import org.eclipse.swt.widgets.Text;

public class GridLayoutSWT {
  public static void main(String[] args) {
    Display display = new Display();
    Shell shell = new Shell(display);
    // Create a new Gridlayout with 2 columns
    // where the 2 column do not have the
    // same size
    GridLayout layout = new GridLayout(2, false);
    // set the layout of the shell
    shell.setLayout(layout);
    // Create a label and a button
    Label label = new Label(shell, SWT.NONE);
    label.setText("A lable");
    Button button = new Button(shell, SWT.PUSH);
```

```
  button.setText("Press Me");

  // Create a new label that will spam two columns
  label = new Label(shell, SWT.BORDER);
  label.setText("This is a label");
  // Create new layout data
  GridData data = new GridData(GridData.FILL,
    GridData.BEGINNING, true, false, 2, 1);
  label.setLayoutData(data);

  // Create a new label which is used as a separator
  label = new Label(shell, SWT.SEPARATOR | SWT.HORIZONTAL);
  // Create new layout data
  data = new GridData(GridData.FILL, GridData.BEGINNING, true,
    false, 2, 1);
  data.horizontalSpan=2;
  label.setLayoutData(data);

  // Create a right aligned button
  Button b = new Button(shell, SWT.PUSH);
  b.setText("New Button");

  data = new GridData(GridData.END, GridData.BEGINNING, false,
    false, 2, 1);
  b.setLayoutData(data);

  Spinner spinner = new Spinner(shell, SWT.READ_ONLY);
  spinner.setMinimum(0);
  spinner.setMaximum(1000);
  spinner.setSelection(500);
  spinner.setIncrement(1);
  spinner.setPageIncrement(100);
  GridData gridData = new GridData(SWT.FILL,
    SWT.FILL, true, false);
  gridData.widthHint = SWT.DEFAULT;
  gridData.heightHint = SWT.DEFAULT;
  gridData.horizontalSpan=2;
  spinner.setLayoutData(gridData);

  Composite composite = new Composite(shell, SWT.BORDER);
  gridData = new GridData(SWT.FILL, SWT.FILL, true, false);
  gridData.horizontalSpan= 2;
  composite.setLayoutData(gridData);
  composite.setLayout(new GridLayout(1, false));


  Text text = new Text(composite, SWT.NONE);
  text.setText("Testing");
  gridData = new GridData(SWT.FILL, SWT.FILL, true, false);
  text.setLayoutData(gridData);

  text = new Text(composite, SWT.NONE);
  text.setText("Another test");
//  gridData = new GridData(SWT.FILL, SWT.FILL, true, false);
```

```
//   text.setLayoutData(gridData);
    Group group = new Group(shell, SWT.NONE);
    group.setText("This is my group");
    gridData = new GridData(SWT.FILL, SWT.FILL, true, false);
    gridData.horizontalSpan= 2;
    group.setLayoutData(gridData);
    group.setLayout(new RowLayout(SWT.VERTICAL));
    text = new Text(group, SWT.NONE);
    text.setText("Another test");


    shell.pack();
    shell.open();
    while (!shell.isDisposed()) {
     if (!display.readAndDispatch())
      display.sleep();
    }
    display.dispose();
   }

}
```

If you start your application, it should look like the following screenshot.

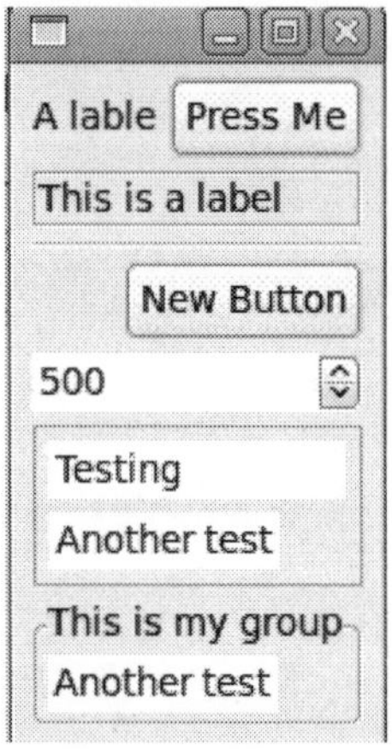

Resize the window and see how the arrangement of the widgets change.

31. SWT Designer (WindowBuilder)

SWT Designer is a visual editor used to create graphical user interfaces. It is a two way parser, e.g. you can edit the source code or use a graphical editor to modify the user interface and SWT Designer will synchronize between both representations.

SWT Designer is part of the WindowBuilder project. WindowBuilder provides the foundation and *SWT Designer* adds the support for working with Eclipse based applications.

SWT Designer supports Eclipse 4 application in the WindowBuilder 1.5 release which is part of the Eclipse Juno release (Eclipse 4.2).

You can install *SWT Designer* via the Eclipse Update Manager from the Eclipse Juno Update site.

After installation you can open your *Parts* in this editor and work on your user interface. *SWT Designer* allows to drag-and-drop *SWT* components into an existing layout, change layout settings and create Event Handlers for your widgets.

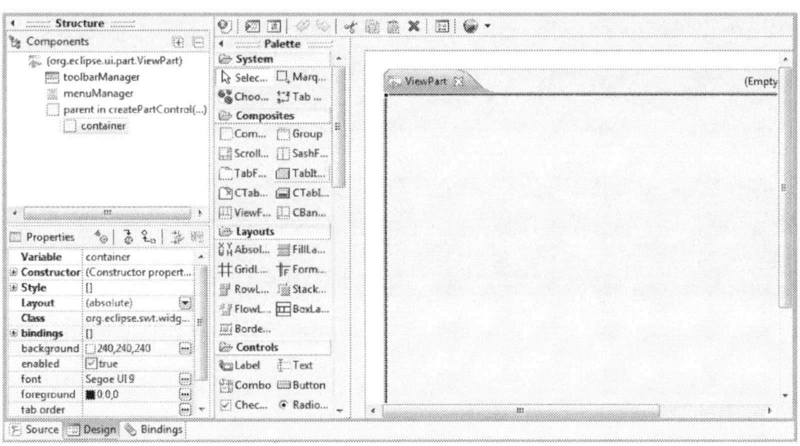

You can also use the *SWT* and *JFace* templates which *SWT Designer* contributes to the Eclipse IDE. For example you can use it to create `Composites` and add these to the Eclipse user interface. To create a new `Composite` select File → New → Other → WindowBuilder → SWT Designer → SWT → Composite.

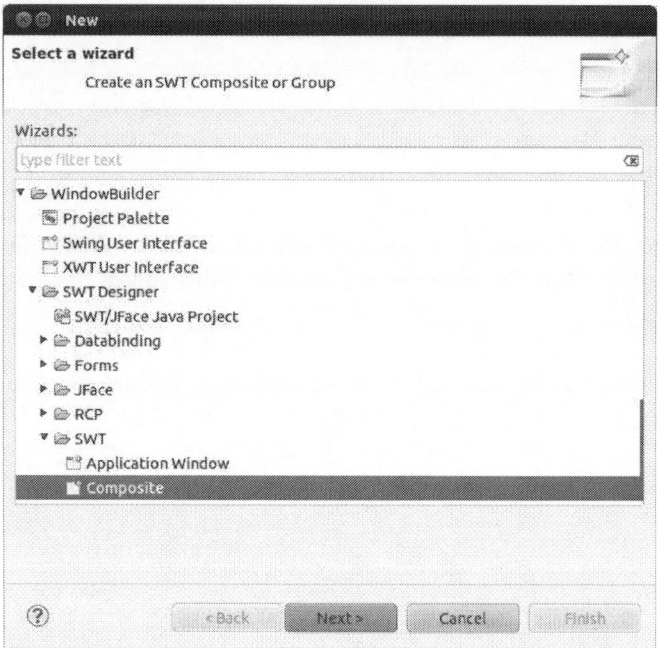

SWT Designer has excellent support for creating databinding between your data model and your user interface components via the *JFace Databinding* framework.

32. Exercise: Getting started with SWT Designer

32.1. Exercise: Install SWT Designer

If you downloaded the *Eclipse for RCP and RAP Developers* package from Eclipse.org than *SWT Designer* is already included. Otherwise use the Eclipse Juno update site to install it.

A word of warning, currently the SWT Designer support for Eclipse 4 is very new, hence it might be that you experience problems using it for Eclipse 4 *Parts* or other components.

You can always switch back to the standard Java editor to work on your code manually.

32.2. Exercise: Using SWT Designer

Right-click on your `PlaygroundPart` class and select Open With → WindowBuilder Editor.

Switch to the *Design* tab in the *Editor*.

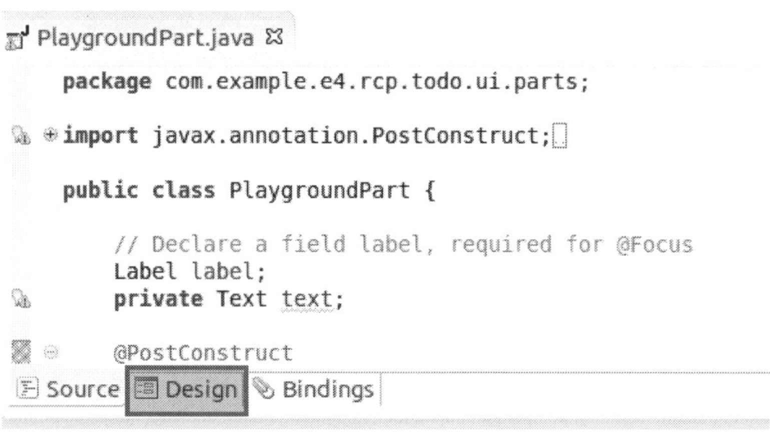

Use SWT Designer to change the layout of the `Composite` of the *Part* to a `GridLayout`.

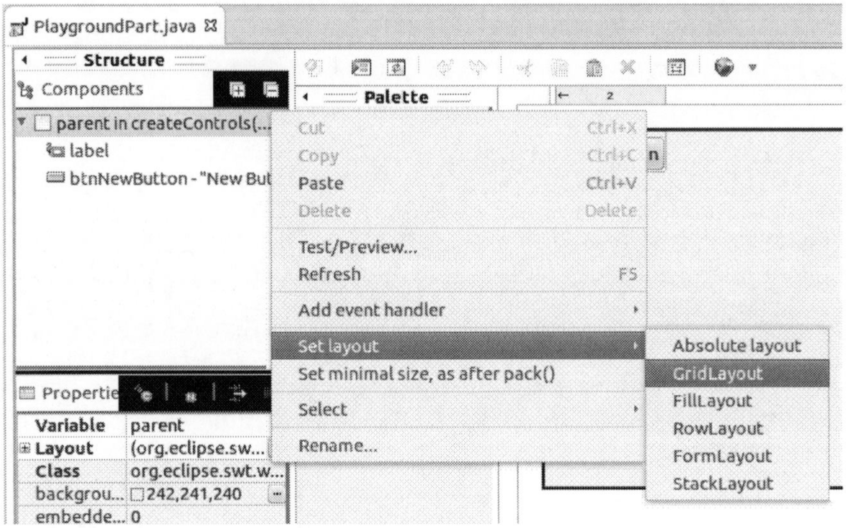

Click in the Palette on *Button* and add a few `Buttons` to your user interface.

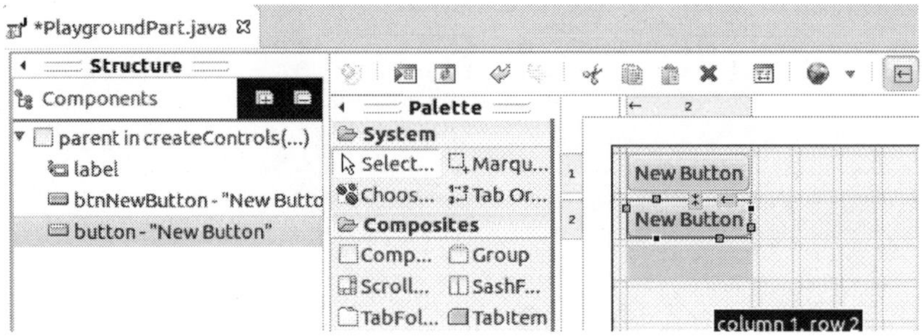

Add a `Label` and a `Text` field.

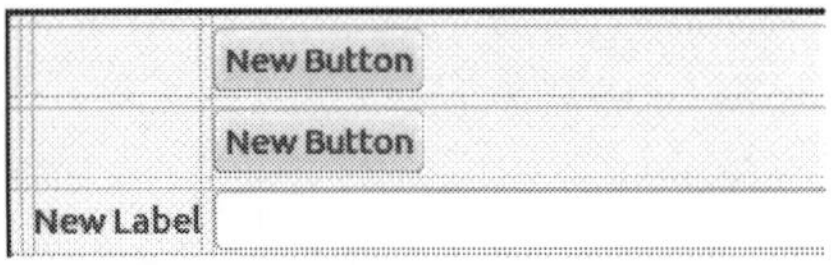

Assign an `EventHandler` to one of your `Buttons`.

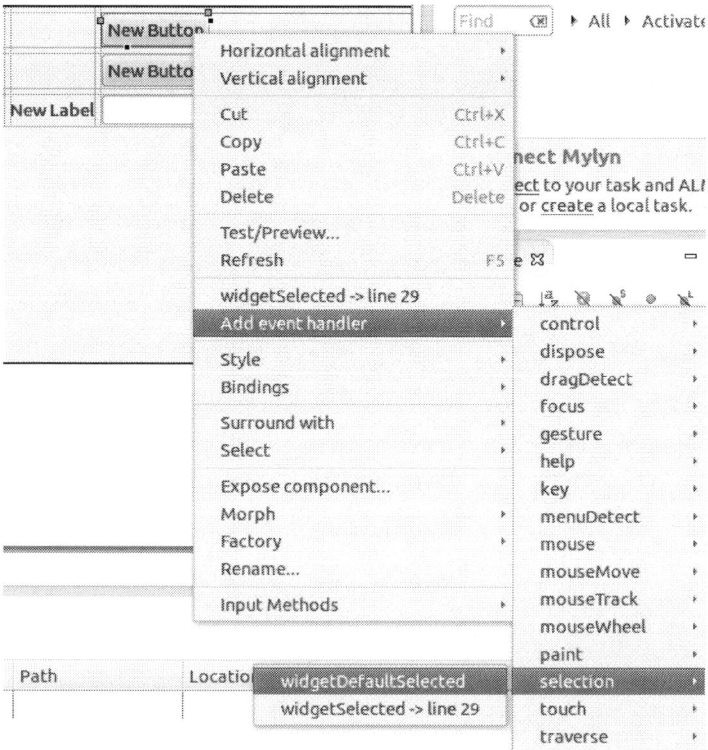

Switch to the *Source* tab and review the changes *SWT Designer* did.

33. Exercise: Build a SWT user interface

The following user interfaces can either be developed manually or via *SWT Designer*.

33.1. TodoOverviewPart

Add a `Button` to your `TodoOverviewPart` class. Add a `Label` beside it with the default text set to: "Data not available."

Add a `SelectionListener` to the `Button`. If the `Button` is pressed the text of the `Label` should change to: "Number of Todo items: 7".

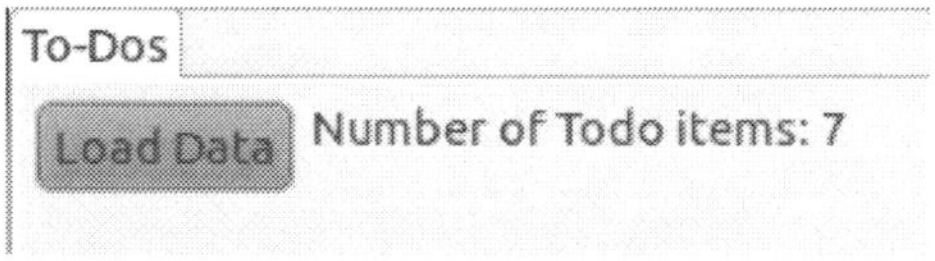

33.2. TodoDetailsPart

Change `TodoDetailsPart` so that you create a user interface similar to the following.

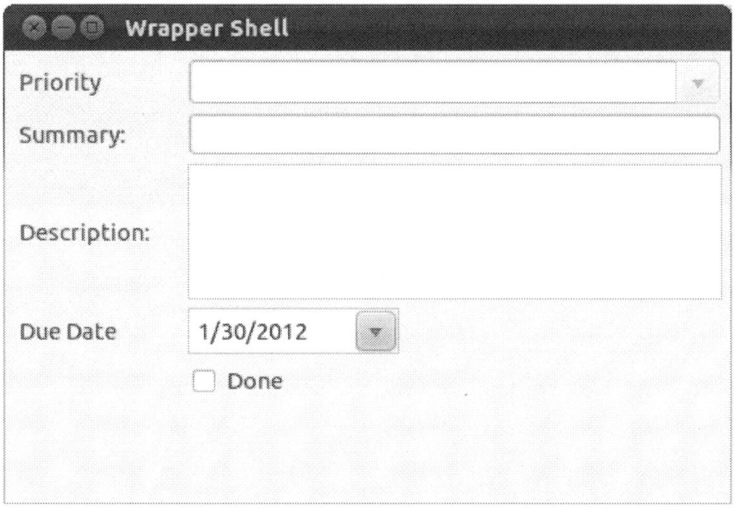

33.3. Implement @Focus

Ensure that your @Focus method sets the focus to one of the *SWT* widgets. This is required by the Eclipse 4 workbench otherwise certain services will not work correctly.

34. Modularity with OSGi

In this chapter we evaluate how other plug-ins can contribute to the Eclipse 4 application model.

34.1. OSGi Overview

34.1.1. What is OSGi

OSGi is a specification. The core of the OSGi specification defines a component and service model for Java. The components and services can be dynamically activated, de-activated, updated and de-installed.

A very practical advantage of OSGi is that every bundle must define its exported Java packages and its required dependencies. This way you can effectively control the provided API and the dependencies of your plug-ins.

34.1.2. Implementations

OSGi has several implementations, for example Equinox, Knopflerfish OSGi or Apache Felix.

34.2. OSGi Bundles and Dependencies

34.2.1. OSGi bundles

The OSGi specification defines the OSGi bundle as the unit of modularization.

A bundle is a cohesive, self-contained unit, which explicitly defines its dependencies to other modules and services. It also explicitly defines its external API.

Technically OSGi bundles are `.jar` files with additional meta information. This meta information is stored in the `META-INF` folder in the `MANIFEST.MF` file.

The `MANIFEST.MF` file is part of a standard jar specification to which OSGi adds additional metadata. Any non-OSGi runtime will ignore the OSGi metadata. Therefore OSGi bundles can be used without restrictions in non-OSGi Java environments.

34.2.2. Bundle-SymbolicName and Version

Each bundle has a symbolic name which is defined via the `Bundle-SymbolicName` property. The name starts by convention with the reverse domain name of the author of the bundle, e.g. if you owned the domain example.com the name of your symbolic name would start with "com.example".

Each bundle has also a version number in the `Bundle-Version` property.

The `Bundle-Version` and the `Bundle-SymbolicName` uniquely identifies a bundle in OSGi.

Both properties are defined in the `MANIFEST.MF` file.

34.2.3. MANIFEST.MF

The following is an example of a `MANIFEST.MF` file.

```
Manifest-Version: 1.0
Bundle-ManifestVersion: 2
Bundle-Name: Popup Plug-in
Bundle-SymbolicName: com.example.myosgi; singleton:=true
Bundle-Version: 1.0.0
Bundle-Activator: com.example.myosgi.Activator
Require-Bundle: org.eclipse.ui,
 org.eclipse.core.runtime
Bundle-ActivationPolicy: lazy
Bundle-RequiredExecutionEnvironment: JavaSE-1.6
```

The following table gives an explanation of the identifiers.

Table 34.1. OSGi Manifest Identifier

Identifier	Description
Bundle-Name	Short descriptive text of the bundle.
Bundle-SymbolicName	The unique identifier for this bundle.
Bundle-Version	Defines the bundle version and must be incremented if a new version of the bundle is published.
Bundle-Activator	Optional, defines an Activator. This class will be notified whenever the bundle is started or stopped.
Bundle-RequiredExecutionEnvironment	Specify which Java version is required to run the bundle. If this requirement is not fulfilled then the OSGi runtime does not load the bundle.

Identifier	Description
Bundle-ActivationPolicy	Setting this to `lazy` will tell the OSGi runtime that this plug-in should only be activated if one of its components, i.e. classes and interfaces are used by other bundles. If not set, the OSGi runtime will activate this bundle by default.

34.2.4. Bundle dependencies and public API

Via the `MANIFEST.MF` file a bundle can define its dependency to other bundles or packages. OSGi will throw a `ClassNotFoundException`, if a class from a bundle tries to access a class without a defined dependency to it.

In the `MANIFEST.MF` file a bundle also defines its API, i.e. via the exported packages. All packages which are not explicitly exported are not visible to other bundles.

All these restrictions are enforced via a specific OSGi `classloader`. Each bundle has its own classloader. Access to restricted classes is not possible, also not via reflection.

A bundle can define that it depends on a certain version (or a range) of another bundle, e.g. bundle A can define that it depends on bundle C in version 2.0, while bundle B defines that it depends on version 1.0 of bundle C.

34.2.5. Provisional API and Friends

Equinox supports that an exported package is declared as provisional via the `x-internal` flag. The following screenshot shows how to set a package as `x-internal` in the `MANIFEST.MF` editor.

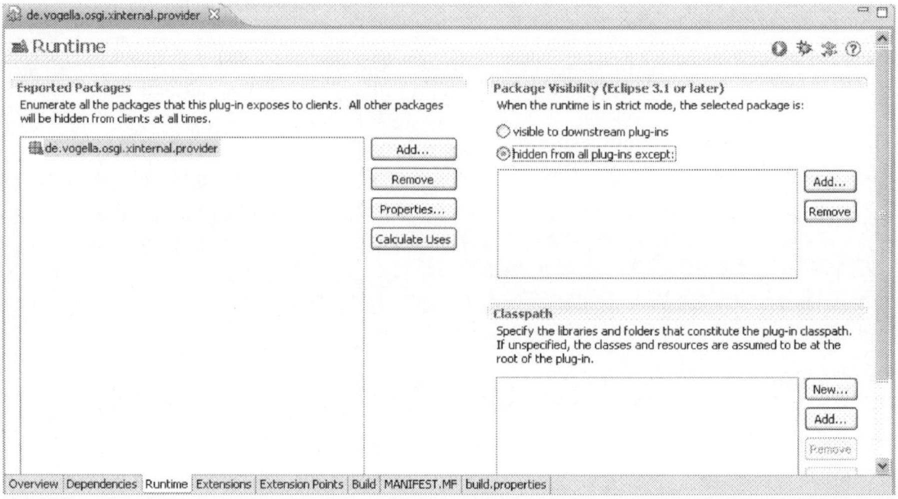

This results in the following MANIFEST.MF file.

```
Manifest-Version: 1.0
Bundle-ManifestVersion: 2
Bundle-Name: Example
Bundle-SymbolicName: osgi.example
Bundle-Version: 1.0.0.qualifier
Bundle-Activator: osgi.example.Activator
Bundle-ActivationPolicy: lazy
Bundle-RequiredExecutionEnvironment: JavaSE-1.6
Import-Package: org.osgi.framework;version="1.3.0"
Export-Package: osgi.example;x-internal:=true
```

Eclipse will show the usage of this API as an error, warning or ignore this, depending on the setting in Window → Preferences → Java → Compiler → Error.

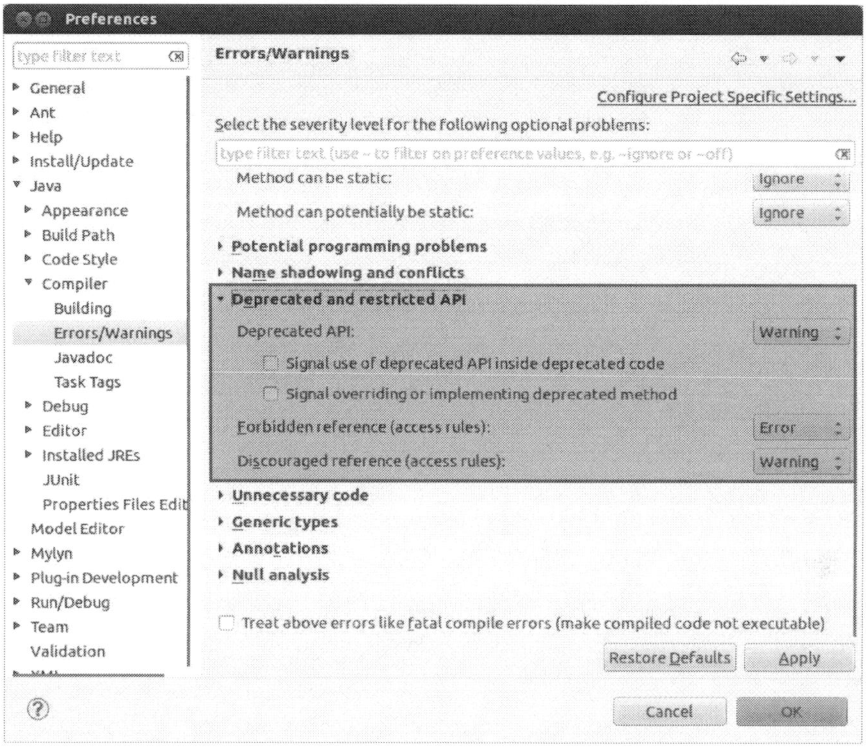

You can also release a package only for a specific plug-in via the `x-friends` directive. This flag is added if you add a plug-in to the *Package Visibility* section on the *Runtime* tab of the `MANIFEST.MF` editor.

```
Manifest-Version: 1.0
Bundle-ManifestVersion: 2
Bundle-Name: Provider
Bundle-SymbolicName: de.vogella.osgi.xinternal.provider
Bundle-Version: 1.0.0.qualifier
Bundle-RequiredExecutionEnvironment: JavaSE-1.6
Export-Package: de.vogella.osgi.xinternal.provider;x-friends:="bundle"
```

34.2.6. OSGi dependency management

OSGi is responsible for the dependency management between the bundles.

OSGi reads the MANIFEST.MF of a bundle during its installation. It ensures that all dependent bundles are also loaded, if the bundle is activated.

If the dependencies are not met, then the bundle is not loaded.

34.2.7. Bundle Lifecycle

With the installation of a bundle in the OSGi runtime this bundle is persisted in a local bundle cache. The OSGi runtime then tries to resolve all dependencies of the bundle.

If all required dependencies are resolved the bundle is in the status *RESOLVED* otherwise it is in the status *INSTALLED*.

If several bundles exist which would satisfy the dependency, then the bundle with the highest version is used. If the versions are the same, then the bundle with the lowest ID will be used. If the bundle is started, its status is *STARTING*. Afterwards it gets the *ACTIVE* status.

34.3. Eclipse Equinox

Eclipse Equinox is the reference implementation of the base OSGi specification.

Eclipse Equinox is the runtime environment on which Eclipse application are based.

In Eclipse the smallest unit of modularization is a plug-in. The terms plug-in and bundle are (almost) interchangeable. An Eclipse plug-in is also an OSGi bundle and vice versa.

Eclipse Equinox extends the concept of bundles with the concept of extension points.

34.4. OSGi console

34.4.1. OSGi console commands

The OSGi console is like an MS-DOS prompt. In this console you can type a command to perform certain OSGi actions. The following is a reference of the most important OSGi commands.

Use for example the command ss to get an overview of all bundles and their status.

Table 34.2. OSGi commands

Command	Description
help	Lists the available commands.

Command	Description
ss	Lists the installed bundles and their status.
ss `vogella`	Lists bundles and their status that have `vogella` within their name.
start `id`	Starts the bundle with the `id` ID
stop `id`	Stops the bundle with the `id` ID
install `URL`	Installs a bundle from a URL
uninstall `id`	Uninstalls the bundle with the `id` ID
bundle `id`	Show information about the bundle with the `id` ID, including the registered and used services.
services `filter`	Show all available services and their consumer. Filter is an optional LDAP filter, e.g. to see all services use "services (objectclass=*ManagedService)".

Bundles can be identified via their id which is displayed by the command ss.

34.4.2. Required bundles

As of Eclipse 4.2 (and Eclipse 3.8) you have to add the following bundles to your runtime configuration to use the OSGi console.

- org.eclipse.equinox.console
- org.apache.felix.gogo.command
- org.apache.felix.gogo.runtime
- org.apache.felix.gogo.shell

34.4.3. Telnet

If you specify the `-console` parameter in your launch configuration Eclipse will allow you to interact with the OSGi console. An OSGi launch configuration contains this parameter as default. Via `-console 5555` you can open a port to which you can telnet. If you telnet to the OSGi console the new console included in Eclipse 4.2 supports tab completion and a history of the commands.

34.4.4. Access to the Eclipse OSGi console

You can also access the OSGi console of your running Eclipse IDE. In the *Console View* of your running Eclipse you find a menu entry with the tooltip *Open*

Console. If you select *Host OSGi Console*, you will have access to your running OSGi instance.

Please note that interfering with your running Eclipse IDE via the OSGi console, may put the Eclipse IDE into a bad state.

35. Exercise: Creating the data model

You will now create a bundle for your data model and make this data model available to other plug-ins.

35.1. Create plug-in

Create a plug-in project called *com.example.e4.rcp.todo.model*. This bundle will make no contribution to the user interface, does not require an Activator and is not a RCP application.

35.2. Create base class

Create the `com.example.e4.rcp.todo.model` package and the following model class.

```
package com.example.e4.rcp.todo.model;

import java.util.Date;

public class Todo {

 private long id;
 private String summary = "";
 private String description = "";
 private boolean done = false;
 private Date dueDate;

}
```

Select Source → Generate Constructor using Fields to generate a constructor using all fields.

Use the Source → Generate Getter and Setter to create getters and setters for all fields.

The resulting class should look like the following listing.

```
package com.example.e4.rcp.todo.model;

import java.util.Date;

public class Todo {

 private long id;
 private String summary = "";
```

```
private String description = "";
private boolean done = false;
private Date dueDate;

public Todo(long id, String summary, String description, boolean done,
  Date dueDate) {
 this.id = id;
 this.summary = summary;
 this.description = description;
 this.done = done;
 this.dueDate = dueDate;

}

public long getId() {
 return id;
}

public void setId(long id) {
 this.id = id;
}

public String getSummary() {
 return summary;
}

public void setSummary(String summary) {
 this.summary = summary;
}

public String getDescription() {
 return description;
}

public void setDescription(String description) {
 this.description = description;
}

public boolean isDone() {
 return done;
}

public void setDone(boolean done) {
 this.done = done;
}

public Date getDueDate() {
 return dueDate;
}

public void setDueDate(Date dueDate) {
 this.dueDate = dueDate;
}
```

```
}
```

Use Eclipse to generate a `toString()` method for the `Todo` class based on the *id* and *summary* field. This can be done via the Eclipse menu Source → Generate toString().

Also use Eclipse to generate a `hashCode()` and `equals()` method based on the *id* field. This can be done via the Eclipse menu Source → Generate hashCode() and equals().

Also add the following `copy()` method to the class.

```
public Todo copy() {
  return new Todo(this.id, this.summary,
    this.description, this.done,
    this.dueDate);
 }
```

35.3. Create model interface

Create the following `ITodoModel` interface.

```
package com.example.e4.rcp.todo.model;

import java.util.List;

public interface ITodoModel {

 List<Todo> getTodos();

 boolean saveTodo(Todo todo);

 Todo getTodo(long id);

 boolean deleteTodo(long id);
}
```

35.4. Export the model

Export the `com.example.e4.rcp.todo.model` package. For this open the `MANIFEST.MF` file and select the *Runtime* tab. Add `com.example.e4.rcp.todo.model` to the exported packages.

35.5. Providing data via a Singleton

Create a new plug-in project called *com.example.e4.rcp.todo.service*. Define the `com.example.e4.rcp.todo.service` package and export this package so that is available for other plug-ins.

Add the `com.example.e4.rcp.todo.model` plug-in as dependency to your service plug-in.

Create the `com.example.e4.rcp.todo.service.internal` package and create the following class.

```
package com.example.e4.rcp.todo.service.internal;

import java.util.ArrayList;
import java.util.Date;
import java.util.List;

import com.example.e4.rcp.todo.model.ITodoModel;
import com.example.e4.rcp.todo.model.Todo;

public class MyTodoModelImpl implements ITodoModel {
 static int current = 1;
 private List<Todo> model;

 public MyTodoModelImpl() {
  model = createInitialModel();
 }

 // Always return a new copy of the data
 @Override
 public List<Todo> getTodos() {
  ArrayList<Todo> list = new ArrayList<Todo>();
  for (Todo todo : model) {
   list.add(todo.copy());
  }
  return list;
 }

 @Override
 public boolean saveTodo(Todo todo) {
  throw new UnsupportedOperationException("Not supported yet");
 }

 @Override
 public Todo getTodo(long id) {
  for (Todo todo : model) {
   if (todo.getId() == id) {
    return todo.copy();
   }
```

```
  }
  return null;
 }

 @Override
 public boolean deleteTodo(long id) {
  throw new UnsupportedOperationException("Not supported yet");
 }

 // Example data, change if you like
 private List<Todo> createInitialModel() {
  ArrayList<Todo> list = new ArrayList<Todo>();
  list.add(createTodo("SWT", "Learn Widgets"));
  list.add(createTodo("JFace", "Especially Viewers!"));
  list.add(createTodo("DI", "@Inject looks interesting"));
  list.add(createTodo("OSGi", "Services"));
  list.add(createTodo("Compatibility Layer","Run Eclipse 3.x"));
  return list;
 }

 private Todo createTodo(String summary, String description) {
  return new Todo(current++, summary, description, false, new Date());
 }
}
```

Create the following class which provides access to the data via the `ITodoModel` interface.

```
package com.example.e4.rcp.todo.service;

import com.example.e4.rcp.todo.model.ITodoModel;
import com.example.e4.rcp.todo.service.internal.MyTodoModelImpl;

/**
 * Provides access to the model service
 *
 * @author vogella
 *
 */
public class TodoService {

 private static ITodoModel todoService = new MyTodoModelImpl();

 public static ITodoModel getInstance() {
  return todoService;
 }

}
```

35.6. Using the model Singleton

In your `com.example.e4.rcp.todo` plug-in define a dependency to the two bundles you created. Also add them to your `com.example.e4.rcp.todo.feature` feature.

In your `TodoOverviewPart` class use the model service to access the data model. Once you press your `Button` write the correct number of todos to the `Label`.

36. JFace

36.1. Eclipse JFace Overview

Eclipse *JFace* is based upon the user interface toolkit *SWT*. JFace provides classes and frameworks which simplify common *SWT* use cases. *JFace* does not hide the *SWT* API; therefore *SWT* knowledge is still required.

It provides the *JFace Viewers* which simplify the mapping of a data model to a visual representation. For example you find Viewers for ComboBoxes, Tables and Trees.

JFace also provides helper classes to effectively manage your system resources, like colors, images and fonts.

In addition *JFace* provides Preferences and Preference pages, Wizards and Dialogs. It also contains functionality to support icon decorations and input help for SWT controls.

JFace Data Binding is a framework which connects properties of objects. It is typically used to synchronize fields of the user interface with properties of model objects and allows you to include validation and conversion in this synchronization process.

36.2. Eclipse JFace Viewers

36.2.1. Eclipse JFace viewers

Eclipse *JFace Viewers* allow you to display a domain model in a standard SWT widget like list, combo, tree or table without converting the domain model beforehand.

A *Viewer* allows you to set a *ContentProvider* which provides the data for the *Viewer*. The *ContentProvider* makes no assumption about the representation of the data model by the *Viewer*.

You can also assign at least one *LabelProvider* to a *Viewer*. The LabelProvider defines how the data from the model will be displayed in the *Viewer*.

36.2.2. Standard JFace Viewers

JFace provides several standard *Viewers*. The following *Viewers* are the most important ones.

- ComboViewer
- ListViewer
- TreeViewer
- TableViewer

These *Viewers* are part of the `org.eclipse.jface.viewers` package.

The related interfaces for defining a *ContentProvider* are:

Table 36.1. Content Providers

Class	Description
IStructuredContentProvider	Used for list, combo and table Viewer. Default implementation: ArrayContentProvider
ITreeContentProvider	Used for trees. Has additional methods to determine the children and the parents of the elements.

`ArrayContentProvider.getInstance()` delivers a default implementation for `IStructuredContentProvider` and can handle Arrays and Collections as Input.

Typical *LabelProviders* are:

Table 36.2. Label providers

Interface	Template class	Description
ILabelProvider	LabelProvider	Used for lists and trees, can return an icon and a label per element.
ColumnLabelProvider	CellLabelProvider	Used for tables. Defines a label provider per column.

36.3. JFace ComboViewer

A simple example for a JFace Viewer framework is the `ComboViewer` class. Assume the following data model.

```
package de.vogella.rcp.intro.first;

public class Person {
```

```
 private String firstName;
 private String lastName;

 public Person(String firstName, String lastName) {
  this.firstName = firstName;
  this.lastName = lastName;

 }

 public String getFirstName() {
  return firstName;
 }

 public void setFirstName(String firstName) {
  this.firstName = firstName;
 }

 public String getLastName() {
  return lastName;
 }

 public void setLastName(String lastName) {
  this.lastName = lastName;
 }

}
```

Given this data model, here is an example snippet which shows how you could use a `ComboViewer` in a *Part*.

```
// This happens in the method which creates the user interface
// parent is the composite which is available

GridLayout layout = new GridLayout(2, false);
parent.setLayout(layout);
Label label = new Label(parent, SWT.NONE);
label.setText("Select a person:");
final ComboViewer viewer = new ComboViewer(parent, SWT.READ_ONLY);

// ArrayContentProvider does not store state,
// therefore you can re-use instances

viewer.setContentProvider(ArrayContentProvider.getInstance());
viewer.setLabelProvider(new LabelProvider() {
 @Override
 public String getText(Object element) {
  if (element instanceof Person) {
   Person person = (Person) element;
   return person.getFirstName();
  }
  return super.getText(element);
 }
```

```
});

Person[] persons = new Person[] { new Person("Lars", "Vogel"),
 new Person("Tim", "Taler"), new Person("Jim", "Knopf") };

// Set set the input to the Viewer.
// This input will be send to the
// content provider

viewer.setInput(persons);

// React to the selection of the viewer
// Note that the viewer return the real object and not just a string
// representation

viewer.addSelectionChangedListener(new ISelectionChangedListener() {
 @Override
 public void selectionChanged(SelectionChangedEvent event) {
  IStructuredSelection selection = (IStructuredSelection) event
   .getSelection();
  System.out.println(((Person) selection.getFirstElement())
   .getLastName());
 }
});
```

You can get and set selections using Java objects based on your domain model.

```
// You can select a object directly via the domain object
Person person = persons[0];
viewer.setSelection(new StructuredSelection(person));

// Get the selection, returns the data model object
IStructuredSelection selection =
  (IStructuredSelection) viewer.getSelection();
Person p = (Person) selection.getFirstElement();
```

36.4. Resource Manager for Colors, Fonts and Images

SWT is based on the native widgets of the OS system. Whenever a *SWT* widget is allocated, a corresponding OS specific widget is created.

The Java garbage collector cannot automatically clean-up these references.

Fortunately all widgets which are created based on a parent widget are automatically disposed when the parent `Composite` is disposed.

If you develop Eclipse plug-ins, the `Composite` of a *Part* is automatically disposed once the Part is closed. Therefore these *SWT* widgets are handled automatically in Eclipse plug-in projects.

This rule does not apply for colors, fonts and images, as these may be re-used in other places. For this reason they need to be explicitly disposed. Fortunately *JFace* provides the `LocalResourceManager` class.

An instance of the `LocalResourceManager` class is created with a reference to a `Composite`. If this `Composite` is disposed, the resources created by the `LocalResourceManager` will also be disposed.

```
// Create the manager and bind to a widget
LocalResourceManager resManager =
 new LocalResourceManager(JFaceResources.getResources(), composite);

// Create resources
Color color = resManager.createColor(new RGB(200, 100, 0));
Font font = resManager.
 createFont(FontDescriptor.createFrom("Arial", 10, SWT.BOLD));
// Get an imageDescriptor and create Image from it
Image image = resManager.createImage(imageDescriptor);
```

The `createImage()` method expects an `ImageDescriptor` class. To get one `ImageDescriptor` from an image file stored in your current plug-in use the following:

```
Bundle bundle = FrameworkUtil.getBundle(this.getClass());
URL url = FileLocator.find(bundle,
 new Path("icons/alt_window_32.gif"), null);
ImageDescriptor image = ImageDescriptor.createFromURL(url);
```

To create the `Image` from the `ImageDescriptor` you can use the `createImage()` method.

36.5. ControlDecorations

The `ControlDecorations` class allows you to place image decorations on SWT controls to show additional information about the control. These decorations can also set a description text which is displayed once the user places the mouse over them.

During the layout of your screen you need to make sure that enough space is available to display these decorations.

The following shows how to create `ControlDecorations` and how to set a description and an icon to it.

```
// Create the decoration for the text UI component
```

```
final ControlDecoration deco =
 new ControlDecoration(text, SWT.TOP | SWT.RIGHT);

// Re-use an existing image
Image image = FieldDecorationRegistry.
 getDefault().
 getFieldDecoration(FieldDecorationRegistry.DEC_INFORMATION).
 getImage();
// Set description and image
deco.setDescriptionText("This is a tooltip text");
deco.setImage(image);
// Hide deco if not in focus
deco.setShowOnlyOnFocus(true);
```

You can also hide and show the decoration.

```
deco.hide();
deco.show();
```

36.6. FieldAssists

The `org.eclipse.jface.fieldassist` package provides assistance to define input help for a widget, e.g. text field or combo box. The `ContentProposalAdapter` class is responsible for providing the possible input values.

In the following example the content proposal should get activated via certain keys ("." and "#") as well as the **Ctrl+Space** key combination.

The following code demonstrates the usage of the `FieldAssists`. It also uses the `ControlDecoration` class.

```
Text text = new Text(parent, SWT.BORDER);

// Create the decoration for the text UI component
final ControlDecoration deco = new ControlDecoration(text, SWT.TOP
 | SWT.RIGHT);

// Re-use an existing image
Image image = FieldDecorationRegistry.getDefault()
 .getFieldDecoration(FieldDecorationRegistry.DEC_INFORMATION)
 .getImage();

// Set description and image
deco.setDescriptionText("Use CNTL + SPACE to see possible values");
deco.setImage(image);

// Always show decoration
```

```
deco.setShowOnlyOnFocus(false);

// Also if the text UI componet is not empty hide the decoration
text.addModifyListener(new ModifyListener() {
 @Override
 public void modifyText(ModifyEvent e) {
  Text text = (Text) e.getSource();
  if (text.getText().length() > 0) {
    deco.hide();
  } else {
    deco.show();
  }
 }
});

// Help the user with the possible inputs
// "." and "#" will also activate the content proposals
char[] autoActivationCharacters = new char[] { '.', '#' };
KeyStroke keyStroke;
//
try {
 keyStroke = KeyStroke.getInstance("Ctrl+Space");
 ContentProposalAdapter adapter = new ContentProposalAdapter(text,
  new TextContentAdapter(),
  new SimpleContentProposalProvider(new String[] {
   "ProposalOne", "ProposalTwo", "ProposalThree" }),
   keyStroke, autoActivationCharacters);
 } catch (ParseException e1) {
 e1.printStackTrace();
}
```

If used the result should look similar to the following.

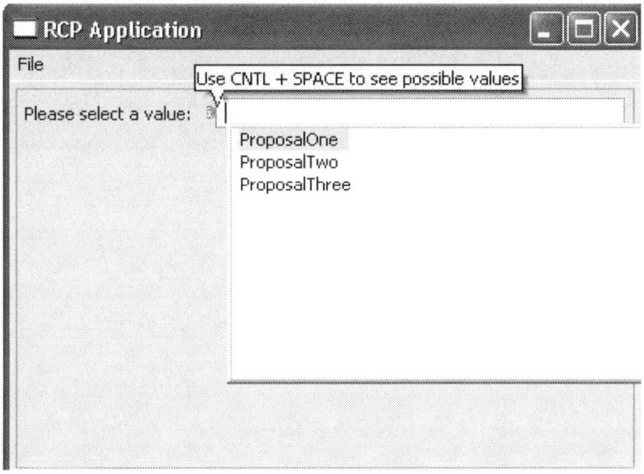

37. Exercise: Build a Part with a ComboViewer

Rearrange the user interface so that the left area of your application contains two *Parts*. The class for the second *Part* should be called `TodoDeletionPart` and it should be below the `TodoOverviewPart` *Part*.

Add the `org.eclipse.jface` plug-in as a dependency to `com.example.e4.rcp.todo` and add it to your product.

Implement a `ComboViewer` which allows you to select a Todo item. Add a `Button` to the *Part*. If this `Button` is pressed the `deleteTodo()` method of your `ITodoModel` should be called.

Also implement the `deleteTodo()` method in `ITodoModel`.

Validate that the number of entries in your data model has been reduced, e.g. via a `System.out` message.

38. JFace Table Viewer

38.1. TableViewer

You can use the `TableViewer` class to create tables using the JFace framework. The SWT `Table` widget is wrapped into the `TableViewer` and can still be accessed to set its properties.

```
// Define the TableViewer
viewer = new TableViewer(parent, SWT.MULTI | SWT.H_SCROLL
    | SWT.V_SCROLL | SWT.FULL_SELECTION | SWT.BORDER);

// Create the columns
// Not yet implemented
createColumns(parent);

// Make lines and make header visible
final Table table = viewer.getTable();
table.setHeaderVisible(true);
table.setLinesVisible(true);
```

38.2. ContentProvider for TableViewer

As with other JFace *Viewers* the `ContentProvider` provides the data which should be displayed in the `TableViewer`.

You can implement your own `ContentProvider` for a table by implementing the interface `IStructuredContentProvider` from the `org.eclipse.jface.viewers` package.

Eclipse provides an implementation of this interface via the `ArrayContentProvider` class. The `ArrayContentProvider` class supports Arrays or Lists as input, containing the domain data. Because `ArrayContentProviders` do not store any data, it is possible to share an instances with several *Viewers*. To get a shared instance use the `ArrayContentProvider.getInstance()` method.

The `getElements()` method of the `ContentProvider` is called by the JFace table `Viewer` to translate the input into an array of elements.

These elements are displayed as individual elements by the table `Viewer`, i.e. as individual rows.

The input to the `ContentProvider` is set via the `setInput()` method of the `Viewer` class.

```
// Continued after the definition of
// the Viewer

// Set the ContentProvider
viewer.setContentProvider(ArrayContentProvider.getInstance());

// Get the content for the Viewer,
// setInput will call getElements in the ContentProvider
viewer.setInput(someData...);
```

38.3. Columns and LabelProviders

Columns for a JFace `TableViewer` are defined by creating instances of `TableViewerColumn`.

You define `LabelProviders` for a `TableViewer` per column.
Each `TableViewerColumn` needs to get a `LabelProvider` assigned via the `setLabelProvider()` method. The `LabelProvider` defines how the data from the model will be displayed. Typically you return the String which should be displayed.

The `setLabelProvider()` method expects an instance of the abstract `CellLabelProvider` class. A default implementation of this class is provided by the `ColumnLabelProvider` class.

```
// First column is for the first name
TableViewerColumn col = new TableViewerColumn(viewer, SWT.NONE);
col.getColumn().setWidth(200);
col.getColumn().setText("Firstname:");
col.setLabelProvider(new ColumnLabelProvider() {
 @Override
 public String getText(Object element) {
  Person p = (Person) element;
  return p.getFirstName();
 }
});

// Maybe more text columns...

// Now the status married
// Uses an getImage instead o getText
// CHECKED and UNCHECK are fields of type Image

col = new TableViewerColumn(viewer, SWT.NONE);
col.getColumn().setWidth(200);
col.getColumn().setText("Lastname:");
col.setLabelProvider(new ColumnLabelProvider() {
@Override
public Image getImage(Object element) {
```

```
  if (((Person) element).isMarried()) {
   return CHECKED;
  }
  return UNCHECKED;
  }
});
```

The code above uses two fields which contain `Image` instances. These fields could for example be initialized via the following code.

```
// Fields for your class
// Assuming your have these two icons
// in your icons folder
private static final Image CHECKED = getImage("checked.gif");
private static final Image UNCHECKED = getImage("unchecked.gif");



// More code...


// Helper Method to load the images
private static Image getImage(String file) {
 Bundle bundle = FrameworkUtil.getBundle(View.class);
 URL url = FileLocator.find(bundle, new Path("icons/" + file), null);
 ImageDescriptor image = ImageDescriptor.createFromURL(url);
 return image.createImage();

}
```

Before Eclipse 3.3 you had to use the `ITableLabelProvider` interface to define label providers. This interface is outdated and should not be used in new projects.

38.4. Reflect data changes in the Viewer

To reflect data changes in the data model which is displayed by the `Viewer`, you can call the `viewer.refresh()` method. This method will update the `Viewer` based on the data which was assigned to it.

To change the data which is displayed use the `viewer.setInput()` method.

38.5. Editing Support

To make a JFace `TableColumn` editable, you need an object of type `EditingSupport`.

The following shows an example of an `EditorSupport` implementation.

```java
package de.vogella.jface.tableviewer.edit;

import org.eclipse.jface.viewers.CellEditor;
import org.eclipse.jface.viewers.EditingSupport;
import org.eclipse.jface.viewers.TableViewer;
import org.eclipse.jface.viewers.TextCellEditor;

import de.vogella.jface.tableviewer.model.Person;

public class FirstNameEditingSupport extends EditingSupport {

 private final TableViewer viewer;

 public FirstNameEditingSupport(TableViewer viewer) {
  super(viewer);
  this.viewer = viewer;
 }

 @Override
 protected CellEditor getCellEditor(Object element) {
  return new TextCellEditor(viewer.getTable());
 }

 @Override
 protected boolean canEdit(Object element) {
  return true;
 }

 @Override
 protected Object getValue(Object element) {
  return ((Person) element).getFirstName();
 }

 @Override
 protected void setValue(Object element, Object value) {
  ((Person) element).setFirstName(String.valueOf(value));
  viewer.refresh();
 }
}
```

The `EditingSupport` implementation defines how the content can be changed. `EditingSupport` returns an object of type `CellEditor` from the `getCellEditor()` method. This object creates the controls to change the data.

The method `setValue()` in `EditingSupport` receives the changed value based on the user input. In this method you assign the value to your data object.

The `getValue()` method receives the current object and returns the value which should be displayed. The `canEdit()` method defines if the cell can be edited.

Eclipse provides default implementations for typical cases, e.g. `TextCellEditor`, `ColorCellEditor`, `CheckboxCellEditor`, `DialogCellEditor` and `ComboBoxViewerCellEditor`.

You can assign the `EditorSupport` class to your `TableColumn` via the `setEditingSupport()` method of your `TableViewerColumn`.

```
col.setEditingSupport(new FirstNameEditingSupport(viewer));
```

From an application design perspective, editing within a table can be cumbersome for the user. If the end user has to edit a lot of data, you should also offer a dialog, wizard or *Part* to edit the data.

38.6. Filtering data

JFace Viewer supports filtering of data via the `setFilters()` or `addFilter()` methods. These methods expect `ViewerFilter` objects as arguments.

For each registered `ViewerFilter` object the `select()` method is called. The methods returns true if the data should be shown and false if it should be filtered.

```
package de.vogella.jface.tableviewer.filter;

import org.eclipse.jface.viewers.Viewer;
import org.eclipse.jface.viewers.ViewerFilter;

import de.vogella.jface.tableviewer.model.Person;

public class PersonFilter extends ViewerFilter {

 private String searchString;

 public void setSearchText(String s) {
  // Search must be a substring of the existing value
  this.searchString = ".*" + s + ".*";
 }

 @Override
 public boolean select(Viewer viewer,
   Object parentElement,
   Object element) {
  if (searchString == null || searchString.length() == 0) {
   return true;
  }
  Person p = (Person) element;
```

```
  if (p.getFirstName().matches(searchString)) {
   return true;
  }
  if (p.getLastName().matches(searchString)) {
   return true;
  }

  return false;
 }
}
```

All filters are checked whenever the input on the `Viewer` changes, or whenever the `refresh()` method is called on the `Viewer`.

If more than one filter is defined for a `Viewer`, all filters must return true for the *Viewer* to display the data.

38.7. ViewerComparator

JFace supports sorting of the table content via the `setComparator()` method on the Viewer object. This method expects a `ViewerComparator` object. By default it will sort based on the `toString()` method of the objects in the viewer.

```
// Sort according to due date
viewer.setComparator(new ViewerComparator() {
 public int compare(Viewer viewer, Object e1, Object e2) {
  Todo t1 = (Todo) e1;
  Todo t2 = (Todo) e2;
  return t1.getDueDate().compareTo(t2.getDueDate());
 };
});
```

38.8. StyledCellLabelProvider

It is also possible to use a `StyledCellLabelProvider` for a very flexible styling of your text. `StyledCellLabelProvider` extends `CellLabelProvider` and allows you to draw via its `update()` method.

The following example shows how to use a `StyledCellLabelProvider`. In this example a part of a pre-defined text is highlighted.

```
column.setLabelProvider(new StyledCellLabelProvider() {
@Override
 public void update(ViewerCell cell) {
  StyledString text = new StyledString();
  StyleRange myStyledRange = new StyleRange(17, 2, null, Display
```

```
      .getCurrent().getSystemColor(SWT.COLOR_YELLOW));
    text.append("This is a test", StyledString.DECORATIONS_STYLER);
    text.append(" (" + 15 + ") ", StyledString.DECORATIONS_STYLER);
    cell.setText(text.toString());

    StyleRange[] range = { myStyledRange };
    cell.setStyleRanges(range);
    super.update(cell);
  }
});
```

As a result the number "15" will be highlighted as presented in the following screenshot.

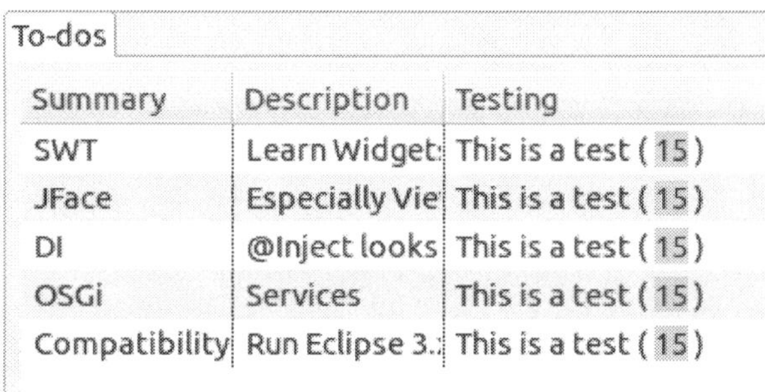

38.9. Show and hide table columns

You can add a `Menu` to your table. This `Menu` can get a `MenuItem` for each column and you can use it for example to hide and show columns based on the width setting.

```
// Define the menu and assign to the table
Menu headerMenu = new Menu(parent.getShell(), SWT.POP_UP);
viewer.getTable().setMenu(headerMenu);
// Create your columns....
// ... as usual


// Now add a MenuItem for the colum to the table menu
createMenuItem(headerMenu, column.getColumn());

// The createMenuItem method add per column a
// new MenuItem to the menu
private void createMenuItem(Menu parent, final TableColumn column) {
  final MenuItem itemName = new MenuItem(parent, SWT.CHECK);
  itemName.setText(column.getText());
  itemName.setSelection(column.getResizable());
  itemName.addListener(SWT.Selection, new Listener() {
    public void handleEvent(Event event) {
```

```
    if (itemName.getSelection()) {
     column.setWidth(150);
     column.setResizable(true);
    } else {
     column.setWidth(0);
     column.setResizable(false);
    }
   }
  });
 }
```

38.10. Tooltips for Viewers

You can use tooltips for the cells of the `Viewer`. You have to activate tooltips for the Viewer to get this working.

```
// Activate the tooltip support for the viewer
ColumnViewerToolTipSupport.enableFor(viewer, ToolTip.NO_RECREATE);
```

In your `CellLabelProvider` you specify the related methods for displaying the tooltip.

```
col.setLabelProvider(new CellLabelProvider() {
 @Override
 public void update(ViewerCell cell) {
  cell.setText(((Person) cell.getElement()).getLastName());
 }

 @Override
 public String getToolTipText(Object element) {
  return "Tooltip (" + element + ")";
 }

 @Override
 public Point getToolTipShift(Object object) {
  return new Point(5, 5);
 }

 @Override
 public int getToolTipDisplayDelayTime(Object object) {
  return 100; //msec
 }

 @Override
 public int getToolTipTimeDisplayed(Object object) {
  return 5000; //msec
 }

});
```

39. Exercise: JFace TableViewer

39.1. Create a JFace TableViewer for the Todo Items

Add the `org.eclipse.jface` plug-in as a dependencies to your `com.example.e4.rcp.todo` plug-in.

Create a JFace `TableViewer` in `TodoOverviewPart` which shows the list of todos. Make columns for all the fields.

Load the data into the `Viewer` once the `Button` is pressed.

39.2. JFace TreeViewer

You will now use the Eclipes 4 platform to build a file browser. This exercise is not related to the Todo example and can be used to repeat the steps of creating an Eclipse 4 application.

Create a new Eclipse plug-in called *com.example.e4.filebrowser* and convert it into an Eclipse 4 application.

Add a *Part* to your application and implement a `TreeViewer` in this *Part*.

Implement a class for the `ITreeContentProvider` interface which allows you to browse the filesystem. Review the Javadoc of this class to understand the methods of this interface.

Also implement your own `LabelProvider` for the tree.

Use `viewer.setInput(File.listRoots());` to set the initial input to the `Viewer`.

40. Dialogs

40.1. Dialogs in Eclipse

Dialogs allow you to prompt the user for additional information or provide the user with feedback. The Eclipse platform offers several different SWT and JFace *Dialogs*.

40.2. SWT System Dialogs

SWT offers an API for the use of the native dialogs from the OS platform. The SWT dialogs are the following:

- `ColorDialog` - For selecting a color
- `DirectoryDialog` - For selecting a directory
- `FileDialog` - For selecting a file
- `FontDialog` - For selecting a font
- `MessageBox` - For opening a Message Dialog to the user

The following example shows how to open the `MessageBox` dialog.

```
// Message with ok and cancel button and info icon
MessageBox dialog =
  new MessageBox(shell, SWT.ICON_QUESTION | SWT.OK| SWT.CANCEL);
dialog.setText("My info");
dialog.setMessage("Do you really want to do this?");
returnCode = dialog.open();
```

40.3. JFace Dialogs

40.3.1. MessageDialog and ErrorDialog

JFace contains additional *Dialogs* which are more flexible then the SWT *Dialogs* It provides static methods to open commonly used dialogs.

You can for example use the `MessageDialog` class which allows you to customize the `Buttons` which should be used.

`MessageDialog` also provides static methods to open commonly used *Dialogs*, e.g. an info or a warning `Dialog`.

```
// Customized MessageDialog with configured buttons
MessageDialog dialog = new MessageDialog(shell, "My Title", null,
    "My message", MessageDialog.ERROR, new String[] { "First",
 "Second", "Third" }, 0);
int result = dialog.open();
System.out.println(result);

// A few standard message dialog
MessageDialog.openConfirm(shell, "Confirm", "Please confirm");
MessageDialog.openError(shell, "Error", "Error occured");
MessageDialog.openInformation(shell, "Info", "Info for you");
MessageDialog.openQuestion(shell, "Question", "Really, really?");
MessageDialog.openWarning(shell, "Warning", "I warn you");
```

JFace also provides the `ErrorDialog` class which allows you to report a `Status` object. `Status` objects are frequently used in Eclipse to report errors.

40.3.2. Own Dialog

The `org.eclipse.jface.dialogs.Dialog` class can be extended to create your own *Dialogs*. This class creates a area in which you can place controls and add an *OK* and *Cancel* button to it.

Your class needs to implement the `createDialogArea` method. This method gets a `Composite` which expects to get a `GridData` object assigned as its layout data. Via the `super.createDialogArea(parent)` method call, you can get an `Composite` to which you can add your controls.

40.3.3. JFace TitleAreaDialog

You can also define your own *Dialogs* based on the `TitleAreaDialog` class.

`TitleAreaDialog` has a reserved space for providing feedback to the user. You can set the text in this space via the `setMessage()` and `setErrorMessage()` methods.

The following example shows a custom defined `TitleAreaDialog`.

```
package de.vogella.rcp.intro.dialogs.custom.dialogs;

import org.eclipse.jface.dialogs.IMessageProvider;
import org.eclipse.jface.dialogs.TitleAreaDialog;
import org.eclipse.jface.resource.JFaceResources;
import org.eclipse.swt.SWT;
import org.eclipse.swt.events.SelectionAdapter;
import org.eclipse.swt.events.SelectionEvent;
import org.eclipse.swt.layout.GridData;
import org.eclipse.swt.layout.GridLayout;
```

```
import org.eclipse.swt.widgets.Button;
import org.eclipse.swt.widgets.Composite;
import org.eclipse.swt.widgets.Control;
import org.eclipse.swt.widgets.Label;
import org.eclipse.swt.widgets.Shell;
import org.eclipse.swt.widgets.Text;

public class MyDialog extends TitleAreaDialog {

 private Text firstNameText;
 private Text lastNameText;
 private String firstName;
 private String lastName;

 public MyDialog(Shell parentShell) {
  super(parentShell);
 }

 @Override
 public void create() {
  super.create();
  // Set the title
  setTitle("This is my first own dialog");
  // Set the message
  setMessage("This is a TitleAreaDialog",
    IMessageProvider.INFORMATION);

 }

 @Override
 protected Control createDialogArea(Composite parent) {
  GridLayout layout = new GridLayout();
  layout.numColumns = 2;
  // layout.horizontalAlignment = GridData.FILL;
  parent.setLayout(layout);

  // The text fields will grow with the size of the dialog
  GridData gridData = new GridData();
  gridData.grabExcessHorizontalSpace = true;
  gridData.horizontalAlignment = GridData.FILL;

  Label label1 = new Label(parent, SWT.NONE);
  label1.setText("First Name");

  firstNameText = new Text(parent, SWT.BORDER);
  firstNameText.setLayoutData(gridData);

  Label label2 = new Label(parent, SWT.NONE);
  label2.setText("Last Name");
  // You should not re-use GridData
  gridData = new GridData();
  gridData.grabExcessHorizontalSpace = true;
  gridData.horizontalAlignment = GridData.FILL;
  lastNameText = new Text(parent, SWT.BORDER);
```

```
  lastNameText.setLayoutData(gridData);
  return parent;
 }

 @Override
 protected void createButtonsForButtonBar(Composite parent) {
  GridData gridData = new GridData();
  gridData.verticalAlignment = GridData.FILL;
  gridData.horizontalSpan = 3;
  gridData.grabExcessHorizontalSpace = true;
  gridData.grabExcessVerticalSpace = true;
  gridData.horizontalAlignment = SWT.CENTER;

  parent.setLayoutData(gridData);
  // Create Add button
  // Own method as we need to overview the SelectionAdapter
  createOkButton(parent, OK, "Add", true);
  // Add a SelectionListener

  // Create Cancel button
  Button cancelButton =
    createButton(parent, CANCEL, "Cancel", false);
  // Add a SelectionListener
  cancelButton.addSelectionListener(new SelectionAdapter() {
   public void widgetSelected(SelectionEvent e) {
    setReturnCode(CANCEL);
    close();
   }
  });
 }

 protected Button createOkButton(Composite parent, int id,
   String label,
   boolean defaultButton) {
  // increment the number of columns in the button bar
  ((GridLayout) parent.getLayout()).numColumns++;
  Button button = new Button(parent, SWT.PUSH);
  button.setText(label);
  button.setFont(JFaceResources.getDialogFont());
  button.setData(new Integer(id));
  button.addSelectionListener(new SelectionAdapter() {
   public void widgetSelected(SelectionEvent event) {
    if (isValidInput()) {
     okPressed();
    }
   }
  });
  if (defaultButton) {
   Shell shell = parent.getShell();
   if (shell != null) {
    shell.setDefaultButton(button);
   }
  }
  setButtonLayoutData(button);
```

```
  return button;
 }

 private boolean isValidInput() {
  boolean valid = true;
  if (firstNameText.getText().length() == 0) {
   setErrorMessage("Please maintain the first name");
   valid = false;
  }
  if (lastNameText.getText().length() == 0) {
   setErrorMessage("Please maintain the last name");
   valid = false;
  }
  return valid;
 }

 @Override
 protected boolean isResizable() {
  return true;
 }

 // Coyy textFields because the UI gets disposed
 // and the Text Fields are not accessible any more.
 private void saveInput() {
  firstName = firstNameText.getText();
  lastName = lastNameText.getText();
 }

 @Override
 protected void okPressed() {
  saveInput();
  super.okPressed();
 }

 public String getFirstName() {
  return firstName;
 }

 public String getLastName() {
  return lastName;
 }
}
```

This `Dialog` can get opened via:

```
MyDialog dialog = new MyDialog(shell);
dialog.create();
if (dialog.open() == Window.OK) {
 System.out.println(dialog.getFirstName());
 System.out.println(dialog.getLastName());
}
```

40.3.4. Selection Dialogs

Eclipse provides several standard selection *Dialogs* in Eclipse 3.x. In Eclipse 3.x you can directly use them, in Eclipse 4.x you may have to copy them into your plug-in and modify them slightly. I still list them here, so that you can use their coding as examples.

A release after Eclipse 4.2 might make the directly available.

Here is a list of these *Dialogs*.

- ElementListSelectionDialog
- ListDialog
- ElementTreeSelectionDialog
- CheckTreeSelectionDialog

For example `ElementListSelectionDialog` allows you to select elements from a list where the dialog provides a filter for the elements.

```
ElementListSelectionDialog dialog =
 new ElementListSelectionDialog(shell, new LabelProvider());
dialog.setElements(new String[] { "Linux", "Mac", "Windows" });
dialog.setTitle("Which operating system are you using");
// User pressed cancel
if (dialog.open() != Window.OK) {
  return false;
}
Object[] result = dialog.getResult();
```

Which operati...
Linux
Mac
Windows
OK
Cancel

41. Exercise: Confirmation Dialog

In your `TodoDetailsPart` class trigger a JFace confirmation dialog if the selection in the table of `TodoOverviewPart` changes and if `TodoDetailsPart` contains modified data.

The confirmation dialog should allow to prevent an update in `TodoDetailsPart`.

42. Wizards

42.1. Overview

Eclipse provides *Wizards* to capture user feedback in a structured way. A *Wizard* guides a user step by step through different pages.

The following screenshot shows the second page of a *Wizard*.

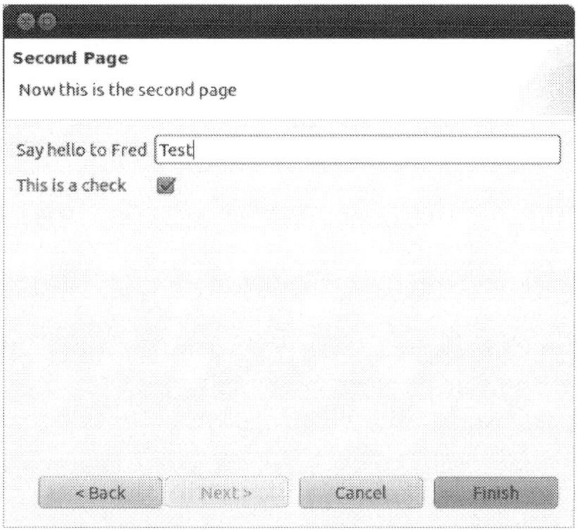

42.2. Wizards and WizardPages

The `Wizard` class from the `org.eclipse.jface.wizard` package provides the functionality to build own wizards. This class controls the navigation between the different pages and provides the base user interface, i.e. a progress bar and an area for error and information messages.

A `Wizard` contains one or several pages of the type `WizardPage`. Such a page is added to a `Wizard` via the `addPage()` method.

A `WizardPage` must create a new `Composite` in the `createControl()` method. This new `Composite` must use the `Composite` of the method parameter as parent. It also must call the `setControl()` method with this new `Composite` as parameter. If this is omitted, Eclipse will throw an error.

42.3. Starting the Wizard

To open a `Wizard` you use the `WizardDialog` class from the `org.eclipse.jface.wizard` package.

```
WizardDialog dialog = new WizardDialog(shell, new YourWizardClass());
dialog.open();
```

Typically a wizard is opened via a menu or toolbar entry or via a `SelectionListener` on a *SWT* `Button`.

42.4. Changing the page order

Frequently you want to jump to a specific page depending on the user input.

A `WizardPage` can override the `getNextPage()` method for this purpose.

If you do this, you would typically access the correct page via the `Wizard`. You get the `Wizard` via the `getWizard()` method. Afterwards you can access via the `Wizard` the page which should be the next one.

42.5. Working with the same data on different pages

To use the same data in different pages in your wizard, add the required objects to the constructor of your wizard page. The `isVisible()` method is called whenever the `WizardPage` either gets visible or invisible. Call the `super.isVisible()` method. and check the current status of the page. If the page is visible, assign the data of your object to the user interface components.

42.6. Tutorial: Wizards Example

The following gives an example of a wizard with two pages.

Create the following `MyPageOne` and `MyPageTwo` classes.

```
package de.vogella.rcp.intro.wizards.wizard;

import org.eclipse.jface.wizard.WizardPage;
import org.eclipse.swt.SWT;
import org.eclipse.swt.events.KeyEvent;
import org.eclipse.swt.events.KeyListener;
import org.eclipse.swt.layout.GridData;
import org.eclipse.swt.layout.GridLayout;
import org.eclipse.swt.widgets.Composite;
import org.eclipse.swt.widgets.Label;
```

```
import org.eclipse.swt.widgets.Text;

public class MyPageOne extends WizardPage {
 private Text text1;
 private Composite container;

 public MyPageOne() {
  super("First Page");
  setTitle("First Page");
  setDescription("Fake Wizard. First page");
 }

 @Override
 public void createControl(Composite parent) {
  container = new Composite(parent, SWT.NULL);
  GridLayout layout = new GridLayout();
  container.setLayout(layout);
  layout.numColumns = 2;
  Label label1 = new Label(container, SWT.NULL);
  label1.setText("Put here a value");

  text1 = new Text(container, SWT.BORDER | SWT.SINGLE);
  text1.setText("");
  text1.addKeyListener(new KeyListener() {

   @Override
   public void keyPressed(KeyEvent e) {
   }

   @Override
   public void keyReleased(KeyEvent e) {
    if (!text1.getText().isEmpty()) {
     setPageComplete(true);

    }
   }

  });
  GridData gd = new GridData(GridData.FILL_HORIZONTAL);
  text1.setLayoutData(gd);
  // Required to avoid an error in the system
  setControl(container);
  setPageComplete(false);

 }

 public String getText1() {
  return text1.getText();
 }
}
```

```
package de.vogella.rcp.intro.wizards.wizard;
```

```
import org.eclipse.jface.wizard.WizardPage;
import org.eclipse.swt.SWT;
import org.eclipse.swt.events.KeyEvent;
import org.eclipse.swt.events.KeyListener;
import org.eclipse.swt.layout.GridData;
import org.eclipse.swt.layout.GridLayout;
import org.eclipse.swt.widgets.Button;
import org.eclipse.swt.widgets.Composite;
import org.eclipse.swt.widgets.Label;
import org.eclipse.swt.widgets.Text;

public class MyPageTwo extends WizardPage {
 private Text text1;
 private Composite container;

 public MyPageTwo() {
  super("Second Page");
  setTitle("Second Page");
  setDescription("Now this is the second page");
  setControl(text1);
 }

 @Override
 public void createControl(Composite parent) {
  container = new Composite(parent, SWT.NULL);
  GridLayout layout = new GridLayout();
  container.setLayout(layout);
  layout.numColumns = 2;
  Label label1 = new Label(container, SWT.NULL);
  label1.setText("Say hello to Fred");

  text1 = new Text(container, SWT.BORDER | SWT.SINGLE);
  text1.setText("");
  text1.addKeyListener(new KeyListener() {

   @Override
   public void keyPressed(KeyEvent e) {
    // TODO Auto-generated method stub

   }

   @Override
   public void keyReleased(KeyEvent e) {
    if (!text1.getText().isEmpty()) {
     setPageComplete(true);
    }
   }

  });
  GridData gd = new GridData(GridData.FILL_HORIZONTAL);
  text1.setLayoutData(gd);
  Label labelCheck = new Label(container, SWT.NONE);
  labelCheck.setText("This is a check");
```

```
    Button check = new Button(container, SWT.CHECK);
    check.setSelection(true);
    // Required to avoid an error in the system
    setControl(container);
    setPageComplete(false);
  }

  public String getText1() {
    return text1.getText();
  }
}
```

Create the following class called *MyWizard*.

```
package de.vogella.rcp.intro.wizards.wizard;

import org.eclipse.jface.wizard.Wizard;


public class MyWizard extends Wizard {

  protected MyPageOne one;
  protected MyPageTwo two;

  public MyWizard() {
    super();
    setNeedsProgressMonitor(true);
  }

  @Override
  public void addPages() {
    one = new MyPageOne();
    two = new MyPageTwo();
    addPage(one);
    addPage(two);
  }

  @Override
  public boolean performFinish() {
    // Print the result to the console
    System.out.println(one.getText1());
    System.out.println(two.getText1());

    return true;
  }
}
```

To show the wizard you could for example add a `Button` to your *Part* and call the Wizard via a `SelectionListener` on the `Button`.

```
Button button = new Button(parent, SWT.PUSH);
button.setText("Open Wizard");
button.addSelectionListener(new SelectionAdapter() {
 @Override
 public void widgetSelected(SelectionEvent e) {
  WizardDialog wizardDialog = new WizardDialog(parent.getShell(),
   new MyWizard());
  if (wizardDialog.open() == Window.OK) {
   System.out.println("Ok pressed");
  } else {
   System.out.println("Cancel pressed");
     }
 }
});
```

43. Exercise: Create a Wizard for new Todos

Create a Wizard in your `com.example.e4.rcp.todo` plug-in which allows you to create a new Todo item. Reuse the `TodoDetailsPart` for defining the user interface in your first `WizardPage`. The second `WizardPage` should only contain a checkbox *Confirm* button.

Call the wizard from your `NewTodoHandler` class, which you already added to the menu.

This exercise demonstrates how you can reuse *Parts* in a *Wizard*, something which was not possible in Eclipse 3.x.

44. Fragments Projects

44.1. Overview

A *fragment project* is always defined for a host project. At runtime the *fragment project* is merged with its host project and for the runtime both projects are just one.

Fragment project are always optional for their host plug-in.

To create a fragment project select File → New → Other → Plug-in Development → Fragment Project.

44.2. Usage

Fragment project are typical used for containing the tests. This way the tests can access the host plug-in classes, even if the host plug-in does not define them as external API. Sometimes tests are also contained in normal plug-ins, in this case they can only test the external API for other plug-ins.

Another typical usage of *fragment projects* is for translations. A new translation can be contributed to a plug-in via a *fragment project*.

45. Internationalization

45.1. Java Resource bundles and selection

The process of preparing an application for being translated into several languages is called internationalization. This term is typically abbreviated to *i18n*.

The process of translating the application is called localization and is abbreviated to *l10n*.

Java applications are typically translated via *Property* files. Based on the language of the user the Java Runtime will search for the corresponding resource bundle using language identifiers. If a certain language identifier is not provided, the Java runtime will fall back to the next general resource bundle.

For example:

- messages.properties: default language file, if nothing else is available
- messages_de.properties: used for German
- message_en.properties: default for English
- message_en_US.properties: US English file
- message_en_UK.properties: British English file

Resource bundles in Java are always LATIN-1 encoded.

45.2. Relevant files for translation

The following table lists the relevant elements for translation of an Eclipse 4 application.

Table 45.1. Translation relevant entities for Eclipse plug-ins

Entity	Description
plugin.xml	Primarily important for Eclipse 3.x based plug-ins.
application model (Application.e4xmi)	Describes the application model in Eclipse 4.
Source Code	The source code contains text, e.g. for label which also must be translated.

45.3. Best practices

It is best practice to have one language plug-in which defines the texts for the main language.

Additional languages for Eclipse plug-ins are typically provided via fragments which extend the host plug-in.

45.4. Setting the language in the launch configuration

By default Eclipse uses the language configured in the Operating System of the user.

For testing you can set the language manually. In your Eclipse launch configuration on the *Arguments* tab you can specify the runtime parameter `-nl` to select the language, e.g. `-nl en`.

45.5. OSGi resource bundles

For the translation Eclipse uses OSGi resource bundles. This is based on the property files in the `OSGi-INF/l10n/` folder. OSGi expects at least one bundle property file, e.g. `bundle.properties`, in this folder.

Via the `Bundle-Localization` attribute in the `MANIFEST.MF` file, you point to these files.

```
Manifest-Version: 1.0
Bundle-ManifestVersion: 2
Bundle-Name: I18n
Bundle-SymbolicName: de.vogella.rcp.i18n; singleton:=true
Bundle-Version: 1.0.0.qualifier
Bundle-Activator: de.vogella.rcp.i18n.Activator
Require-Bundle: org.eclipse.ui,
 org.eclipse.core.runtime
Bundle-ActivationPolicy: lazy
Bundle-RequiredExecutionEnvironment: JavaSE-1.6
Bundle-Localization: OSGI-INF/l10n/bundle
```

The `bundle.properties` file contains key/values.

```
#Properties file
TodoOverviewPart=Overview of Todos
TodoDetailPart=Todo Details
```

Alternative languages are defined via additional property files. The filename of these files include a language indicator, e.g. `bundle_en.properties`.

45.6. Translating plugin.xml

The key in your property file can be used for contribution to extensions points in the `plugin.xml` file via the *%key* reference. This is used mainly in the label attribute.

The Eclipse tooling supports extracting existing strings from the `plugin.xml` file. Select your `plugin.xml` file, right-click on it and select PDE Tools → Externalize Strings.

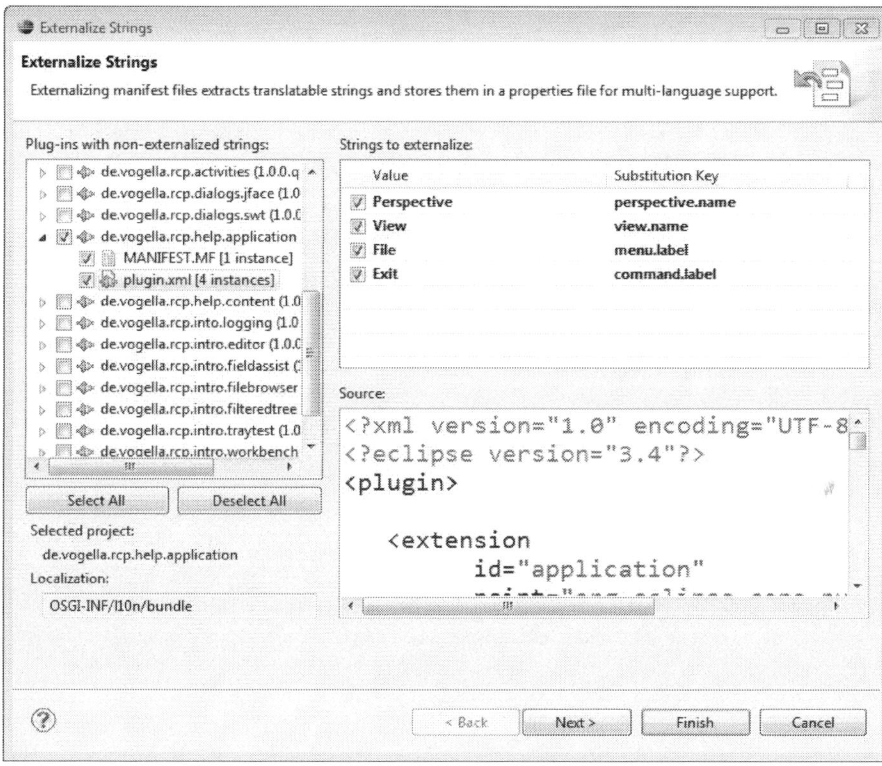

Via PDE Tools → Internationalize you can also directly create one or several fragments for the result of the internationalization.

45.7. Translating the application model

The translation of model element is similar to the translation to the `plugin.xml` file. Use *%key* for labels in the model.

Currently the application model includes rudimentary support for extracting Strings. Press the right mouse key in the application model editor and select, *Externalize Strings*.

You can also manually replace the hard-coded strings with a *%key* placeholder and create the `bundle.property` file.

To create the bundle.property file and the OSGi reference you can use the PDE wizard.

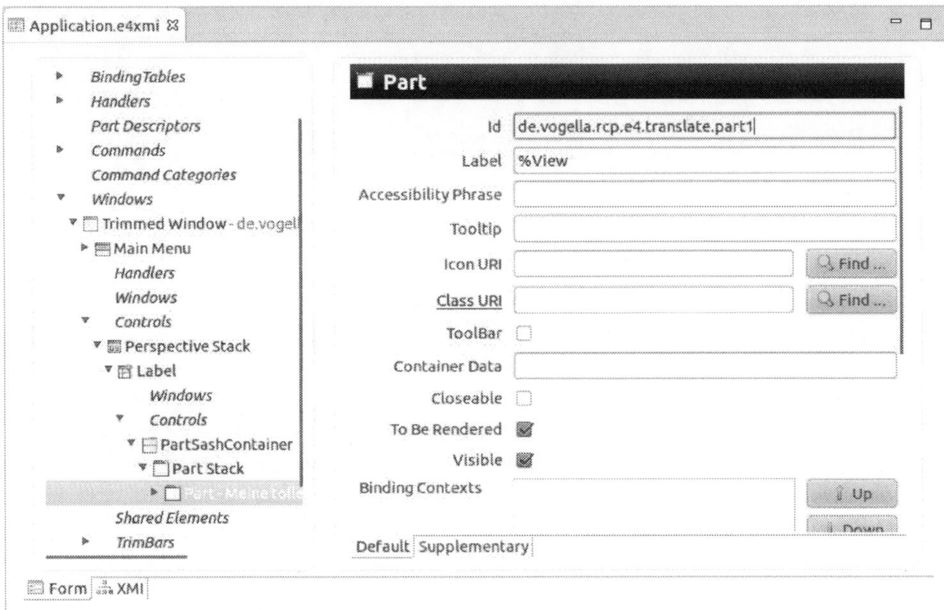

45.8. Translating your source code

To translate String in the source code, select the file you want to translate and select Source → Externalize Strings.

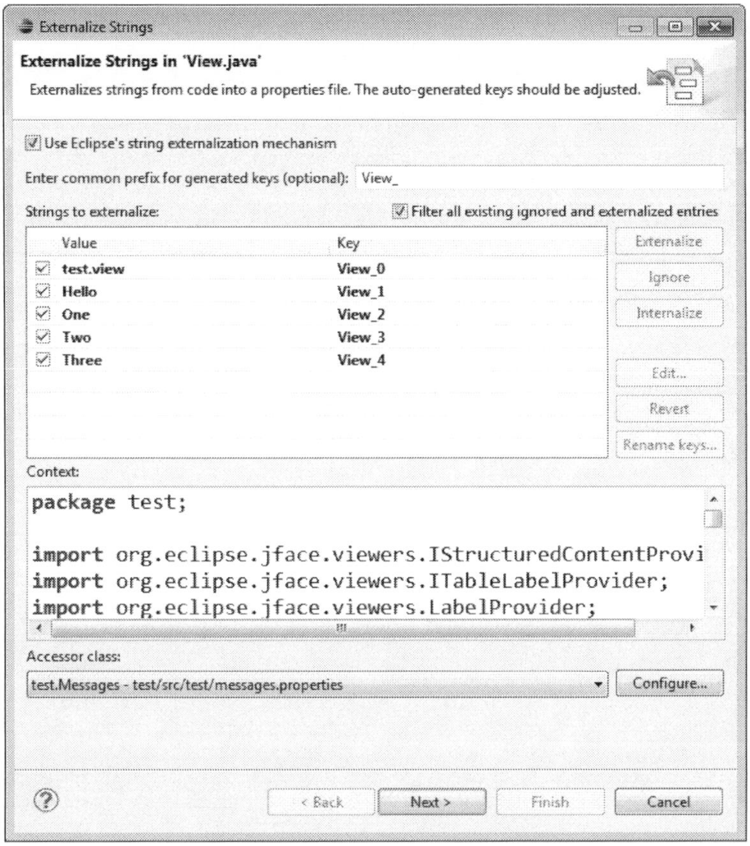

In this wizard you can select which strings should be translated, which can be skipped for the translation and which strings should be marked as not translatable.

If you select that a string should not be translated Eclipse will mark these strings with a `$NON-NLS` comment in the source code.

As the result a `Messages` class is generated which serves as an access point for the properties file.

```
package test;

import org.eclipse.osgi.util.NLS;

public class Messages extends NLS {
 private static final String BUNDLE_NAME
  = "test.messages"; //$NON-NLS-1$
 public static String View_0;
 public static String View_1;
```

```
  static {
    // initialize resource bundle
    NLS.initializeMessages(BUNDLE_NAME, Messages.class);
  }

  private Messages() {
  }
}
```

Via the BUNDLE_NAME constant it points to a resource `message*.properties` file in the `test` package. * is a placeholder for your locale, e.g. _de,_en, etc.

```
View_0=test.view
View_1=Hello
```

In your code you access the translations via the `Message` class.

```
label.setText(Messages.View_1);
```

You can also use placeholder in the messages and evaluate them with the `NLS.bind()` method.

```
MyMessage = {0} says {1}
```

```
// NLS bind will call the toString method on obj
NLS.bind(Message.MyMessage, obj, obj);
```

If Strings should be consistently used over several plug-ins, it is best practice to create a separate plug-in or fragment for the Messages. All plug-ins which wants to use the Messages define a dependency to this plug-in.

Additional languages are typically contributed via Eclipse fragment projects to this message plug-in.

45.9. Exporting Plug-ins and Products

The `build.properties` file in a plug-in defines which of the files are included in the exported product.

You must include your property files in the `build.properties` file otherwise your translations will be missing in the exported product.

45.10. Flexible Eclipse 4 Internationalization

The translation based on property files was hard-coded into Eclipse 3.x. Eclipse 4 replaces this with a flexible approach.

Eclipse 4 introduced a translation service via the `TranslationService` interface. The default implementation of this class is the `BundleTranslationProvider` which will work on property files but you can provide your own OSGi service which uses a different source, e.g. a database to get the translations.

This service is stored in the Application Context. You can replace it here, e.g. via a lifecyle hook. By storing it in the Eclipse Context you can have different translation services for different local contexts, e.g. for different Windows you can use different translation services.

45.11. Common problems with i18n

- Translations not available in the exported product: Check the `build.properties` file of the plug-in which provides the property files, if the property files are included in the export.
- Translations are not displayed in the application: OSGi caches text information, select *Clear Configuration* in your launch configuration.

46. Exercise: Internationalization

Externalize your relevant Strings in your `com.example.e4.rcp.todo` plug-in and provide them in English and in and in another language of your choice.

Using the *`-nl`* start parameter in your launch configuration, ensure that the application work well in English and in your other language.

Part V. Eclipse 4 Advanced Development

Table of Contents

47. Model dynamics at runtime

47.1. Overview

We have learned that the model elements can be injected. As the model is interactive, you can change it at runtime, for example you can change the size of the current window, add Parts to your application or remove menu entries. This chapter lists a few examples.

47.2. Example: Dynamically create a new Window

To create new model objects you can use the `MBasicFactory.INSTANCE` class. This is a factory used to create new model objects via typed `create*()` methods. For example you can create a new Window at runtime as shown in the following snippet.

```
// Create a new window and set its size
MWindow window = MBasicFactory.INSTANCE.createTrimmedWindow();
window.setWidth(200);
window.setHeight(300);

// Add new Window to the application
application.getChildren().add(window);
```

47.3. Example: Dynamically create a new Part

For example the following adds a new part to the currently active window.

```
package testing.handlers;

import org.eclipse.e4.core.di.annotations.Execute;
import org.eclipse.e4.ui.model.[CONTINUE...]
  .application.descriptor.basic.MPartDescriptor;
import org.eclipse.e4.ui.model.application.ui.basic.MBasicFactory;
import org.eclipse.e4.ui.model.application.ui.basic.MPart;
import org.eclipse.e4.ui.model.application.ui.basic.MWindow;

public class AddPartHandler {
 @Execute
 public void execute(MWindow window) {

  MPart part = MBasicFactory.INSTANCE.createPart();
  part.setLabel("New part");
  part.setContributionURI("platform:/plugin/" +
    "testing/testing.MyView");
  window.getChildren().add(part);
```

```
  }
}
```

47.4. Example: Implement Editor behavior

The following snippet demonstrates how to use the `MDirtyable` model property in a part to flag it as a Part which should be saved by the corresponding workbench action.

```
import javax.annotation.PostConstruct;
import javax.inject.Inject;

import org.eclipse.e4.ui.di.Persist;
import org.eclipse.e4.ui.model.application.ui.MDirtyable;
import org.eclipse.swt.SWT;
import org.eclipse.swt.events.SelectionAdapter;
import org.eclipse.swt.events.SelectionEvent;
import org.eclipse.swt.widgets.Button;
import org.eclipse.swt.widgets.Composite;

public class MySavePart {

 @Inject
 MDirtyable dirty;

 @PostConstruct
 public void createControls(Composite parent) {
  Button button = new Button(parent, SWT.PUSH);
  button.addSelectionListener(new SelectionAdapter() {
   @Override
   public void widgetSelected(SelectionEvent e) {
    dirty.setDirty(true);
   }
  });
 }

 @Persist
 public void save() {
  System.out.println("Saving data");
  // Save the data
  // ...
  // Now set the dirty flag to false
  dirty.setDirty(false);
 }

}
```

48. Eclipse 4 Platform Services

48.1. Overview

Services are software components which provide functionality. The Eclipse platform defines several services, which can be used in an Eclipse plug-in. To access them you can use dependency injection.

Services are technically defined as OSGi services.

To use an Eclipse service you specify the service dependency via an `@Inject` annotation and the Eclipse framework will inject this component into your class.

The typical naming convention for Eclipse services is that they start with an *E* " and end with *Service* e.g. *E*Service*. The most important services are:

Table 48.1. Platform Services

Service	Description
EModelService	Find elements in the model, create or clone snippets and insert new elements model structures
ESelectionService	Retrieve and set the current workbench selection.
ECommandService	Access, create, change and trigger commands.
EHandlerService	Access, change and trigger handlers.
EPartService	Provides API to access parts, e.g. find parts by their ID. It allows you to switch Perspectives and to hide and show Parts.
IEventBroker	Provides functionality to send event data and to register for certain events.
StatusReporter	Allows you uto report Status objects, concise interface compared to standard IStatus reporting.
EContextService	Activate and deactivate keybindings defined as `BindingContext` in the application model.
IThemeEngine	Define themes and switch the styling at runtime.

Other available services are:

- org.eclipse.e4.core.services.Adapter - An adapter can adapt an object to the specified type, allowing clients to request domain-specific behavior for an object. It integrates `IAdaptable` and `IAdapterManager`.
- org.eclipse.e4.core.services.Logger - Provides logging functionality

There are additional services available which depends on SWT.

- EMenuService - Registers a popup menu (MPopupMenu) for an SWT control.
- org.eclipse.jface.window.IShellProvider - allows access to a `Shell`

48.2. Model Service

The `EModelService` service gives access to the model and allows you to modify it, e.g. add and remove model elements.

It can get injected via `@Inject EModelService`.

The `findElements()` method allows you to search for specific model elements. The following code shows an example for using the `findElements()` method.

```
package com.example.e4.rcp.todo.handlers;

import java.util.ArrayList;
import java.util.List;
import java.util.concurrent.TimeUnit;

import org.eclipse.e4.core.di.annotations.Execute;
import org.eclipse.e4.ui.model.application.MApplication;
import org.eclipse.e4.ui.model.application.ui.MUIElement;
import org.eclipse.e4.ui.model.application.ui.basic.MPart;
import org.eclipse.e4.ui.model.application.ui.basic.MWindow;
import org.eclipse.e4.ui.workbench.modeling.EModelService;
import org.eclipse.swt.widgets.Display;

public class ModelServiceExampleHandler {

 @Execute
 public void execute(MApplication application,
   EModelService service,
   Display display) {
  System.out.println("Got Model Service: "
   + (service != null));

  // Alternatively to get the model service
  // via the application
  EModelService modelService =
    (EModelService) application.getContext()
    .get(EModelService.class.getName());

  // both services are identical
  System.out.println("Got Model Service: "
    + (service != modelService));
```

```
    // Find objects by ID
    findObjectsById(application, service);

    // Find objects by type
    findObjectsByType(application, service);

    // Find objects by tags
    findObjectsByTag(application, service);

    // Get the MWindow and change its size
    getWindowAndChangeSize(application, service, display);

  }


  // Example for search by ID
  private void findObjectsById(MApplication application,
    EModelService service) {
   List<MPart> findElements = service.findElements(application,
     "mypart",MPart.class, null);
   System.out.println("Found part(s) : " + findElements.size());

  }

  // Example for search by Type
  private void findObjectsByType(MApplication application,
    EModelService service) {
   List<MPart> parts = service.findElements(application, null,
     MPart.class, null);
   System.out.println("Found parts(s) : " + parts.size());

  }

  // Example for search by Tag
  private void findObjectsByTag(MApplication application,
    EModelService service) {
   List<String> tags = new ArrayList<String>();
   tags.add("justatag");
   List<MUIElement> elementsWithTags = service.findElements(application,
     null, null, tags);
   System.out.println("Found parts(s) : " + elementsWithTags.size());
  }

  // Example: Get the MWindow and change its size
   private void getWindowAndChangeSize(MApplication application,
     EModelService service, Display display) {
    List<MWindow> windows = service.findElements(application, null,
      MWindow.class, null);
    if (windows.size() >= 1) {
     MWindow mWindow = windows.get(0);
     System.out.println("Got the window");
     for (int i = mWindow.getWidth();
       i >= mWindow.getWidth() - 100; i--) {
```

```
      while (!display.readAndDispatch()) {
       mWindow.setWidth(i);
       wait10();
      }
     }
    }

   }

 private void wait10() {
   try {
    TimeUnit.SECONDS.sleep(10);
   } catch (InterruptedException e) {
    e.printStackTrace();
   }
  }
}
```

Here is an example of how to find the *Perspective* for a *Part*.

```
package com.example.e4.rcp.todo.handlers;

import org.eclipse.e4.core.di.annotations.Execute;
import org.eclipse.e4.ui.model.application.MApplication;
import org.eclipse.e4.ui.model.application.ui.MUIElement;
import org.eclipse.e4.ui.model.application.ui.advanced.MPerspective;
import org.eclipse.e4.ui.workbench.modeling.EModelService;

public class FindPerspectiveHandler{
 @Execute
 public void execute(MApplication application, EModelService service) {
  System.out.println("Called save");
  MUIElement element = service.
    find("com.example.e4.rcp.parts.tododetail",
       application);
  MPerspective perspective = service.getPerspectiveFor(element);
  System.out.println(perspective);
 }
}
```

The following example shows how to access a `PartSashContainer` with the `mypartsashcontainer` ID and how to set the *`container data`* parameter for its children. This will re-arrange (layout) the *Parts* in the container.

```
@Execute
public void execute(EModelService service, MWindow window) {
 MPartSashContainer find = (MPartSashContainer) service.
  find("mypartsashcontainer", window);
 List<MPartSashContainerElement> list = find.getChildren();
```

```
 int i = 0;
 // Make the first part in the container larger
 for (MPartSashContainerElement element : list) {
  element.setContainerData("80");
  if (i > 0) {
   element.setContainerData("20");
  }
  i++;
 }
}
```

In Eclipse 4.2 the model service does not find menu and toolbar model entries as well as handlers. It is expected that this will be changed in a release after Eclipse 4.2.

48.3. Part service

`EPartService` allows you to find and perform actions on *Parts* in the application model. It also allows you to switch *Perspectives* and to create new *Parts* based on *PartDescriptors*.

The following example shows how you can find *Parts*, hide them or show them. If the `Visible` attribute of the *Part* was initially set to `false` (not visible), you need to call the `setVisible(true)` method of the model element to ensure that the *Part* gets displayed.

```
@Inject private EPartService partService;

// Get the part
detailsTodoPart = partService.findPart("de.vogella.e4.tododetails");

// Hide the part
partService.hidePart(detailsTodoPart);

// Required if initial not visible
detailsTodoPart.setVisible(true);

//Show the part
partService.showPart(detailsTodoPart, PartState.VISIBLE);
```

The following example shows, how to save all *Parts* in the application model which are marked as dirty.

```
package com.example.e4.rcp.todo.handlers;

import org.eclipse.e4.core.di.annotations.Execute;
```

```
import org.eclipse.e4.ui.workbench.modeling.EPartService;

public class SaveHandler {

 @Execute
 void execute(EPartService partService) {
  partService.saveAll(false);
 }
}
```

The following example shows how you can switch to another *Perspective*.

```
package com.example.e4.rcp.todo.handlers;

import java.util.List;

import org.eclipse.e4.core.di.annotations.Execute;
import org.eclipse.e4.ui.model.application.MApplication;
import org.eclipse.e4.ui.model.application.ui.MUIElement;
import org.eclipse.e4.ui.model.application.ui.advanced.MPerspective;
import org.eclipse.e4.ui.model.application.ui.basic.MPart;
import org.eclipse.e4.ui.workbench.modeling.EModelService;
import org.eclipse.e4.ui.workbench.modeling.EPartService;
import org.eclipse.e4.ui.workbench.modeling.EPartService.PartState;

public class SwitchPerspectiveHandler {
 @Execute
 public void execute(MApplication app,
    EModelService modelService,
    EPartService partService) {
   List<MPerspective> list =
     modelService.findElements(app,
       "secondperspective",
       MPerspective.class,
       null);

   // Alternatively direct access via the ID
   // Result not used
     MPerspective element =
    (MPerspective) modelService.find("secondperspective", app);

   // Now switch perspective
   partService.switchPerspective(list.get(0));


 }
}
```

If you defined a *PartDescriptor* in your application model you can use the `EPartService` to create a Part from this template.

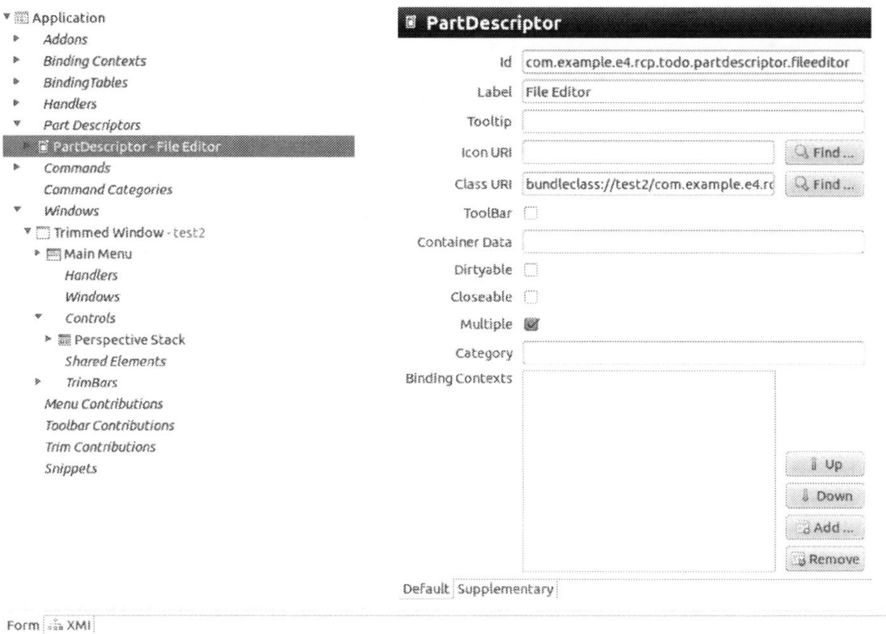


```
package com.example.e4.rcp.todo.handlers;

import org.eclipse.e4.core.di.annotations.Execute;
import org.eclipse.e4.ui.model.application.ui.basic.MPart;
import org.eclipse.e4.ui.workbench.modeling.EPartService;
import org.eclipse.e4.ui.workbench.modeling.EPartService.PartState;

public class OpenPartHandler {

 @Execute
 public void execute(EPartService partService) {

  // Create a new Part based on a PartDescriptor
  // in the Application model
  MPart part = partService
    .createPart("com.example.e4.rcp.todo.partdescriptor.fileeditor");
  part.setLabel("New Dynamic Part");

  // If multiple parts of this type is allowed
  // in the application model,
  // then the provided part will be shown
  // and returned
  partService.showPart(part, PartState.ACTIVATE);
 }
}
```

48.4. Selection service

48.4.1. Getting the selection service

The `ESelectionService` service allows you to retrieve the current workbench selection.

A client can get the selection service via: `@Inject ESelectionService`.

The `getSelection()` method allows to get the last global selection. The `getSelection(partId)` method allows you to retrieve the selection of a specific *Part*.

48.4.2. Changing the current selection

You can change the current selection with the `setSelection()` method.

The consumer defines a method with a named (`@Named`) parameter (`IServiceConstants.ACTIVE_SELECTION`) and a type. The Eclipse framework makes sure that selections are only injected if they have the fitting type.

```
@Inject ESelectionService selectionService;

// viewer is a JFace Viewer
viewer.addSelectionChangedListener(new ISelectionChangedListener() {
 @Override
 public void selectionChanged(SelectionChangedEvent event) {
  IStructuredSelection selection = (IStructuredSelection)
    viewer.getSelection();
  Object firstElement = selection.getFirstElement();
  selectionService.setSelection(selection.getFirstElement());
 }
});
```

```
@Inject
public void setTodo(@Optional
  @Named(IServiceConstants.ACTIVE_SELECTION) Todo todo) {
 if (todo != null) {
  // Do something with the value
 }
}
```

48.5. Command and Handler service

The `ECommandService` and `EHandlerService` provide the functionality to work with commands and handlers, e.g. create and change them.

A client can get these services injected via dependency injection.

For example via the handler service you could add a handler to the IEclipseContext of a perspective, even though the application model does not foresee this.

The following example shows how to add a new handler to an existing command. It assumes that the `AboutHandler` handler class already exists.

```
Command command = commandService.getCommand("com.example.mycommand");

//Returns true
System.out.println(command.isDefined());

// Activate Handler, assume AboutHandler() class exists already
handlerService.activateHandler("com.example.mycommand",
  new AboutHandler());

ParameterizedCommand cmd =
 commandService.createCommand("com.example.mycommand", null);

//Some methods on command are only there for legacy reasons
//and return nonsense
//Return null and false
System.out.println(command.getHandler());
System.out.println(command.isEnabled());

// Test if execution works fine
System.out.println(handlerService.canExecute(cmd));
handlerService.executeHandler(cmd);
```

Currently some methods are only used in the compatibility layer.

49. Exercise: Selection and part service

49.1. SelectionService

In this section you will propagate the selection of the viewer in the `TodoOverviewPart` to your `TodoDetailsPart`.

In your `TodoOverviewPart` acquire the selection service.

Use the selection service to set the selection in the selection service, once the user selects an entry in the list.

Define a method which will be called by the Eclipse framework if the selection is set with an object of type "Todo". If the selection is set update your user interface.

```
@Inject
public void setTodo(@Optional
  @Named(IServiceConstants.ACTIVE_SELECTION) Todo todo) {
  if (todo != null) {
    this.todo = todo;
    updateUserInterface(todo);
  }
}

private updateUserInterface(Todo todo){
  // Check if Ui is available
  if (summary!=null){
    summary.setText(todo.getSummary());
    description.setText(todo.getDescription());
  }
}
```

If you now select a `Todo` item in your table, this selection is propagated via the selection service to the `TodoDetailsPart` class.

Please keep in mind that ALL injections run before `@PostConstruct`, e.g. the annotated constructor, the annotated fields and the annotated setter methods. `@PostConstruct` will be executed afterwards. Hence you need to check if your user interface is already available.

49.2. Set TodoDetailsPart to dirty

Use the `MDirtyable` attribute to mark the `TodoDetailsPart` as dirty once the user changes data via the user interface.

Implement the *save* command so that the user changes can be saved.

```
package com.example.e4.rcp.todo.handlers;

import org.eclipse.e4.core.di.annotations.Execute;
import org.eclipse.e4.ui.workbench.modeling.EPartService;

public class SaveAllHandler {

  @Execute
  void execute(EPartService partService) {
   partService.saveAll(false);
  }
}
```

49.3. PartService in a Handler

Change your `SaveAllHandler` class so that the *save* handler is only active if there is a *Part* in the model which has its `dirty` attribute set to true.

```
@CanExecute
boolean canExecute(@Optional MWindow window) {
 if (window == null) return false;

 IEclipseContext context = window.getContext();
 if (context == null) return false;

 EPartService partService = context.get(EPartService.class);
 if (partService == null) return false;

 return !partService.getDirtyParts().isEmpty();
}
```

49.4. PartService in a Part

In this exercise you make the `TodoDetailsPart` initially not visible. Once the user selects an entry, the Part is set to visible.

In your application model, change the visibility of your `TodoDetailsPart` to initially not visible.

In your `TodoOverviewPart` acquire the part service.

If the user selects an entry in the list, set the `TodoDetailsPart` to visible via the part service. Please note that you also have to set the model attribute of the Part to visible to make this work.

50. Asynchronous processing

50.1. User Interface Thread

By default Eclipse uses one `Thread` to run all the code instructions. This `Thread` also creates the event loop for the user interface (UI) and is the only `Thread` that is allowed to interact with the UI.

This `Thread` is called the *UI thread* or *main thread*. It is created by the `org.eclipse.swt.widgets.Display` class.

If another `Thread`, which is not the *UI thread*, tries to update the UI, the *SWT* framework will raise a `SWTException` exception.

```
org.eclipse.swt.SWTException: Invalid thread access
```

All events in the user interface will be executed one after another. If you perform a long running operation in the *UI thread*, the user interface will not respond to any user interaction.

Therefore it is important not to block this thread, e.g. with network or file access otherwise the user interface will appear frozen.

All long running operations should be performed in a separate `Thread`.

The Eclipse framework provides ways for a `Thread` to synchronize itself with the user interface. It also provides the Eclipse Jobs Framework which allows you to run operations in the background using the Eclipse platform.

50.2. Using syncExec() and asyncExec()

If you need to update the user interface from another `Thread`, you can use the `syncExec()` and `asyncExec()` methods of the `Display` object.

```
// Update the user interface asynchronously
Display.getDefault().asyncExec(new Runnable() {
 public void run() {
  // ... do any work that updates the screen ...
 }
});

// Update the user interface synchronously
```

```
Display.getDefault().syncExec(new Runnable() {
 public void run() {
  // Do any work that updates the screen ...
  // Remember to check if the widget
  // still exists
  // Might happen if the Part was closed
 }
});
```

50.3. Eclipse 4 UISynchronize

The `org.eclipse.e4.ui.di` plug-in contains the `UISynchronize` class. An instance of this class is in the Eclipse 4 context and can be injected into an Eclipse 4 application via dependency injection.

`UISynchronize` also provides the `syncExec()` and `asyncExec()` methods to synchronize with the main thread.

Using `UISynchronize` is the preferred method rather than using the `Display` class, as this allows a consistent programming model using dependency injection.

50.4. Eclipse Jobs API

The Eclipse Jobs API provides support for running background processes. It allows you to provide feedback about the progress of the `Job` to the user via a progress indicator.

The important parts of the Job API are:

- IJobManager - Schedules the jobs
- Job - The individual task to perform
- IProgressMonitor - Interface to communicate information about the status of your Job.

You create a `Job` via the following:

```
Job job = new Job("My Job") {
 @Override
 protected IStatus run(IProgressMonitor monitor) {
  // Do something long running
  //...

  // If you want to update the UI
  Display.getDefault().asyncExec(new Runnable() {
```

```
    @Override
    public void run() {
      // Do something in the user interface
      // e.g. set a text field
    }
  });
  return Status.OK_STATUS;
 }
};

// Start the Job
job.schedule();
```

If you want to update the UI from a `Job` you still need to use the `Display.syncExec()` or `asyncExec()` methods.

50.5. Priorities of Jobs

You can set the `Job` priority via the `job.setPriority()` method using the constants defined in the `Job` class, e.g. `Job.SHORT`, `Job.LONG`, `Job.BUILD` and `Job.DECORATE`.

The job scheduler will use these priorities to determine in which order the `Jobs` are scheduled. For example `Jobs` with the priority `Job.SHORT` are scheduled before jobs with `Job.LONG`. `Jobs` with the priority `Job.DECORATE` are scheduled after all other jobs are finished. Check the JavaDoc of the `Job` class for details.

50.6. Blocking the UI and providing feedback

Sometimes you simply want to give the user the feedback that something is running without using `Threads`.

The easiest way to provide feedback is to change the cursor via the `BusyIndicator.showWhile()` method call.

```
// Show a busy indicator while the runnable is executed
BusyIndicator.showWhile(display, runnable);
```

If this code is executed, the cursor will change to a busy indicator until the `Runnable` is done.

A more advanced approach is to use a `ProgressMonitorDialog` together with an `IRunnableWithProgress`.

50.7. IProgressMonitor

The `IProgressMonitor` object can be used to report progress. Use the `beginTask()` method to define the total units of work and the `worked()` method to report the additional units of work.

```
Job job = new Job("My Job") {
 @Override
 protected IStatus run(IProgressMonitor monitor) {
  // Set total number of work units
  monitor.beginTask("Doing something time consuming here", 100);
  for (int i = 0; i < 5; i++) {
   try {
     // Sleep a second
     TimeUnit.SECONDS.sleep(1)

     monitor.subTask("I'm doing something here " + i);

     // Report that 20 units are done
     monitor.worked(20);
    } catch (InterruptedException e1) {
     e1.printStackTrace();
     break;
    }
   }
  System.out.println("Called save");
  return Status.OK_STATUS;
  }
 };
job.schedule();
```

50.8. Reporting Progress in Eclipse 4

In Eclipse 4 you can report progress by implementing the `IProgressMonitor` interface.

You can for example add a `ToolItem` to a Toolbar of your Window Trim in your application model. This `ToolItem` can implement the `IProgressMonitor` interface.

This is demonstrated in the following example.

```
package com.example.e4.rcp.todo.ui.composites;

import javax.annotation.PostConstruct;

import org.eclipse.core.runtime.IProgressMonitor;
import org.eclipse.swt.SWT;
import org.eclipse.swt.widgets.Composite;
```

```
import org.eclipse.swt.widgets.Display;
import org.eclipse.swt.widgets.ProgressBar;

public class MyToolItem implements IProgressMonitor {
 private ProgressBar progressBar;

 @PostConstruct
 public void createControls(Composite parent) {
  System.out.println("ToolItem");
  progressBar = new ProgressBar(parent, SWT.SMOOTH);
  progressBar.setBounds(100, 10, 200, 20);
 }

 @Override
 public void worked(final int work) {
  Display.getDefault().asyncExec(new Runnable() {
   @Override
   public void run() {
    System.out.println("Worked");
    progressBar.setSelection(progressBar.getSelection() + work);
   }
  });
 }

 @Override
 public void subTask(String name) {

 }

 @Override
 public void setTaskName(String name) {

 }

 @Override
 public void setCanceled(boolean value) {

 }

 @Override
 public boolean isCanceled() {
  return false;
 }

 @Override
 public void internalWorked(double work) {
 }

 @Override
 public void done() {
  System.out.println("Done");

 }
```

```
  @Override
  public void beginTask(String name, int totalWork) {
   System.out.println("Starting");
  }
 }
```

This new element can be accessed via the model service and used as an `IProgressMonitor` for the job.

```
// EModelService injected as service
// Mapplication injected as application

Job job = new Job("My Job") {
 // As before
};

// Setting the progress monitor
IJobManager manager = job.getJobManager();

// ToolItem has the ID "statusbar" in the model
MToolControl element = (MToolControl) service.find("statusbar",
 application);

Object widget = element.getObject();
final IProgressMonitor p = (IProgressMonitor) widget;
ProgressProvider provider = new ProgressProvider() {
 @Override
 public IProgressMonitor createMonitor(Job job) {
  return p;
 }
};

manager.setProgressProvider(provider);
job.schedule();
```

A more advanced implementation could for example implement a Progress Monitoring OSGi Service and report progress to the user interface via the EventAdmin service.

51. Exercise: Using asynchronous processing

Change your `getTodos()` method in `MyTodoModelImpl` to the following example. This code simulates a slow server access with the `TimeUnit` class.

```
// Always return a new copy of the data
@Override
public List<Todo> getTodos() {
  // Simulate Server access delay
  try {
   TimeUnit.SECONDS.sleep(5);
  } catch (InterruptedException e) {
   e.printStackTrace();
  }

  List<Todo> list = new ArrayList<Todo>();
  for (Todo todo : model) {
   list.add(todo.copy());
  }
  return list;
}
```

Start your application. What happens? What happens if you press the `Button` to fill the JFace table?

Change your user interface so that the content of the table in `TodoOverviewPart` is automatically loaded via a Job in the background.

Once the data is loaded, update the JFace `Viewer` with the new data. Make sure that this happens in the user interface thread.

After finishing this exercises and validating that everything works correctly, change the delay to one second.

52. OSGi services

52.1. Overview

A bundle can register and use OSGi services. An OSGi service registered Java class provides a certain functionality.

OSGi provides the central OSGi Service Registry for this purpose.

A service in OSGi is defined by a standard Java class or interface. Typically a Java interface is used to define the service interface.

A service in OSGi can be dynamically started and stopped, therefore the bundles must manage these dependencies themselves. The bundles can register listeners to be informed, if a service is started or stopped.

52.2. BundleContext

Access to the service registry is performed via the `BundleContext` class.

A bundle can define a `Bundle-Activator` (Activator) in its declaration. This class must extend the `BundleActivator` interface.

If defined, OSGi injects the `BundleContext` into the start() and stop() methods of the implementing `Activator` class.

```
import org.osgi.framework.BundleActivator;
import org.osgi.framework.BundleContext;

public class Activator implements BundleActivator {

 public void start(BundleContext context) throws Exception {
  System.out.println("Starting bundle");
  // Do something with the context, e.g.
  // register services
 }

 public void stop(BundleContext context) throws Exception {
  System.out.println("Stopping bundle");
  serviceTracker.close();
  // Do something with the context, e.g.
  // deregister service
 }
```

```
}
```

If you do not have an `Activator`, you can use the `FrameworkUtil` class from the OSGi framework which allows you to retrieve the `BundleContext` for a class.

```
BundleContext bundleContext =
    FrameworkUtil.
    getBundle(this.getClass()).
    getBundleContext();
```

52.3. Registering services

A bundle can also register itself for the events (`ServiceEvents`) of the `BundleContext`. These are, for example, triggered if a new bundle is installed or de-installed or if a new service is registered.

To publish a service in your bundle use:

```
public class Activator implements BundleActivator {
 // ...
 public void start(BundleContext context) throws Exception {
  context.
    registerService(IMyService.class.getName(),
        new ServiceImpl(), null);

 }
 // ...
}
```

Once the service is no longer used you must unregister the service with OSGi. OSGi counts the usage of services to enable the dynamic replacement of services.

```
context.ungetService(serviceReference);
```

52.4. Accessing a service

A bundle can acquire a service via the `BundleContext` class. The following example demonstrates that.

```
ServiceReference<?> serviceReference = context.
 getServiceReference(IMyService.class.getName());
IMyService service = (IMyService) context.
 getService(serviceReference);
```

52.5. Selection of OGSi services

If several services are available and valid then the OSGi runtime will by default select the service with the lowest bundle ID. You can also set a service ranking for your services via a property. OSGi assigns by default a value of zero as the service ranking and selects the service with the highest ranking.

The `Constants` class from the `org.osgi.framework` package defines via `Constants.SERVICE_RANKING` the *`service.ranking`* constant. This constant can be used to set the integer property of the service ranking.

In the `registerService()` method from the `BundleContext` class you can specify arbitrary properties in the Dictionary.

You can use the `getProperty()` method of the `org.osgi.framework.ServiceReference` class, to access a specific property.

52.6. Best practices for defining services

It is common practice to define the service via a bundle which only contains the interface definition. Another bundle would provide the implementation for this service. This allows you to change the implementation of the service via a different bundle.

52.7. OSGi Service Tracker

OSGi allows services that are dynamically defined, stopped and updated. To use this you can use the `ServiceTracker` class. `ServiceTracker` has the `addingService()` and `removedService()` methods in which you can define your code to react to the change.

The class ServiceTracker can be either used directly or via the ServiceTrackerCustomizer interface.

```
MyQuoteServiceTrackerCustomizer customer =
 new MyQuoteServiceTrackerCustomizer(context);

serviceTracker = new ServiceTracker(context,
  IQuoteService.class.getName(),
  customer);

serviceTracker.open();
```

OSGi provides a service to track service events, e.g. new service registered, service stopped, service started. For this the `org.osgi.util.tracker` package from the `org.eclipse.osgi` bundle can be used.

52.8. Problems with service tracker

The problem with service trackers is that they still obey Java rules. In the case where your service consumer keeps a reference to the service, this service cannot be removed via the OSGi framework. The other disadvantage is that the service tracker requires a lot of boilerplate code. To solve these issues declarative services were developed.

OSGi *declarative services* simplify the handling of OSGi services.

53. Declarative OSGi services

53.1. Overview

The *OSGi declarative services* (DS) functionality allows you to define and consume services via metadata (XML). Via DS you can define OSGi services without extending or implementing OSGi classes. This allows for these services to be tested independently of the OSGi runtime.

The *OSGi service component* is responsible for starting the service (service component). For the service consumer it is not visible if the service has been created via declarative service or via other means.

Service Components consists of an XML description (Component Description) and an object (Component Instance). The component description contains all information about the service component, e.g. the class name of the component instance and the service interface.

A reference to the component description is maintained in the `MANIFEST.MF` file. This file is read by the OSGi runtime. If a component description is found, the corresponding service is created. The component description in the `MANIFEST.MF` file looks for example like the following:

```
Service-Component: OSGI-INF/component.xml
```

53.2. Required bundles

To run declarative services you require the following bundles.

- org.eclipse.equinox.util
- org.eclipse.equinox.ds - Declarative service

53.3. Definition of a DS service

Typically component definitions are created in the project `OSGi-INF` folder via New → Other → Plug-in Development → Component Definition. The wizard will also add the `Service-Component` entry to the `MANIFEST.MF` file.

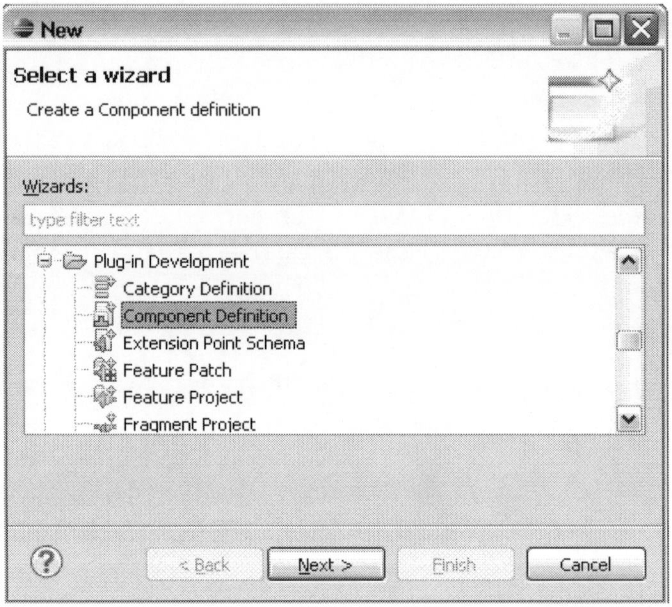

On the next page of the wizard, you can maintain the name of the component definition file, a name and the class which implements the services (or consumes the services).

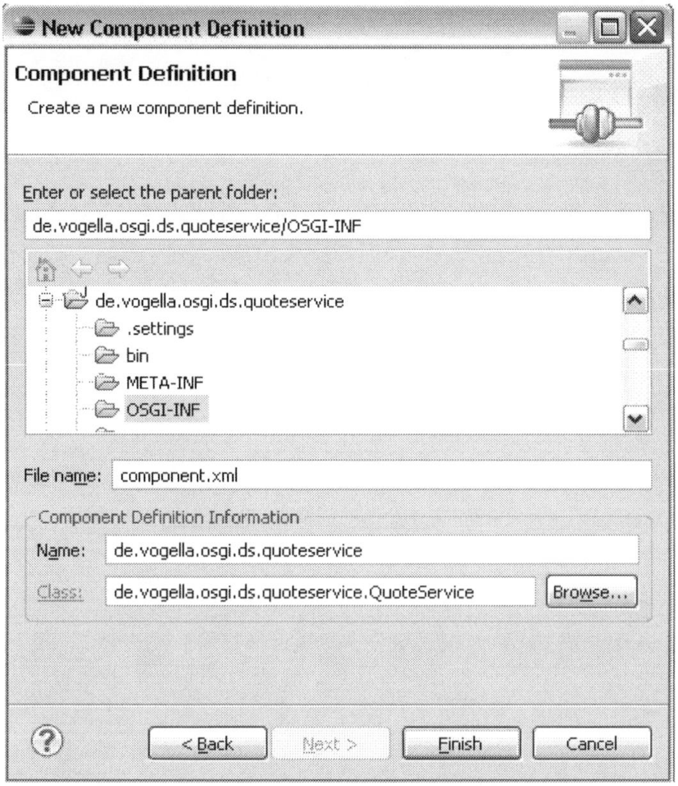

If you press finish, the service editor opens.

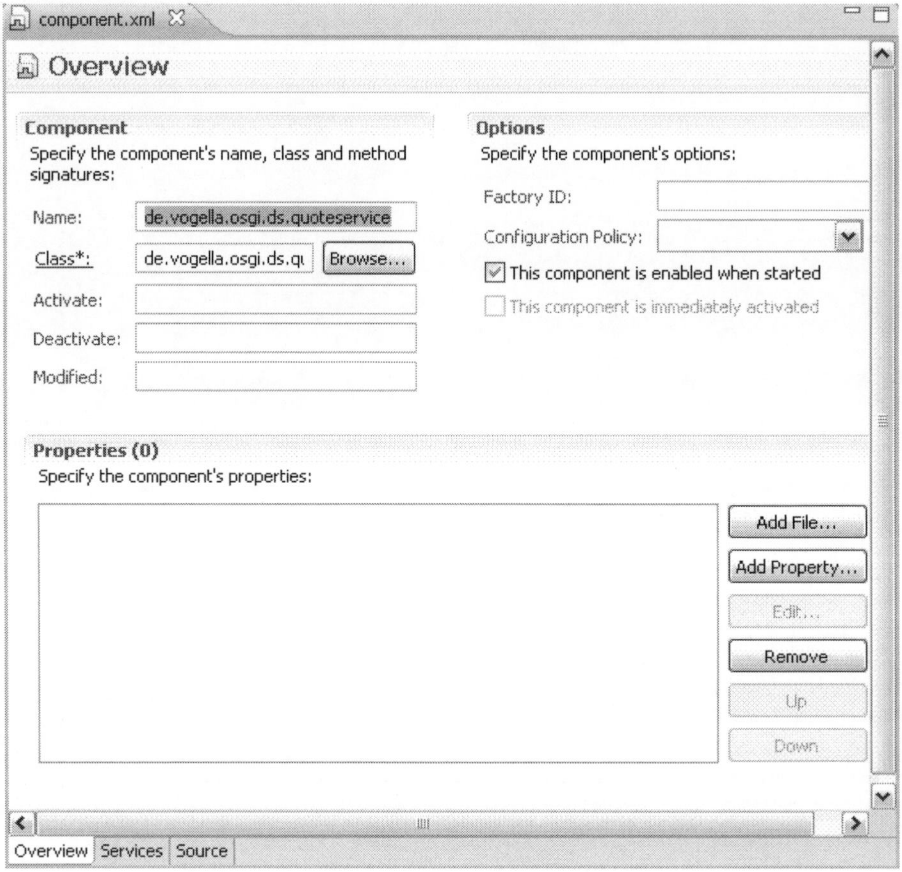

On the *Services* tab you can maintain provided services or referred services. For example to provide a service you would press the *Add* button under *Provided Services* and select the service interface you want to implement.

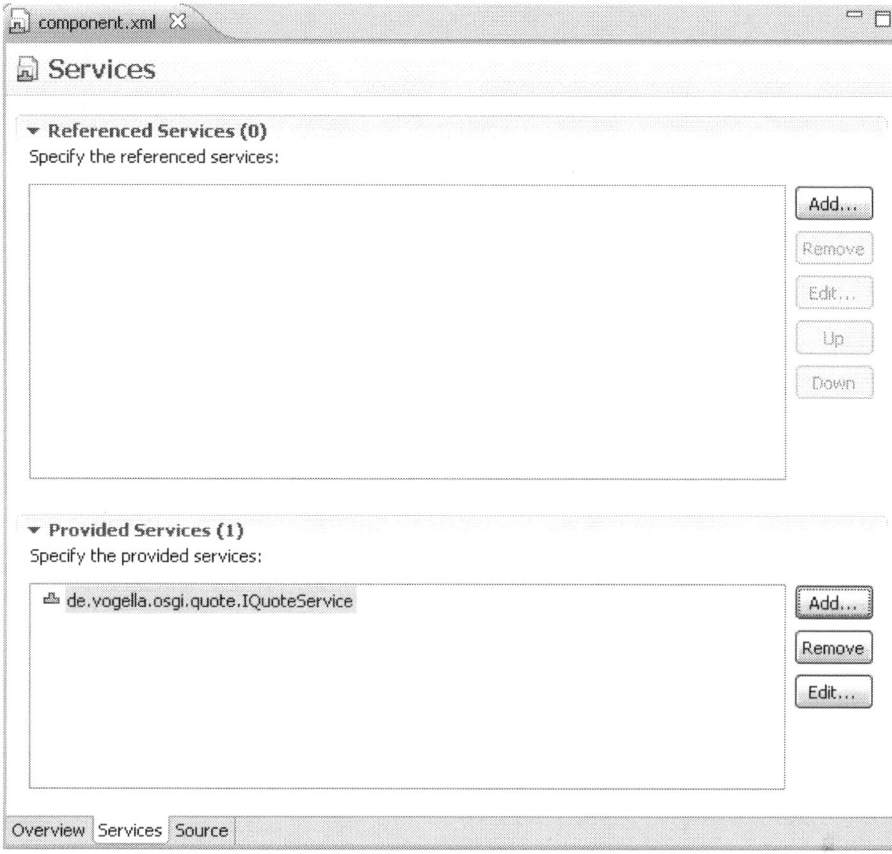

As a final step you would implement the class which would provide the service.

A correctly maintained `component.xml` XML file would look like the following.

```
<?xml version="1.0" encoding="UTF-8"?>
<scr:component xmlns:scr="http://www.osgi.org/xmlns/scr/v1.1.0"
 name="de.vogella.osgi.ds.quoteservice">
<implementation class="de.vogella.osgi.ds.quoteservice.QuoteService"/>
   <service>
      <provide interface="de.vogella.osgi.quote.IQuoteService"/>
   </service>
</scr:component>
```

This means that there is a component called *de.vogella.osgi.ds.quoteservice* which provides a service to the OSGi Service Registry under the

`IQuoteService` interface. This component is implemented by the `QuoteService` class.

After the definition of the component your `MANIFEST.MF` file would contain an entry to the service component.

```
Manifest-Version: 1.0
Bundle-ManifestVersion: 2
Bundle-Name: Quoteservice
Bundle-SymbolicName: de.vogella.osgi.ds.quoteservice
Bundle-Version: 1.0.0.qualifier
Bundle-RequiredExecutionEnvironment: JavaSE-1.6
Import-Package: de.vogella.osgi.quote
Service-Component: OSGI-INF/component.xml
```

53.4. Defining start levels

The `org.eclipse.equinox.ds` bundle is the bundle which is responsible for reading the component meta data and registering services.

Therefore this bundle needs to start before the service becomes available.

You can ensure this in your run configuration by setting `.ds` bundle and the bundle which contains the new service to auto start.

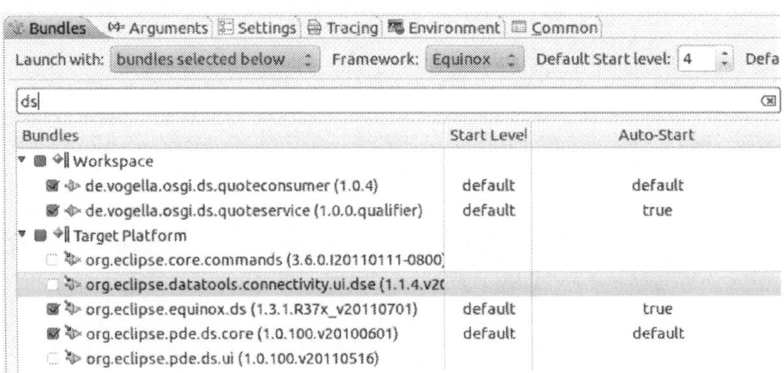

Please note that using start levels to ensure the correct starting of the OSGi bundles is not a good approach. Alternatively you can define a plug-in dependency but this is even worse as it prevents the flexibel replacement of plug-ins which provide the service.

53.5. Start level in Eclipse Products

In Eclipse 4 applications you can ensure the right start level by setting the `.ds` bundle and the bundle which contains the new service to auto start in your product definition file.

You also need to ensure that the service is available before your Eclipse 4 application starts otherwise the dependency injection framework will throw an error. You can ensure this by using a lower start level then the default one for your service and the .ds bundle.

The following screenshot shows an example for defining a start-level.

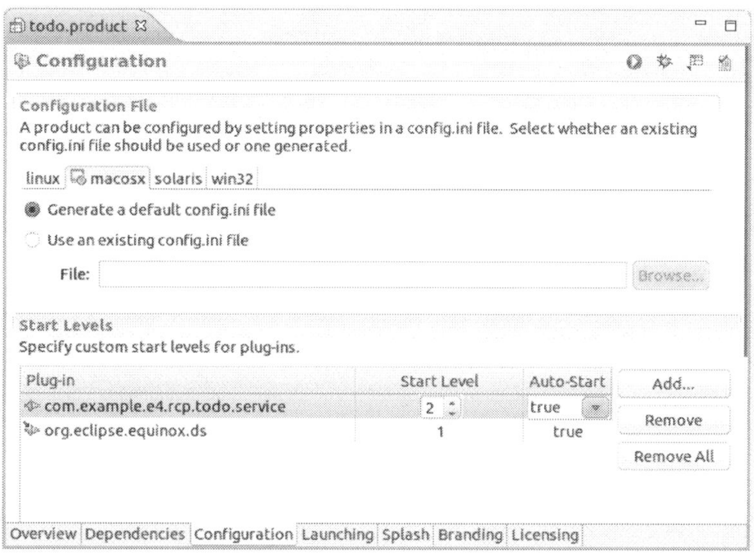

Please note that you may have to set the start-level for `org.eclipse.core.runtime` also, this should not be necessary but without this, an export application sometimes does not start. `org.eclipse.core.runtime` need to have the lowest start-level.

53.6. OSGi Services and Eclipse Context

OSGi Services are available for dependency injection in Eclipse 4. If you define your own OSGi services, you can inject them into your model objects. This removes the need to create Singletons in your application for accessing data.

54. Exercise: Define and use an OSGi service

You require that the following bundles are included in your product definition file. They are part of the `org.eclipse.e4.rcp` feature which your product is already based on.

- org.eclipse.equinox.util
- org.eclipse.equinox.ds

Via OSGi declarative services you define that the `com.example.e4.rcp.todo.service` plug-in provides a service for the `ITodoModel` interface via the existing `MyTodoModelImpl` class. The `component.xml` should look like the following example.

```
<?xml version="1.0" encoding="UTF-8"?>
<scr:component xmlns:scr="http://www.osgi.org/xmlns/scr/v1.1.0"
   name="com.example.e4.rcp.todo.service">
<implementation
 class="com.example.e4.rcp.todo.service.internal.MyTodoModelImpl"/>
<service>
 <provide interface="com.example.e4.rcp.todo.model.ITodoModel"/>
</service>
</scr:component>
```

Set the following plug-ins to `auto-start` in your product configuration file. You do this on the *Configuration* tab.

- org.eclipse.equinox.ds
- com.example.e4.rcp.todo.service

Assign the start-level 3 to these bundles and set them to auto-start, so that they are available before the application's plug-ins try to inject them.

Make sure that `com.example.e4.rcp.todo.service` does not export any packages. This should create syntax errors in the classes which use the `TodoService` Singleton. Change your relevant Parts so that the new OSGi service is injected into them.

Once all Parts are changed, test if everything works.

Afterwards delete the `TodoService` class from your `*.service` plug-in, this class is not required anymore.

55. Exercise: Create an Image Loader Service

55.1. Loading Images

You can load an image from your plug-in via the following code.

```
Bundle bundle = FrameworkUtil.getBundle(this.getClass());
URL url = FileLocator.find(bundle,
 new Path("icons/alt_window_32.gif"), null);

ImageDescriptor imageDescr = ImageDescriptor.createFromURL(url);
imageDescr.createImage();
```

Create a service for your application which performs this automatically based on a class and a path defined via a String.

55.2. Create Bundle

Create a new bundle called *com.example.e4.bundleresourceloader* with one interface called `IBundleResourceLoader`. This interface should define the `loadImage(Class, path)` method.

55.3. Create OSGi bundle

Implement a service in the new `*.bundleresourceloader` bundle.

Extend your table to also display an icon. Use your new OSGi service to load the icon.

56. Using dependency injection for your own Java objects

56.1. Overview

Using dependency injection for your own Java objects has two flavors. First you want the Eclipse dependency container to create your own objects and then get them injected into your model objects. Secondly you want to create objects which declare their dependencies with `@Inject` and want to create it via dependency injection.

Both approaches are described here.

56.2. Using dependency injection to get your own objects

If you want the Eclipse framework to create your objects for you, annotate them with `@Creatable`. This way you are telling the Eclipse DI container that it should create a new instance of this object if it does not find an instance in the context.

The Eclipse DI container will use the constructor with the highest number of parameters of this class for which the Eclipse DI container can find values in the Eclipse context. You can also use `@Inject` on the constructor to indicate that Eclipse should try to run dependency injection also for this constructor.

For example, assume that you have the following domain model.

```
@Creatable
class Todo {
 @Inject
 public Todo(Dependent depend, YourOSGiService service) {
      // placeholder
 }
}

@Creatable
class Dependent {
 public Dependent() {
 // placeholder
 }
}
```

If no fitting constructor is found, the Eclipse framework will throw an exception.

Assuming that you have defined the `YourOSGiService` service in your application, you can get an instance of your Todo data model injected in a Part.

```
// Field Injection
@Inject Todo todo
```

56.3. Using dependency injection to create objects

Using dependency injection is not limited to the objects created by the Eclipse runtime. You can use `@Inject` in a Java class and use the dependency injection framework to create your class.

```
// Create instance of class
ContextInjectionFactory.make(MyJavaObject.class, context);
```

The `ContextInjectionFactory.make()` method creates the object and puts it into the context with `*.class` as the key. If you want to retrieve the object from the `Context`, you can use the `context.get(*.class)` method call. Alternative you could also use the `context.get(*.class.getName())` method.

For this you can either use an existing context as described in the last section or a new context. Using a new context is preferred to avoid collision of keys and to isolate your changes in a local context.

```
IEclipseContext context = EclipseContextFactory.create();

// Add your Java objects to the context
context.set(MyDataObject.class.getName(), data);
context.set(MoreStuff.class, moreData);
```

57. Accessing and extending the Eclipse context

57.1. Accessing the context

To access an existing context you can use dependency injection, if the relevant object is managed by the Eclipse runtime, i.e. if you are using a model object.

```
package com.example.e4.rcp.todo.handlers;

import org.eclipse.e4.core.contexts.IEclipseContext;
import org.eclipse.e4.core.di.annotations.Execute;

public class ShowMapHandler {
 @Execute
 public void execute(IEclipseContext context) {
  // Add objects to this local context of this handler
  // ...
 }

}
```

Alternatively if your model object extends `MContext` you can use DI to get the model object injected and use the `getContext()` method to access its context. For example MPart, MWindow, MApplication and MPerspective extend MContext.

```
package com.example.e4.rcp.todo.ui.parts;

import javax.annotation.PostConstruct;
import javax.annotation.PreDestroy;

import org.eclipse.e4.core.contexts.IEclipseContext;
import org.eclipse.e4.ui.model.application.ui.basic.MPart;
import org.eclipse.swt.widgets.Composite;

// Getting the application context
// via the MApplication object

public class TodoDetailsPart {

 @PostConstruct
 public void createControls(Composite parent,
  MApplication application) {
  IEclipseContext context = application.getContext();
  // Add or access objects to and from the application context
  // ...
```

```
  }
}
```

If you are outside of a model object, you still can access the OSGi context via the following:

```
public Object start() {
  // Get Bundle Information
  Bundle bundle = FrameworkUtil.getBundle(getClass());
  BundleContext bundleContext = bundle.getBundleContext();
  IEclipseContext eclipseCtx =
      EclipseContextFactory.getServiceContext(bundleContext);

  // Fill Context with information using set(String,Object)
  // ....

  // Create instance of class
  ContextInjectionFactory.make(MyPart.class, eclipseCtx);
}
```

57.2. OSGi services

You can add objects to the context via OSGi services. OSGi services are automatically available in the context. But OSGi services are global to the framework runtime — they can not access the workbench model or its context.

57.3. Objects and Context Variables

You can add key / value pairs directly to the `IEclipseContext`, for example a todo object under the *active* key. Adding objects to a Context can be done via the `set()` method on `IEclipseContext`. The following example creates a new context via the `EclipseContextFactory.create()` factory method call and adds some objects to it.

```
@Inject
public void addingContext(IEclipseContext context) {
  // We want to add objects to context

  // Create instance of class
  IEclipseContext myContext = EclipseContextFactory.create();

  // Putting in some values
  myContext.set("mykey1", "Hello1");
  myContext.set("mykey2", "Hello2");

  // Adding a parent relationship
```

```
  myContext.setParent(context);

  // Alternatively you can also
  // establish a parent/child
  // relationship via the
  // context.createChild() method call

}
```

A *Context variable* can be declared as *modifiable* via the `declareModifiable(key)` method call.

```
@Inject
public void addingContext(IEclipseContext context) {
  // Putting in some values
  context.set("mykey1", "Hello1");
  context.set("mykey2", "Hello2");

  //  Declares the named value as modifiable
  // by descendants of this context. If the value does not
  // exist in this context, a null value is added for the name.
  context.declareModifiable("mykey1");

}
```

Modifiable *Context variables* are added to particular levels of the `IEclipseContext` hierarchy and can also be modified using the `modify()` method rather than `set()` method of the `IEclipseContext`.

The `modify()` methods searches up the chain to find the `Context` defining the variable. If none of the `Context` on the parent chain have a value set for the name, the value will be set in this `Context`. If the key already exists in the context, then `modify()` requires that the key has been set to modifiable with the `declareModifiable()` method, if not, the method throws an exception.

You can add key/values pairs and *Context variables* at different levels of the context hierarchy so supply your application with different objects.

57.4. Model Addons

You can add *Addons* to the application model. These *Addons* contain a reference to Java classes, which can extend the context or interact with other Eclipse platform services, e.g. the EventAdmin.

For example you could register a model *Addon* to put some values into the context.

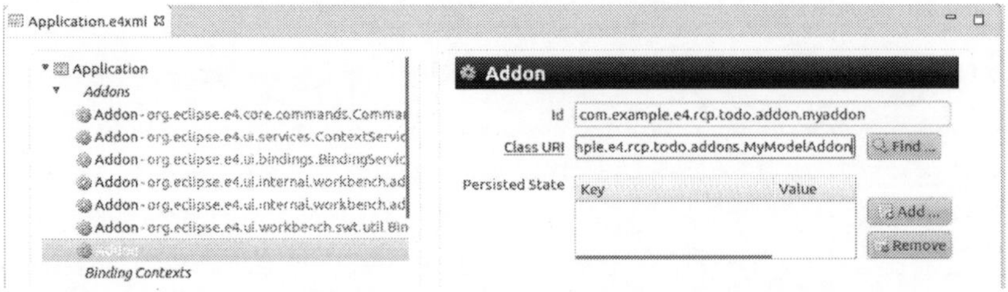

The following code shows an example implementation for the *Addon*.

```
package com.example.e4.rcp.todo.addons;

import javax.annotation.PostConstruct;

import org.eclipse.e4.core.contexts.IEclipseContext;

public class MyModelAddon {
 @PostConstruct
 public void init(IEclipseContext context) {
  context.set("test1", "Hello");
 }
}
```

57.5. RunAndTrack

The `IEclipseContext` allows you via the `runAndTrack()` method to register a Java object of type `RunAndTrack`.

A `RunAndTrack` is basically a `Runnable` which has access to the context. If the runnable accesses any values in this context during its execution, the runnable will be executed again after any of those values change.

The `runAndTrack()` method allows a client to keep some external state synchronized with one or more values in this context.

The runnable does not need to be explicitly unregistered from this context when it is no longer interested in tracking changes. If a subsequent invocation of this runnable does not access any values in this context, it is automatically unregistered from change tracking on this context.

57.6. Context Functions

Context Functions implement the `IContextFunction` interface and allow you to lazily create an object.

In Eclipse 4 you would extend the `ContextFunction` class to receive an `IEclipseContext` in the `compute()` method as input.

Context Functions are contributed as OSGi Services. They implement the `IContextFunction` interface from the `org.eclipse.e4.core.contexts` package. The Eclipse 4 runtime adds them by default to the application context but you could add *Context Functions* to any context in the context hierarchy.

Via the *`service.context.key`* property, they define their key under which they are added to the context.

The following example shows the declaration of a *Context Function*. This function is available in the application context under the `com.example.e4.rcp.todo.contextservice.test` key and can be injected via the `@Inject @Named` annotation.

```
<?xml version="1.0" encoding="UTF-8"?>
<scr:component xmlns:scr="http://www.osgi.org/xmlns/scr/v1.1.0"
 name="com.example.e4.rcp.todo.contextservice.translate">

<implementation class="com.example.e4.rcp.todo.contextservice.Test"/>

 <service>
   <provide interface="org.eclipse.e4.core.contexts.IContextFunction"/>
 </service>

 <property name="service.context.key" type="String"
   value="com.example.e4.rcp.todo.contextservice.test"/>

</scr:component>
```

Using *Context Functions* instead of plain OSGi services have the advantage that these functions has access to the application context, that they can be lazily created and that they are available in the application context. OSGi services are singletons and could not be used in a multi user environment.

58. Exercise: Dependency injection for your own objects

The following demonstrates the usage of dependency injection and the flexible model. This is not a real world example but serves primarily to demonstrate the programming interface which you have learned in the last chapters.

Create a `TitleDialog` re-using the `TodoDetailsPart` for the user interface. Add a menu entry called *Edit* to your Popup-Menu on the JFace table. If this menu entry is selected open your `TitleDialog`. `TitleDialog` should reuse the `TodoDetailPart` for its user interface.

Use `@Inject` to get the `MApplication` object. Retrieve the context from this object.

Create a new local `IEclipseContext` and assign the injected `IEclipseContext` as the parent to this local `IEclipseContext`. Add the selected `Todo` to your local context.

Use the `@Inject` annotation in conjunction with the `@Named` annotation in your `TitleDialog` class to indicate that the fields should be injected.

Create a new instance of your `TitleDialog` via dependency injection.

Edit the data, if the *OK* button is pressed, update the `Todo` item.

59. JFace Databinding

59.1. Overview

JFace Data Binding is a framework which connects properties of objects. It is typically used to synchronize properties of user interface widgets with properties of other Java objects. These Java objects are typically called the data model or the domain model.

Data Binding synchronizes changes of these properties. It allows you to include validation and conversion into this synchronization process.

For example you could bind the String property called *firstName* of a Java object to a *text* property of the *SWT* `Text` widget. If the user changes the text in the user interface, the corresponding property in the Java object is updated.

JFace Data Binding is mainly used in Eclipse applications and Eclipse Plug-ins. The models are typically Java POJOs or Java Beans but other technologies are also supported, e.g. the *Eclipse Modeling Framework* (EMF) or *Google Web Toolkit* (GWT).

59.2. PropertyChangeSupport

To be able to react to changes in an attribute of a Java objects, JFace Data Binding needs to be able to register itself as a listener to the attribute. The *SWT* and *JFace* widgets support this.

JFace Data Binding can be used to observe attribute of a domain model. This requires that the domain model objects follow the Java Bean specification. This specification requires that the class implements property change support via the `PropertyChangeSupport` class and propagates changes to registered listeners.

Bean implementers need to implement the methods outlined in the bean specification, which are unfortunately not represented by a Java interface. A Java class which provides `PropertyChangeSupport` looks like the following example.

```
package de.vogella.databinding.example;

import java.beans.PropertyChangeListener;
import java.beans.PropertyChangeSupport;
```

```
public class ModelObject {
 private PropertyChangeSupport changeSupport =
   new PropertyChangeSupport(this);

 public void addPropertyChangeListener(PropertyChangeListener
   listener) {
  changeSupport.addPropertyChangeListener(listener);
 }

 public void removePropertyChangeListener(PropertyChangeListener
   listener) {
  changeSupport.removePropertyChangeListener(listener);
 }

 public void addPropertyChangeListener(String propertyName,
   PropertyChangeListener listener) {
  changeSupport.addPropertyChangeListener(propertyName, listener);
 }

 public void removePropertyChangeListener(String propertyName,
   PropertyChangeListener listener) {
  changeSupport.removePropertyChangeListener(propertyName, listener);
 }

 protected void firePropertyChange(String propertyName,
   Object oldValue,
   Object newValue) {
  changeSupport.firePropertyChange(propertyName, oldValue, newValue);
 }
}
```

Other domain classes could extend this class. The following example demonstrates that.

```
package de.vogella.databinding.example;

public class Person extends ModelObject {
 private String name;

 public String getName() {
  return name;
 }

 public void setName(String name) {
  firePropertyChange("name", this.name, this.name = name);
 }
}
```

The JFace Data Binding framework can register listeners for these Java objects and gets notified if a change in the model happens.

59.3. Observables

The `IObservableValue` interface is used to observe properties of objects.

JFace Data Binding contains the *Properties API* as the recommended way of using the framework. The *Properties API* provides factories to create `IObservableValue` objects.

The main factories are `PojoProperties`, `BeanProperties` and `WidgetProperties`.

Table 59.1. Factories

Factory	Description
`PojoProperties`	Used to create `IObservableValues` for Java objects.
`BeanProperties`	Used to create `IObservableValue` objects for Java Beans.
`WidgetProperties`	Used to create `IObservableValues` for properties of *SWT* widgets.

The following demonstrates how to create an `IObservableValue` for the *firstName* property of a Java object called *person*.

```
IObservableValue myModel = PojoProperties.value("firstName").
 observe(person)
```

The following demonstrates how to create an `IObservableValue` for the *text* property of a SWT `Text` widget called *firstNameText*.

```
IObservableValue target = WidgetProperties.text(SWT.Modify).
 observe(firstNameText);
```

JFace Data Binding allows you to observe arbitrary attributes. For widgets you typically observe the *text* property but you can also observe other values. For example, you could bind the *enabled* property to a boolean value of the data model.

You can also observe nested model properties, e.g. attributes of classes which are contained in another class. The following demonstrates how to access the *country* property in the *address* field of the object *person*.

```
IObservable model = PojoProperties.value(Person.class,
  "address.country").observe(person);
```

59.4. DataBindingContext and Bindings

The `DataBindingContext` class provides the functionality to bind `IObservableValues`.

Via the `DataBindingContext.bindValue()` method two `IObservableValues` objects are connected. The first parameter is the target and the second is the model. During the initial binding the value from the model will be copied to the target.

```
// Create new Context
DataBindingContext ctx = new DataBindingContext();

// Define the IObservables
IObservableValue target = WidgetProperties.text(SWT.Modify).
 observe(firstName);
IObservableValue model= BeanProperties.
 value(Person.class,"firstName").observe(person);

// Connect them
ctx.bindValue(target, model);
```

It creates as a result an object of type `Binding`.

59.5. UpdateValueStrategy

The `bindValue()` method allows you to specify `UpdateValueStrategy` objects as third and fourth parameters. These objects allow you to control how and when the values are updated. If no `UpdateValueStrategy` is specified, defaults will be used.

59.6. Converters and Validators

You can also add `IValidator` and `IConverter` objects to the `UpdateValueStrategy`.

Validators allow you to implement validation of the data before it is propagated to the other connected property. A class which wants to provide this functionality must implement the `org.eclipse.core.databinding.validation.IValidator` interface.

```
// Define a validator to check that only numbers are entered
IValidator validator = new IValidator() {
 @Override
 public IStatus validate(Object value) {
  if (value instanceof Integer) {
   String s = String.valueOf(value);
   if (s.matches("\\d*")) {
    return ValidationStatus.ok();
   }
  }
  return ValidationStatus.error("Not a number");
 }
};

// Create UpdateValueStratgy and assign
// to the binding
UpdateValueStrategy strategy = new UpdateValueStrategy();
strategy.setBeforeSetValidator(validator);

Binding bindValue =
 ctx.bindValue(widgetValue, modelValue, strategy, null);
```

Converters allow you to convert the values between the model and the target.

59.7. ControlDecorators

JFace Data Binding allows you to use icon decorators in the user interface which reflect the status of the field validation. This allows you to provide immediate feedback to the user.

```
// Assume that a validator is already set
Binding bindValue =
  ctx.bindValue(widgetValue, modelValue, strategy, null);

// Add some decorations to the control
ControlDecorationSupport.create(bindValue, SWT.TOP | SWT.LEFT);
```

59.8. WritableValues

You can create bindings to a `WritableValue` object. `WritableValue` can hold a reference to another object.

You can exchange the reference object in `WritableValue` and the databinding will use the new (reference) object for its binding. This way you can create the binding once and still exchange the object which is bound by databinding.

To bind to `WritableValue` you use the `observeDetail()` method, to inform the framework that you would like to observe the contained object.

```
WritableValue value  = new WritableValue();

// Create the binding
DataBindingContext ctx = new DataBindingContext();
IObservableValue target = WidgetProperties.
 text(SWT.Modify).observe(text);
IObservableValue model = BeanProperties.value("firstName").
  observeDetail(value);

ctx.bindValue(target, model);

// Create a person object called p
// Make the binding valid for this new object
value.setValue(p);
```

59.9. Listening to all changes in the binding

You can register a listener to all bindings of the `DataBindingContext` class. Your listener will be called when something has changed.

This can for example to be used to determine the status of a *Part* which behaves like an *Editor*. If something is changed, it will mark itself as dirty.

```
// Define your change listener
// dirtable holds the state for the changed status of the editor
IChangeListener listener = new IChangeListener() {
 @Override
 public void handleChange(ChangeEvent event) {
  dirtable.setDirty(true);
  }
};


// Get the validation status provides
IObservableList bindings =
 context.getValidationStatusProviders();

// Not all validation status providers
// are bindings, e.g. MultiValidator
// Otherwise you could use
// context.getBindings()

//Register the listener to all bindings
for (Object o : bindings) {
 Binding b = (Binding) o;
 b.getTarget().addChangeListener(listener);
```

```
}
```

59.10. JFace Data Binding Plug-ins

Include the following plug-ins as a dependency in your project to use JFace Data Binding.

- org.eclipse.core.databinding
- org.eclipse.core.databinding.beans
- org.eclipse.core.databinding.property
- org.eclipse.jface.databinding

60. Exercise: Databinding

Add the necessary databinding plug-ins to main plug-in.

Change your implementation of `TodoDetailsPart` to use databinding.

61. Data Binding for JFace Viewer

61.1. Binding Viewers

JFace Data Binding provides functionality to bind the data of JFace *Viewers*, e.g. for `TableViewers`.

Data binding for *Viewers* distinguish between changes in the collection and changes in the individual object.

In the case that Data Binding observes a collection, it requires a `ContentProvider` which notifies it, once the data in the collection changes.

`ObservableListContentProvider` is a `ContentProvider` which requires a list implementing the `IObservableList` interface. The `Properties` class allows you to wrap another list with its `self()` method into an `IObservableList`.

The following snippet demonstrates the usage:

```
// Use ObservableListContentProvider
viewer.setContentProvider(new ObservableListContentProvider());

// Create sample data
List<Person> persons = createExampleData();

// Wrap the input into a writable list
IObservableList input =
   Properties.selfList(Person.class).observe(persons);

// Set the IObservableList as input for the viewer
viewer.setInput(input);
```

61.2. Observing list details

You can also use the `ObservableMapLabelProvider` class to observe changes of the list elements.

```
ObservableListContentProvider contentProvider =
 new ObservableListContentProvider();

// Create the label provider including monitoring
// of the changes of the labels
IObservableSet knownElements = contentProvider.getKnownElements();
```

```
final IObservableMap firstNames = BeanProperties.value(Person.class,
  "firstName").observeDetail(knownElements);
final IObservableMap lastNames = BeanProperties.value(Person.class,
  "lastName").observeDetail(knownElements);

IObservableMap[] labelMaps = { firstNames, lastNames };

ILabelProvider labelProvider =
 new ObservableMapLabelProvider(labelMaps) {
  public String getText(Object element) {
 return firstNames.get(element) + " " + lastNames.get(element);
  }
};
```

61.3. ViewerSupport

`ViewerSupport` simplifies the setup for JFace Viewers in cases where all columns should be displayed. It registers changes listener on the collection as well as on the individual elements.

`ViewerSupport` creates via its `bind()` the `LabelProvider` and `ContentProvider` automatically.

```
// MyModel.getPersons() gives a List of Person objects
// Writable list wraps them in an IObservableList

input = new WritableList(MyModel.getPersons(), Person.class);

// The following will create and bind the data
// for the table based on the input
// No extra label provider /
// content provider / setInput required

ViewerSupport.bind(viewer, input,
  BeanProperties.
  values(new String[] { "firstName", "lastName", "married" }));
```

61.4. Observing Viewer properties

The `ViewerProperties` class allows you to create `IObservableValues` for properties of the viewer. For example you can track the current selection, e.g. which data object is currently selected.

To access fields in the selection you can use the `PojoProperties` or the `BeanProperties` class. Both provide the `value().observeDetail()` method chain. which allows you to observe a detail value of an `IObservableValues` object.

For example the following will map the *summary* property of the `Todo` domain object to a `Label` based on the selection of a `ComboViewer`.

```
// Assume we have Todo domain objects
// todos is a List<Todo>
final ComboViewer viewer = new ComboViewer(parent, SWT.DROP_DOWN);
viewer.setContentProvider(new ArrayContentProvider());
viewer.setLabelProvider(new LabelProvider() {
 public String getText(Object element) {
   Todo todo = (Todo) element;
      return todo.getSummary();
 };
});
viewer.setInput(todos);

// A label to map to
Label label = new Label(parent, SWT.BORDER);
// parent has a GridLayout assigned
label.setLayoutData(new GridData(SWT.FILL, SWT.CENTER, true, false));


DataBindingContext dbc = new DataBindingContext();

// For binding to the label
IObservableValue target = WidgetProperties.text().observe(label);

// Observe the selection
IViewerObservableValue selectedTodo = ViewerProperties
  .singleSelection().observe(viewer);
// We want to get the summary attribute of the selection
IObservableValue detailValue =
 PojoProperties
  .value("summary", String.class)
  .observeDetail(selectedTodo)

dbc.bindValue(target, detailValue);
```

61.5. Chaining properties

You can chain properties together to simplify observing nested properties. The following snippets show examples for this.

```
IObservableValue viewerSelectionSummaryObservable =
 ViewerProperties.singleSelection()
     .value(BeanProperties.value("summary", String.class))
     .observe(viewer);
```

```
IListProperty siblingNames = BeanProperties.
 value("parent").list("children").values("name");
```

```
IObservableList siblingNamesObservable =
 siblingNames.observe(node);
```

62. Exercise: Databinding Advanced

Change your implementation of `TodoOverviewPart` to use databinding.

63. Eclipse Preferences

63.1. Preferences and Scopes

Preferences are key / value pairs, where the key is an arbitrary name for the preference. The value can be a boolean, string, int or another primitive type. For example a user name might be stored via a key called *user* . The actual value for this key might be "Lars Vogel".

Eclipse *Preferences* are based on the `Preferences` class from the `org.osgi.service.prefs` package. Eclipse *Preferences* are very similar to standard Java Preferences with some support of additional features. They use the Eclipse framework to save and retrieve the configuration.

The Eclipse runtime defines three so-called scopes. The scope defines how the preference data is stored and how it is changeable.

Table 63.1. Eclipse Preference scope

Scope	Description
Instance scope	If the user runs the same program twice, the settings between the two programs may be different.
Configuration scope	If the user runs the same program twice then the settings between the two programs are the same.
Default scope	Default values which can not be changed. Supplied via configuration files in plug-ins and product definitions.

63.2. Eclipse Preference API

You can create and manipulate preferences directly in your coding. Preferences are read and saved by `get()` and `put()` methods. In the `get()` method you specify a default value in case the key can not be found. The `clear()` method allows to delete a preference value.

```
// We access the Configuration Scope
Preferences preferences = ConfigurationScope.INSTANCE
 .getNode("de.vogella.preferences.test");

Preferences sub1 = preferences.node("node1");
Preferences sub2 = preferences.node("node2");
sub1.put("h1", "Hello");
sub1.put("h2", "Hello again");
```

```
sub2.put("h1", "Moin");
try {
 // Forces the application to save the preferences
 preferences.flush();
 } catch (BackingStoreException e) {
  e.printStackTrace();
 }
}
```

```
// Read values from the configuration scope
Preferences preferences = ConfigurationScope.INSTANCE
 .getNode("de.vogella.preferences.test");
Preferences sub1 = preferences.node("node1");
Preferences sub2 = preferences.node("node2");
sub1.get("h1", "default");
sub1.get("h2", "default");
sub2.get("h1", "default");
```

63.3. plugin_customization.ini

You can use the file plugin_customization.ini to set preference values. The format to use is <plugin id>/<setting>=<value>, e.g. de.vogella.test.preference/check=true.

To find the right values, just start your Eclipse application, switch to the `.metadata` directory in your workspace directory (by default the directory your application is starting in) and search for files ending with `.pref`.

63.4. Eclipse 4 Preferences

Eclipse 4 provides dependency injection to simplify the handling of preferences. It allows you to access *Preferences* via dependency injection and to track changes.

Eclipse will track changes for *Preferences* in the `InstanceScope` and `ConfigurationScope`. *Preferences* in the `DefaultScope` will not be tracked.

```
// Instance Scope is tracked
Preferences node = InstanceScope.INSTANCE.
 getNode("de.vogella.e4.todo");
node.put("key", "2012");

// Injection will be called
@Inject
@Preference(value = "key", nodePath = "de.vogella.e4.todo")
String year;
```

```
//
@Inject
public TestView() {
    Preferences node = DefaultScope.INSTANCE.getNode("test.project");
 node.put("key", "2010");
}

// Setting the preference via DI
@Inject
public void createControl(final Composite composite,
 @Preference final
 IEclipsePreferences node) {
  Button store = new Button(composite, SWT.PUSH);
        store.addSelectionListener(new SelectionAdapter() {
            @Override
            public void widgetSelected(SelectionEvent e) {
                node.put("key", "myValue");
            }
        });

    }
```

64. Exercise: Preferences

We will simulate that the todo items are fetched from a server.

Create a *Dialog* to enter a user and password which are stored as preferences. Create a menu entry (and a command with a handler) which allows you to open this dialog.

Add a `setCredentials(String user, String password)` method to your services for the `ITodoModel` interface.

After you change the values in your dialog update the information in your service.

Use the application lifecycle hooks to set the user and password in the service during startup of your application.

65. Eclipse Event Notifications

65.1. Event based communication

In your application you frequently have the need to communicate between application components.

For example the user selects an object in a `Tree` widget and a *Part* is updated with this information.

This example can be handled by the selection service. But frequently you want to propagate more than just a selection between the different components of your application. For example a non-visual component wants to send a data update to all relevant visual components.

For this purpose the Eclipse platform provides a global event based communication system, called the event bus. Software components can register for certain events and other components can send new events to the event bus.

The Eclipse platform will make sure that registered components will receive the messages. Eclipse 4 uses this event system for the complete internal communication.

65.2. IEventBroker Service

The Eclipse framework uses the event notification system for its internal communication based on the `IEventBroker` service. This communication service can also be used to communicate between your own application components.

`IEventBroker` is based on the OSGi `EventAdmin` service but has been wrapped with a simpler API. It also automatically removes any event subscriptions when the defining `IEclipseContext` is disposed.

The following plug-ins contain the `IEventBroker` functionality:

- `org.eclipse.e4.core.services`
- `org.eclipse.osgi.services`

Using the `IEventBroker` service the classes in your application can register as event listeners for specific events. Other classes in your application use the service to send events.

65.3. Usage

65.3.1. Sending

The `IEventBroker` service can be injected via dependency injection.

```
@Inject
private IEventBroker eventBroker;
```

The `IEventBroker` service collects all events and sends them to the registered classes. This can be done asynchronously or synchronously.

```
// Asynchronous delivery
// Caller will not be blocked until delivery
IEventBroker.post(String topic, Object data)
```

```
// Synchronous Delivery
// Caller will block until delivery
IEventBroker.send(String topic, Object data)
```

You can now send arbitrary Java objects or primitives through the event bus. The following example shows how to send an object and a String.

```
// Constant for event registration
public static final String TOPIC_NEWDATA = "TOPIC_NEWDATA";

@Execute
public void sendEvent(IEventBroker eventBroker){
 if (eventBroker != null) {
  // Assume there is an object Todo
  Todo todo = new Todo("Event Brooker");
  todo.setDescription("Details");
  Map<String, Object> map = new HashMap<String, Object>();
  map.put("TEST1", "This is the message of the test1");
  map.put("NEWTODO", todo);
  // Do now block via post (asynchronously)
  eventBroker.post(TOPIC_NEWDATA, map);
 }
}
```

65.3.2. Receiving

You can use dependency injection to register and respond to events. This is the preferred way to register for an event as it requires less code then subscribing to the `IEventBroker` directly.

The `@EventTopic` and `@UIEventTopic` annotations tag methods and fields that should be notified on event changes. The `@UIEventTopic` ensures the event notification is performed in the user interface thread.

```
// Constant for event registration
public static final String TOPIC_NEWDATA = "TOPIC_NEWDATA";

// Register to the topic TOPIC_NEWDATA for
// objects of type Todo
@Inject @Optional
void closeHandler(@UIEventTopic(TOPIC_NEWDATA) Todo todo) {
    // Do something
}

//Register to the topic TOPIC_NEWDATA for
//objects of type String
@Inject @Optional
void closeHandler(@UIEventTopic(TOPIC_NEWDATA) String s) {
 // Do something
}
```

Alternatively an object can also get the event broker injected and register for updates via an event handler.

```
// Called for example in @PostConstruct
private void hookToEvents() {
 EventHandler eventHandler = new EventHandler() {
  @Override
  public void handleEvent(Event event) {
   // get the information from the event
   String text = (String) event.getProperty("TEST1");
   Todo todo = (Todo) event.getProperty("NEWTODO");
   // Now do something with this information
   //.....
  }

 };
 eventBroker.subscribe("NEWDATA", eventHandler);
}
```

65.3.3. Eclipse Framework Events

It is also possible to register for Eclipse framework events. The `UIEvents` class from the `org.eclipse.e4.ui.workbench` contains all framework events. This class also contains in its Javadoc information about the purpose of events.

For example the `UIEvents.UILifeCycle.ACTIVATE` event is triggered if a *Part* is activated.

```
@Inject
@Optional
public void partActivation(@UIEventTopic(UIEvents.UILifeCycle.ACTIVATE)
 Event event) {
 // Do something
 System.out.println("Got Part");
}
```

This allows you for example to put a Context variable called *myactivePartId* on every part change into the application context.

```
// Set a context variable
@Inject
@Optional
public void partActivation(@UIEventTopic(UIEvents.UILifeCycle.ACTIVATE)
 Event event,
 MApplication application) {

 MPart activePart = (MPart) event.
   getProperty(UIEvents.EventTags.ELEMENT);
 IEclipseContext context = application.getContext();
 if (activePart != null) {
  context.set("myactivePartId", activePart.getElementId());
 }
}
```

This context variable can be used to define a visible-when clause which can be used to restrict the visibility of menus and toolbars.

```
<?xml version="1.0" encoding="UTF-8"?>
<?eclipse version="3.4"?>
<plugin>

   <extension
         id="product"
         point="org.eclipse.core.runtime.products">
      <product
        application="org.eclipse.e4.ui.workbench.swt.E4Application"
        name="to-do">
         <property
          name="applicationXMI"
          value="com.example.e4.rcp.todo/Application.e4xmi">
         </property>
         <property
               name="appName"
               value="to-do">
         </property>
      </product>
   </extension>
```

```
  <extension
         point="org.eclipse.core.expressions.definitions">
      <definition
            id="com.example.e4.rcp.todo.todooverviewselected">
         <with
               variable="myactivePartId">
            <equals
                  value="com.example.e4.rcp.ui.parts.todooverview">
            </equals>
         </with>
      </definition>
   </extension>

</plugin>
```

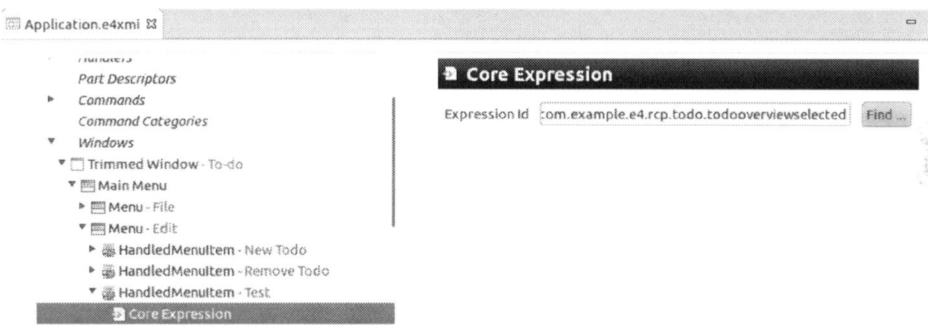

The Eclipse platform places several ContextVariables into the context. Several keys are defined in the `IServiceConstants` interface.

65.4. Evaluation

65.4.1. Context Variables

Context variables can be used to share your application state, instead of the `IEventBroker` service.

If you put *Context variables* into a context which is available to other objects, for example the application context, these other objects can use `@Inject` to get these *Context variables* injected.

The `IEventBroker` is a global event bus and is unaware of the `IEclipseContext` hierarchy. *Context variables* provide an improved way to manage scoped shared application state.

65.4.2. Conclusion

The advantage of the `IEventBroker` Service is that it supports sending event information without knowing who is receiving it. Interested classes can register for events without knowing who is going to provide them. This is known as the whiteboard pattern and this pattern supports the creation of very loosely coupled application components.

The disadvantage is that it is a global bus, i.e. there is no scoping of the events. Publishers have to ensure they provide enough information in the event for subscribers to discriminate and decide that the particular event is applicable to them.

66. Exercises: Event Notifications

66.1. Exercise: Notifications for new Todos

Create a `MyEventConstants` class. This class stores the constants for the event topics. Define the following constant in this class.

```
public static final String TOPIC_TODO_DATA_UPDATE
 = "TOPIC_TODO_DATA_UPDATE";
```

In your `TodoOverviewPart` class register for this event. If this event is received, reload the data from your service into your `Viewer`.

Add a menu item to your model with a handler assigned to it. If the menu item is selected, add a new Todo to the service and send out the event. The `TodoOverviewPart` class should receive this event and refresh the `TableViewer`.

66.2. Exercise: Splash Screen

Register a lifecycle handler in your `plugin.xml` file and show a small `Shell` until the first Part gets activated. You could extend this `Shell` for example to a login screen for your application.

```
<?xml version="1.0" encoding="UTF-8"?>
<plugin>
   <extension
         id="product"
         point="org.eclipse.core.runtime.products">
      <product
        name="testing"
        application="org.eclipse.e4.ui.workbench.swt.E4Application">
         <property
               name="appName"
               value="to-do">
         </property>
   <property
     name="lifeCycleURI"
     value="bundleclass://com.example.e4.rcp.todo/[CONTINUE...]
     com.example.e4.rcp.todo.lifecycle.LifeCycleManager">
    </property>
      </product>
   </extension>

</plugin>
```

```
package com.example.e4.rcp.todo.lifecycle;

import org.eclipse.e4.core.services.events.IEventBroker;
import org.eclipse.e4.ui.workbench.UIEvents;
import org.eclipse.e4.ui.workbench.lifecycle.PostContextCreate;
import org.eclipse.swt.SWT;
import org.eclipse.swt.widgets.Shell;
import org.osgi.service.event.Event;
import org.osgi.service.event.EventHandler;

// For a extended example see
// https://bugs.eclipse.org/382224

public class LifeCycleManager {
 @PostContextCreate
 void postContextCreate(final IEventBroker eventBroker) {
  final Shell shell = new Shell(SWT.TOOL | SWT.NO_TRIM);

  // Will close the shell once a part gets activated
  // Should be easier
  // See the following bug reports
  // https://bugs.eclipse.org/376821

  eventBroker.subscribe(UIEvents.UILifeCycle.ACTIVATE,
    new EventHandler() {
     @Override
     public void handleEvent(Event event) {
      shell.close();
      shell.dispose();
      System.out.println("Closed");
      eventBroker.unsubscribe(this);
     }
    });
  shell.open();

 }

}
```

67. Contributing to the application model

67.1. Eclipse 4 Modularity

67.1.1. OSGi modularity

Eclipse 4 is based on OSGi and therefore supports its modularity. Plug-ins define their external API, and consume API from other plug-ins.

The modularity provided by OSGi is completely available in Eclipse 4. Consuming OSGi services is very well supported in Eclipse 4, as OSGi services can get injected into other components via dependency injection.

67.1.2. Application model and model contributions

In Eclipse 4 the application is described via an application model with the `Application.e4xmi` default filename.

Other plug-ins can extend this base application model with *contributions*.

These model contributions are registered in Eclipse 4 via the `org.eclipse.e4.workbench.model` extension point. This extension point is defined in the `org.eclipse.e4.ui.workbench` plug-in.

67.2. Extending the application model

67.2.1. Contributing to the application model

The `org.eclipse.e4.workbench.model` extension point allows you to define contributions to the application model.

Model contributions can be done via files (*fragments*) or via code (*processors*).

The model contributions are read during startup and the contained information is used to build the runtime application model.

67.2.2. Fragments and Processors

A model *fragment* is a file which typically ends with the `.e4xmi` extension. It specifies additional model elements.

It defines which model element it extends and the new model elements which should be added to this model element. For example a fragment can define that it extends a certain menu with additional menu entries.

A *processor* allows you to contribute to the model via program code. A processor allows the dynamic creation of model elements, therefore this approach has the highest flexibility.

67.2.3. Position of new model elements

Fragments contribute new model elements to existing containers, e.g. new menu entries to existing menus.

Fragments allow to define the position of these new model elements via the `Position in List` attribute. The following values are allowed:

Table 67.1. Position in List attribute

Value	Description
first	Positions the element on the beginning of the list.
index: *`theindex`* Example index:0	Places the new model elements at position *`theindex`*.
before: *`theotherelementsid`*	Places the new model elements before the model element with the ID *`theotherelementsid`*.
after: *`theotherelementsid`*	Places the new model elements after the model element with the ID *`theotherelementsid`*.

Fragments of independent plug-ins are processed in arbitrary order by the Eclipse runtime, therefore *`first`* or *`index`* might not always result in the desired outcome.

67.2.4. Usage of IDs

If you want to contribute to an element of the application model you must specify the ID of the element to which you are contributing.

In general it is good practice to always define IDs in your application model.

67.2.5. Comparison with Eclipse 3.x

The programming model of Eclipse 3.x primarily uses extension points to define contributions to the application. These extensions define new parts, new menus, etc.

This approach is no longer used in Eclipse 4 applications. All contributions are made via fragments or processors.

67.3. Constructing the runtime application model

67.3.1. Components

The application model of a running application consists of different components: the base application model and model contributions via other plug-ins. In addition to that user changes are also recorded and applied to the runtime model.

67.3.2. User Changes

Changes during runtime, e.g. the user moves a part, are written back to the model. While the application is running, the model objects can be changed. For example, *Parts* are closed or opened.

Theses changes are recorded and saved independently in a `workbench.xmi` file in the `.metadata/.plugins/org.eclipse.e4.workbench` folder.

If user changes should be deleted, you can specify the *`clearPersistedState`* parameter as a launch parameter.

67.3.3. Merging model elements at startup

The different components of the runtime application model need to be combined.

Eclipse 4 creates the application model at first based on the base application model and applies the model contributions to it. User deltas are applied afterwards. If these deltas do not apply anymore, e.g. because the base model has changed, they will be skipped.

The deltas are applied to the model based on the IDs of the user interface component.

67.4. Fragment extension elements

In fragments you contribute to an existing model element which is defined via its ID. You also have to specify the *Featurename* to which you want to contribute. A *Featurename* is a direct link to the structure of the application model.

The following table lists some *Featurename* values and their purposes.

Table 67.2. Contribution, Featurename and Element id

You want to contribute to	Featurename	Element id
Command to the application	commands	ID of your application
Handler to the application	handlers	ID of your application
New MenuItem / HandledMenuItem to existing menu	children	ID of the menu
New Menu to the application	children	ID of your application
New Part to existing PartStack	children	ID of your PartStack

68. Tutorial: Fragments

68.1. Create Project and Java classes

In this section you will add a menu entry, a command and a handler to your main application model via fragments.

Create a plug-in project called *com.example.e4.rcp.todo.contribute* without a template and without an `Activator`.

Add a dependency to the following plug-ins:

- javax.inject
- org.eclipse.swt
- org.eclipse.jface
- org.eclipse.e4.core.di
- org.eclipse.e4.ui.workbench
- org.eclipse.e4.ui.di

Create the `de.vogella.e4.todo.contribute.handler` package and the following class.

```
package de.vogella.e4.todo.contribute.handler;

import org.eclipse.e4.core.di.annotations.Execute;
import org.eclipse.jface.dialogs.MessageDialog;
import org.eclipse.swt.widgets.Shell;

public class OpenMapHandler {

 @Execute
 public void run(Shell shell){
  MessageDialog.openInformation(shell, "Just testing", "Test");
 }
}
```

68.2. Create model fragment

Use the Eclipse 4 wizard to create a new fragment via the following menu: File → New → Other → Eclipse 4 → Model → New Model Fragment. Select the `com.example.e4.rcp.todo.contribute` plug-in as the container and use `fragment.e4xmi` as the name for the file.

Select the *Model Fragment* node and press the *Add* button.

Use `com.example.e4.rcp.todo.application` as the *Element id*. This is the ID of the *`Application`* model element in your `Application.e4xmi` file.

You also need to define to which feature you will be adding to. Use *commands* as *Featurename*. Make sure you still have the *Model Fragment* selected and use the *Add* button to add a *Command* to your model fragment.

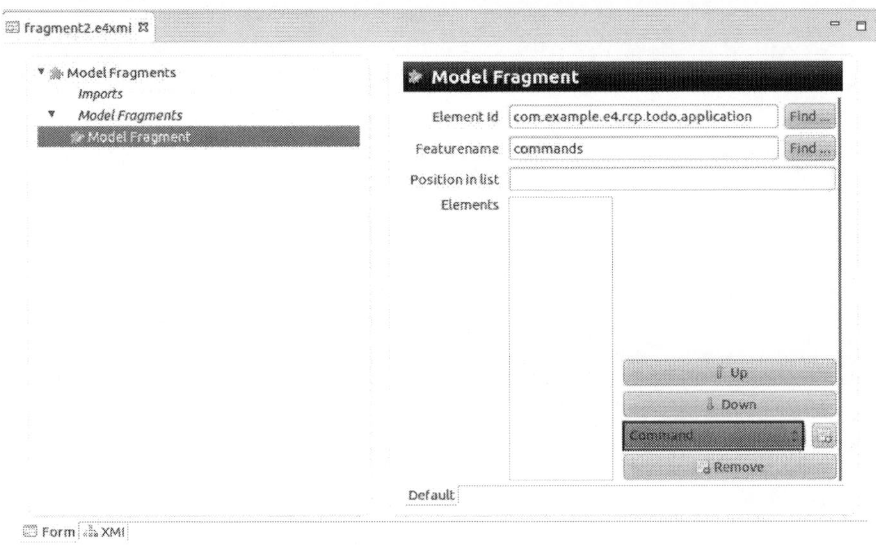

Use *com.example.e4.rcp.todo.contribute.command.openmap* as ID and *Open Map* as name for the corresponding attributes of the command.

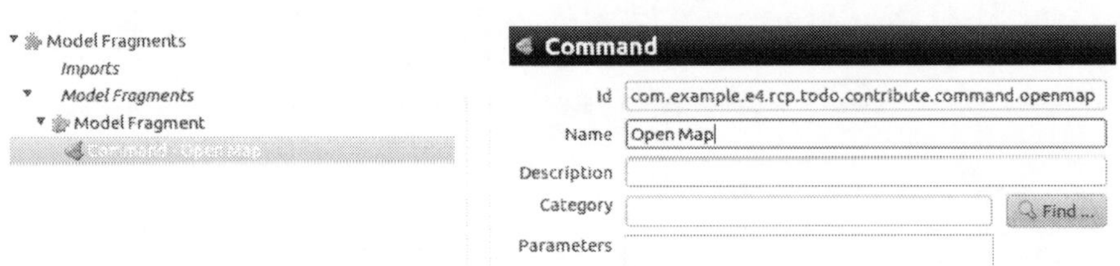

Create a new model fragment for the handler. The *Element id* is again the ID of your application ID, the Featurename is *handlers*. Add a *Handler* to this model fragment.

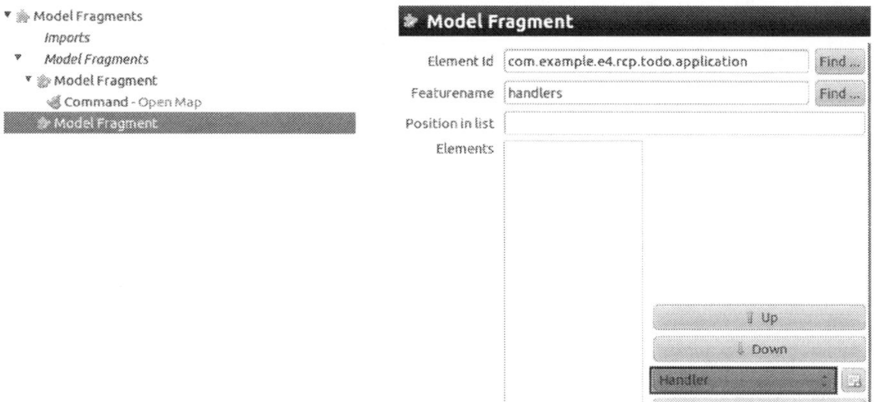

Use *com.example.e4.rcp.todo.contribute.handler.openmap* as ID for the handler. Point to the `OpenMapHandler` class and your *Open Map* command.

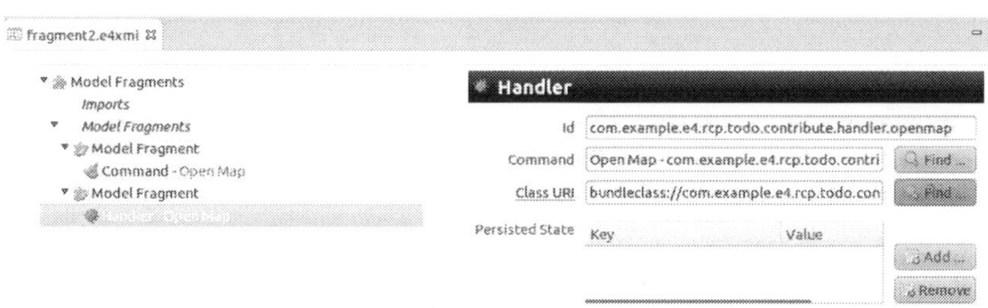

Add another *Model Fragment* to contribute a new menu to your application model. You will contribute to the main menu with the `org.eclipse.ui.main.menu` ID. The Featurename is *children*.

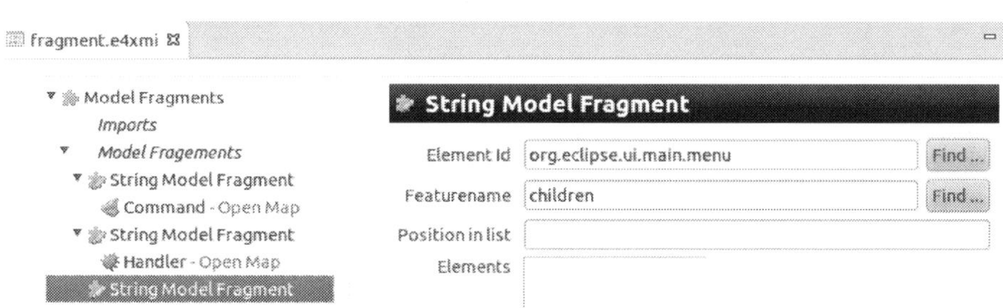

Add a *Menu* with the *Map* label and the *com.example.e4.rcp.todo.contribute.menu.map* ID.

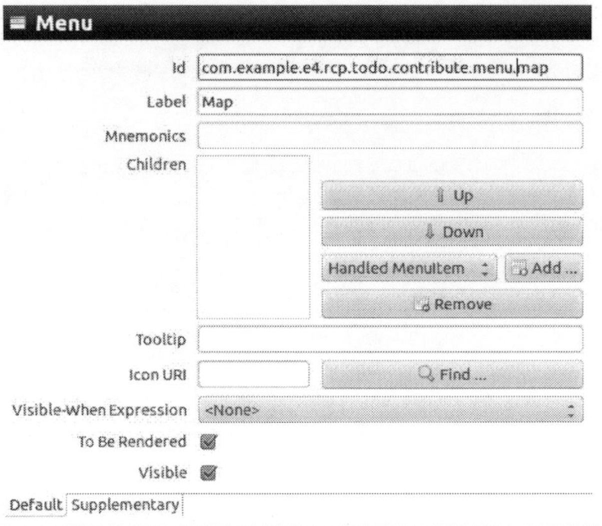

Add a *HandledMenuItem* which points to your command. The process of defining these entries is the same as defining menus in the `Application.e4xmi` and is therefore not described here in detail.

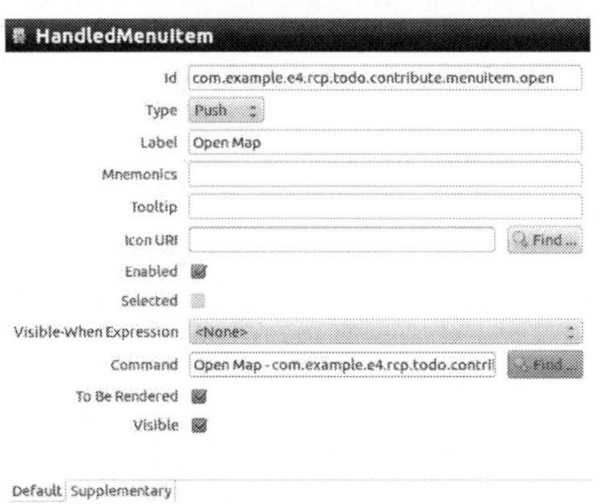

68.3. Register Fragment via extension point

In your `com.example.e4.rcp.todo.contribute` plug-in add the `org.eclipse.e4.workbench.model` extension point.

Right click on the extension point and select New → fragment.

```
<?xml version="1.0" encoding="UTF-8"?>
<?eclipse version="3.4"?>
<plugin>
   <extension
      id="modelContribution"
         point="org.eclipse.e4.workbench.model">
      <fragment
            uri="fragment.e4xmi">
      </fragment>
   </extension>

</plugin>
```

68.4. Update Feature and test

Add the `com.example.e4.rcp.todo.contribute` plug-in to your `com.example.e4.rcp.todo.feature` feature.

Run the Todo product. You should see the new *Map* entry in the application menu. If you select this entry a message dialog opens.

If the menu entry is not displayed ensure that your IDs are correctly entered and that you either use the `clearPersistedState` flag or clear the workspace data in your *Launch configuration*.

Please note that your model entries should all have IDs.

68.5. Extend example: Contributing a Part

Define a new model fragment which contributes a *Part* to an existing *PartStack*.

69. Tutorial: Processors

69.1. Enter dependencies and create Java classes

In the following example you will replace an existing menu entry in the Eclipse 4 application.

Continue to use *com.example.e4.rcp.todo.contribute* plug-in for this tutorial.

Add the `org.eclipse.e4.ui.services` plug-in as dependency to your `MANIFEST.MF` file. You need the `IServiceConstants` interface from this plug-in.

Also add the `org.eclipse.e4.core.contexts` plug-in as dependency.

Create the following dialog and handler classes. The handler will be used later on in the new menu entry.

```
package de.vogella.e4.todo.contribute.dialogs;

import javax.inject.Inject;
import javax.inject.Named;

import org.eclipse.e4.ui.services.IServiceConstants;
import org.eclipse.jface.dialogs.Dialog;
import org.eclipse.swt.SWT;
import org.eclipse.swt.widgets.Composite;
import org.eclipse.swt.widgets.Control;
import org.eclipse.swt.widgets.Label;
import org.eclipse.swt.widgets.Shell;

public class ExitDialog extends Dialog {
 @Inject
 public ExitDialog(@Named(IServiceConstants.
   ACTIVE_SHELL) Shell shell) {
  super(shell);
 }

 @Override
 protected Control createDialogArea(Composite parent) {
  Label label = new Label(parent, SWT.NONE);
  label.setText("Closing this application may result in data loss. "
    + "Are you sure you want that");
  return parent;
 }

}
```

```
package de.vogella.e4.todo.contribute.handler;

import org.eclipse.e4.core.contexts.ContextInjectionFactory;
import org.eclipse.e4.core.contexts.IEclipseContext;
import org.eclipse.e4.core.di.annotations.Execute;
import org.eclipse.e4.ui.workbench.IWorkbench;
import org.eclipse.jface.window.Window;

import de.vogella.e4.todo.contribute.dialogs.ExitDialog;

public class ExitHandlerWithCheck {
 @Execute
 public void execute(IEclipseContext context, IWorkbench workbench) {
  ExitDialog dialog = ContextInjectionFactory.
     make(ExitDialog.class, context);
  dialog.create();
  if (dialog.open() == Window.OK) {
   workbench.close();
  }
 }
}
```

Create now the model processor class.

```
package de.vogella.e4.todo.contribute.processors;

import java.util.ArrayList;
import java.util.List;

import javax.inject.Inject;
import javax.inject.Named;

import org.eclipse.e4.core.di.annotations.Execute;
import org.eclipse.e4.ui.model.application.ui.menu.MDirectMenuItem;
import org.eclipse.e4.ui.model.application.ui.menu.MMenu;
import org.eclipse.e4.ui.model.application.ui.menu.MMenuElement;
import org.eclipse.e4.ui.model.application.ui.menu.MMenuFactory;

public class MenuProcessor {

 // I get this via the parameter
 // of the process definition
 @Inject
 @Named("org.eclipse.ui.file.menu")
 private MMenu menu;

 @Execute
 public void execute() {
//  System.out.println("Starting processor");
  // Remove the old exit menu entry
  if (menu != null && menu.getChildren() != null) {
   List<MMenuElement> list = new ArrayList<MMenuElement>();
```

```
    for (MMenuElement element : menu.getChildren()) {
     System.out.println(element);

     // Separaters have no label hence we
     // need to check for null
     if (element.getLabel() != null) {
      if (element.getLabel().contains("Exit")) {
       list.add(element);
      }
     }
    }
    menu.getChildren().removeAll(list);
   }

   // Now add a new menu entry
   MDirectMenuItem menuItem = MMenuFactory.INSTANCE.
     createDirectMenuItem();
   menuItem.setLabel("Another Exit");
   menuItem.setContributionURI("bundleclass://"
     + "com.example.e4.rcp.todo.contribute/"
     + "de.vogella.e4.todo.contribute.handler.ExitHandlerWithCheck");
   menu.getChildren().add(menuItem);
  }
}
```

69.2. Register processor via extension point

In your `com.example.e4.rcp.todo.contribute` plug-in add a `processor` for the `org.eclipse.e4.workbench.model` extension point.

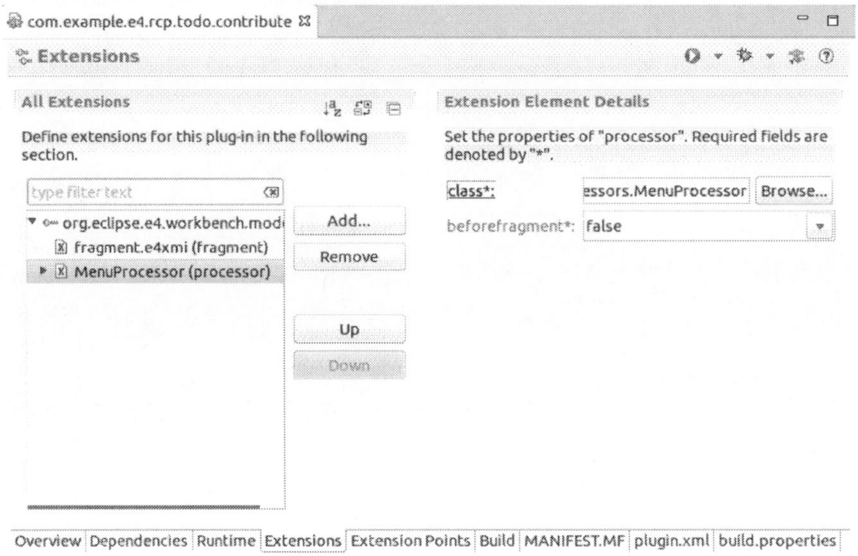

The following assumes that you used *org.eclipse.ui.file.menu* as ID for your *File* menu in the main application model

Right click on the processor and select New → element. The parameter with the ID is the model element which is later on injected into your Java class for the processor. Use `org.eclipse.ui.file.menu` as `id*` parameter.

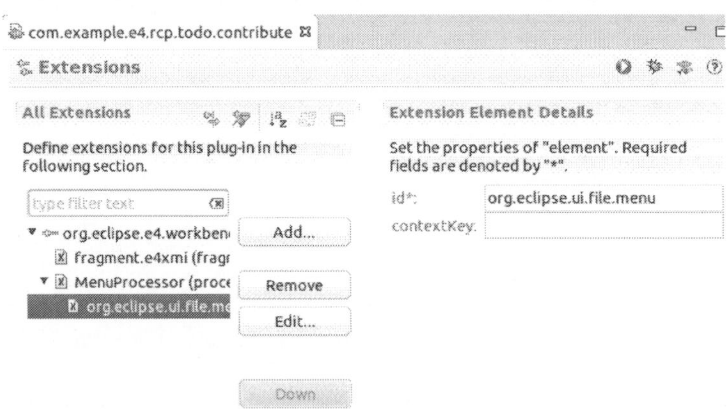

Add this plug-in to your product and run your product. The old exit menu entry should be removed and you should see the new menu entry.

70. Declarative Styling with CSS files

70.1. Cascading Style Sheets (CSS)

70.1.1. Overview

Cascading Style Sheets (CSS) is a mechanism for defining styles and layouts, e.g. fonts, colors and spacing. This layout information is typically maintained in an external file. Other code, e.g. HTML, can refer to this file and therefore use the layout defined in the external file.

CSS is defined as a standard. Currently the versions *CSS 2.1* and *CSS 3* are most widely used.

70.1.2. CSS syntax

CSS defines selectors that contain certain values for properties. The syntax is defined as follows:

```
selector { property:value; }
```

For example the following CSS file defines the size of a color for the `h1` tag.

```
h1 { color:red; font-size:48px; }
```

70.2. Eclipse 4 styling

The Eclipse platform provides the functionality to style an Eclipse application via an external file, using a CSS file.

In the CSS file for Eclipse applications you use identifiers, to relate to SWT widgets or predefined pseudo classes, e.g. application model classes. The styling is similar to the CSS 2.1 standard. Non-standard properties are prefixed with either *swt-* or *eclipse-*.

The following example shows a CSS file which defines the styling of some SWT widgets.

```
Label {
 font: Verdana 8px;
 color: black;
```

```
}

Composite Label {
 color: black;
}

Text {
 font: Verdana 8px;
}

/* Identifies only those SWT Text elements
   appearing within a Composite */

Composite Text {
 background-color: white;
 color: black;
}

SashForm {
 background-color: #c1d5ef;
}


/* background uses a gradient */

.MTrimBar {

 background-color: #e3efff #c1d5ef;
 color: white;
 font: Verdana 8px;
}

Shell {
    background-color: #e3efff #c1d5ef 60%;
}
```

To define the styling for your application, you have two options:

- Fixed styling: Using the a property on the extension point which defines the product
- Dynamic or fixed styling: The *Theme Manager* allows you to register themes and supports switching styles at runtime

70.3. Fixed styling via the applicationCSS parameter

You can specify a fixed styling of your application via the `org.eclipse.core.runtime.products` extension point in the `plugin.xml` file. For this you set the `applicationCSS` property to the CSS file.

The value of the *applicationCSS* property should point to your CSS file via an URI. The URI follows the `platform:/plugin/BundleSymbolicName/path/file` convention. For example:

```
platform:/plugin/com.example.e4.rcp.todo/css/default.css
```

The following listing shows an example for the `plugin.xml` file which the *applicationCSS* property defined.

```
<?xml version="1.0" encoding="UTF-8"?>
<?eclipse version="3.4"?>
<plugin>

 <extension
   id="product"
   point="org.eclipse.core.runtime.products">
  <product
    application="org.eclipse.e4.ui.workbench.swt.E4Application"
     name="to-do">
   <property
      name="applicationXMI"
      value="com.example.e4.rcp.todo/Application.e4xmi">
   </property>
   <property
      name="appName"
      value="to-do">
   </property>
   <property
     name="applicationCSS"
     value="platform:/plugin/com.example.e4.rcp.todo/css/default.css">
   </property>
  </product>
 </extension>

</plugin>
```

70.4. Using the Theme Manager

The *Theme Manager* allows you to define several themes which define different styles for the application and to change these themes at runtime.

The `org.eclipse.e4.ui.css.swt.theme` extension point supports the creation of extensions for themes. This extension defines an ID for the style and a pointer to the CSS file.

You can also define the default theme via the *cssTheme* property in your `org.eclipse.core.runtime.products` extension point. This can also be used to define a fixed styling.

To switch the styling you use the `IThemeEngine`.

```
import javax.inject.Named;

import org.eclipse.e4.core.di.annotations.Execute;
import org.eclipse.e4.ui.css.swt.theme.IThemeEngine;
import org.eclipse.e4.ui.workbench.IWorkbench;


public class ThemeSwitchHandler {
 @Execute
 public void switchTheme(IThemeEngine engine) {
  // The last argument controls
  // whether the change should be persisted and
  // restored on restart
  engine.setTheme("de.vogella.e4.todo.redtheme", true);
 }
}
```

70.5. Limitations

SWT currently has some limitations for styling. For example it is not possible to style menus and table headers. In addition some platforms do not allow the styling of certain widgets, e.g. the `Button` or the `ScrollBar` widget.

70.6. CSS Attributes

The CSS attributes for SWT which can be styled are listed in the Eclipse 4 CSS wiki under the following link: http://wiki.eclipse.org/E4/CSS/SWT_Mapping

Eclipse application model elements, e.g. PartStacks or Parts can also be styled. The CSS selectors are based on the Java classes for example the following:

Table 70.1. Model Elements

Model Element	CSS Selector
MPart	.MPart
MPartStack	.MPartStack
MPartSashContainer	.MPartSashContainer

70.7. CSS Spy

CSS spy is a very useful tool to see the possible styling options. *CSS spy* is part of the *e4 tooling* project and can be installed from its update site. See the Eclipse 4 installation description for details.

Once installed, you can open the *CSS spy* via the **Shift**+**Alt**+**F4** shortcut.

CSS spy allows you to see the available properties and the current style settings.

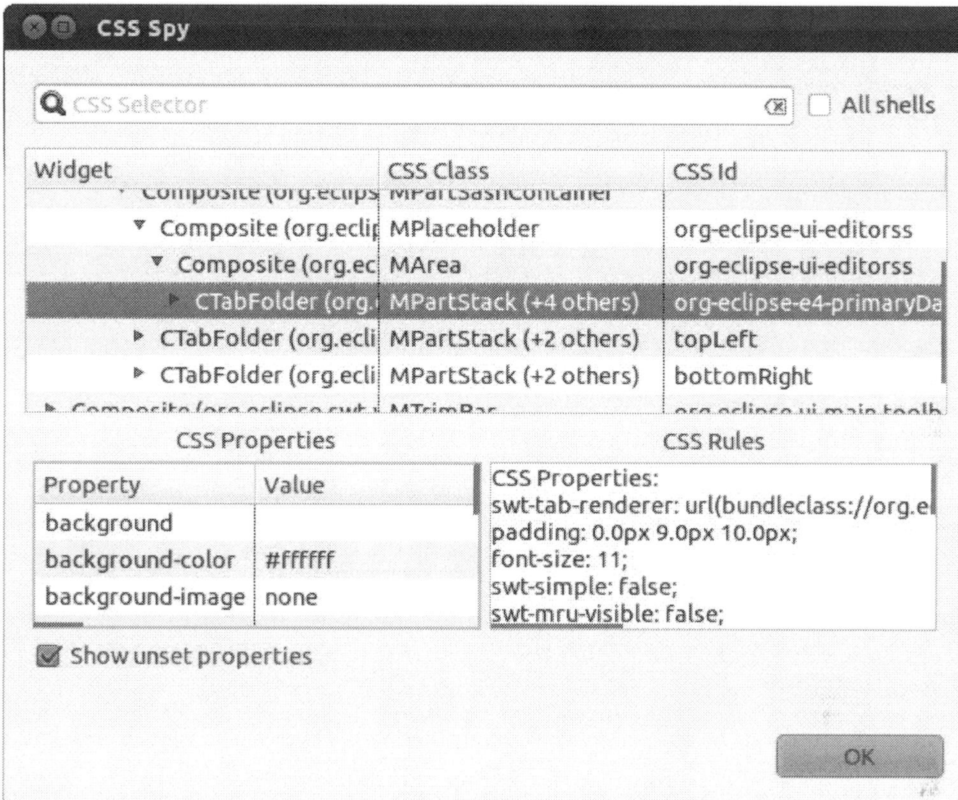

70.8. Styling specific widgets

In your Java code you can specify tags on certain widgets and use these tags in your CSS file to style these widgets. You can specify an ID or a class. In CSS an ID is supposed to be unique across all of the elements in a page (or window in our case) while a class can be assigned to several elements.

The following example shows how to set the ID and the class for specific SWT widgets.

```
// IStylingEngine was injected
// via @Inject
```

```
Label label = new Label(parent, SWT.NONE);
Text text = new Text(parent, SWT.BORDER);

// Set the ID, must be unique in the same window
IStylingEngine.setID(label, "MyCSSTagForLabel");

// Set the class, can be used several times
IStylingEngine.setClassname(text, "error");
```

These elements can be addressed in the CSS file via:

```
#MyCSSTagForLabel{
 color:#blue;
}

.error {
 border: 1px red;
}
```

70.9. Colors and Gradients

Colors can be defined in different ways, e.g. the color white can be described as `#white`, `rgb(255,255,2555)` or `#ffffff`.

Styling supports gradients for the background color of UI controls. Linear and radial gradients are supported. The definition of gradients is demonstrated in the following listing.

```
// linear gradient
background-color: gradient linear color_1 [color_2]* [percentage]*

// For example
background-color: gradient linear white black
background-color: gradient linear white black blue
background-color: gradient linear white black 50%
background-color: gradient linear white black 50% 20%

// radial gradient
background-color: gradient linear color_1 color_2 [percentage]

// For example
background-color: gradient radial white black
background-color: gradient radial white black 50%
```

If you use the optional percentage in the definition, then the color change will be done after the defined percentage. The following picture shows the result of different settings.

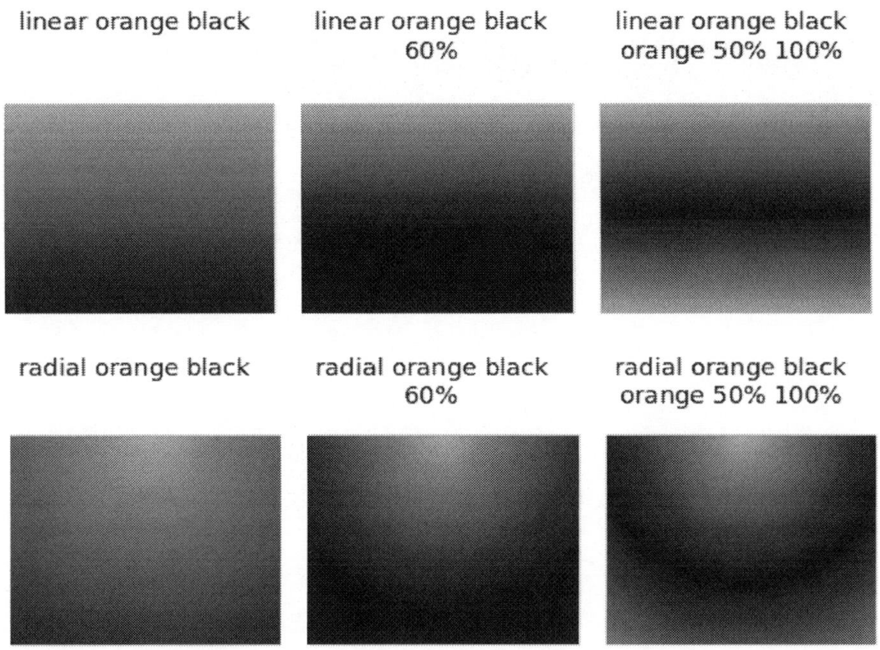

Please note that the current gradient specification is not compliant with the CSS specification and that it is planned to change this definition (after the Eclipse 4.2 release).

70.10. CSS support for custom widgets

It is also possible to implement CSS support for custom widgets. See the Eclipse 4 CSS Wiki for further details description. This can be found under the following URL.

```
http://wiki.eclipse.org/Eclipse4/RCP/CSS
```

71. Exercise: Styling with CSS files

71.1. Create CSS file

Create a folder called `css` in your `com.example.e4.rcp.todo` project and create the following `default.css` file.

```
Label {
 font: Verdana 8px;
 color: black;
}

Composite Label {
 color: black;
}

Text {
 font: Verdana 8px;
}

/* Identifies only those SWT Text elements
   appearing within a Composite */

Composite Text {
 background-color: white;
 color: black;
}

SashForm {
 background-color: #c1d5ef;
}


/* background uses a gradient */

.MTrimBar {

 background-color: #e3efff #c1d5ef;
 color: white;
 font: Verdana 8px;
}

Shell {
    background-color: #e3efff #c1d5ef 60%;
}
```

71.2. Define applicationCSS property

Open the plugin.xml file in your `com.example.e4.rcp.todo` plug-in. Select the *Extensions* tab and add the `applicationCSS` property to the `org.eclipse.core.runtime.products` extension point. The value of this property should use the following identifier.

```
platform:/plugin/com.example.e4.rcp.todo/css/default.css
```

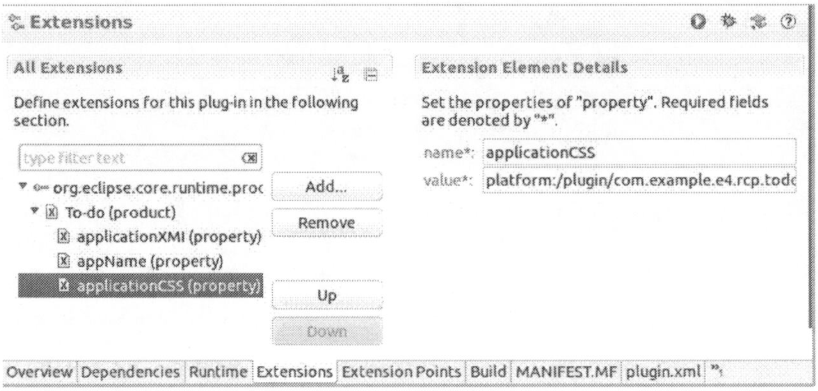

Start your application. The application should be styled.

71.3. Theme Manager and switching styles

You will now use the *Theme Manager* to introduce the ability to switch the application styling at runtime.

Create the following `css/red.css` file.

```
CTabItem, ToolBar, Button, CBanner, CoolBar {
 font-size: 9;
 background-color: red;
}
```

Remove the `applicationCSS` property and create two extensions for the `org.eclipse.e4.ui.css.swt.theme` extension point.

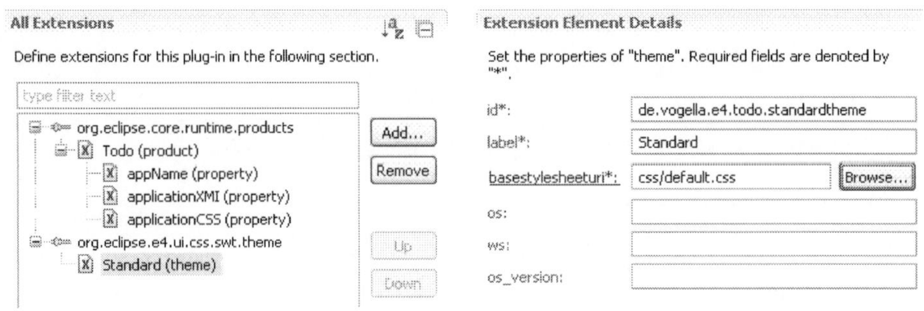

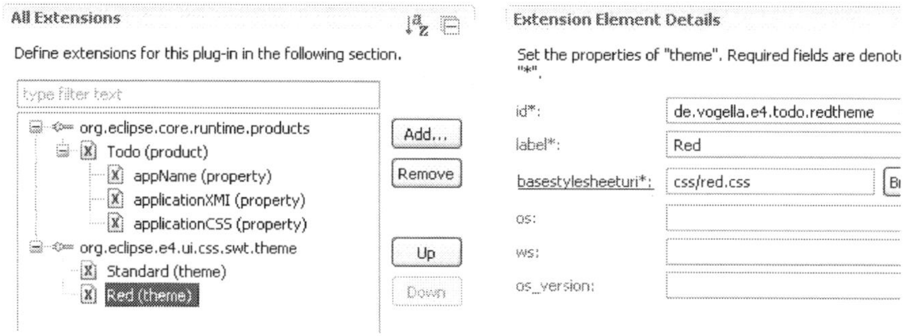

Add the `cssTheme` parameter to your product.

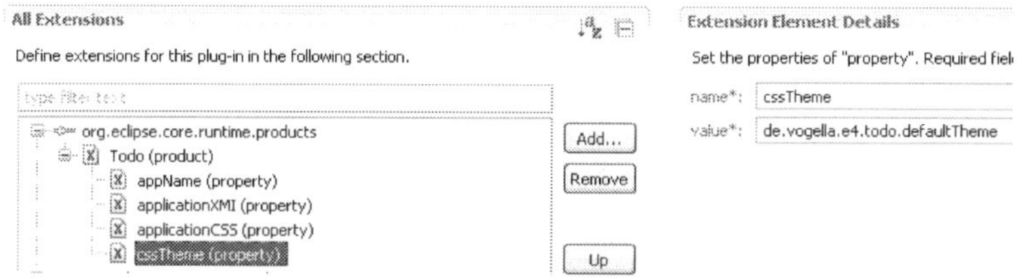

Create a new handler class, which allows you to switch the theme.

```
import javax.inject.Named;

import org.eclipse.e4.core.di.annotations.Execute;
import org.eclipse.e4.ui.css.swt.theme.IThemeEngine;
import org.eclipse.e4.ui.workbench.IWorkbench;


public class ThemeSwitchHandler {
 @Execute
 public void switchTheme(IThemeEngine engine) {
  // The last argument controls
  // whether the change should be persisted and
  // restored on restart
  engine.setTheme("de.vogella.e4.todo.redtheme", true);
 }
}
```

Define a new command and a handler for switching the style. Assign the above class to the handler.

Add a menu entry to your application model which uses your handler for switching the style.

If you run the application and select your new menu entry, the styling of your application should use the *red* color similarly to the following screenshot.

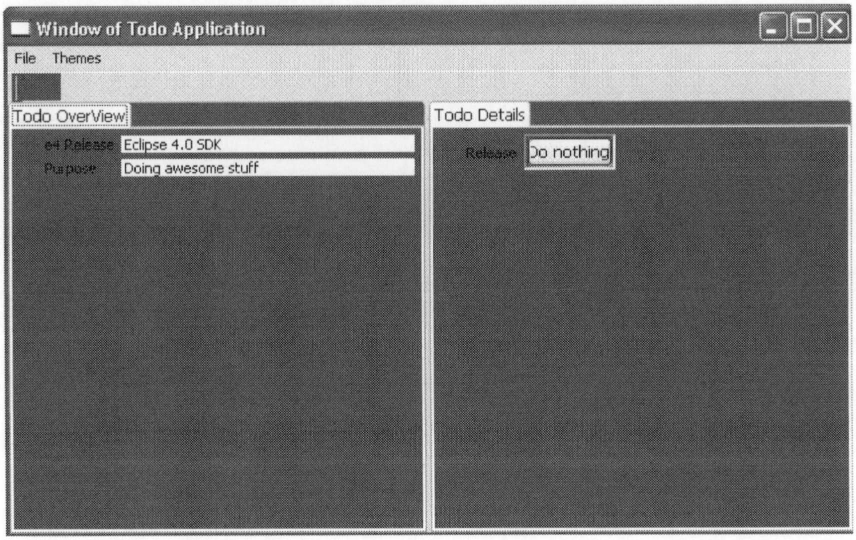

Please note that changes in styling my require a restart of your application.

72. Eclipse application updates with p2

72.1. Eclipse application Updates

The Eclipse platform provides an installation and update mechanism called *Eclipse p2* (short: *p2*). This update mechanism allows you to update Eclipse applications and to install new functionalities into them.

The update and installation of functionalities with *p2* is based on *Eclipse Features* projects (short: *features*). *Features* basically describe a list of plug-ins and other features and represent a logical grouping of plug-ins. In the terminology of *p2* these *features* are *installable Units*.

Eclipse p2 allows you to group *installable Units* into a *p2* repository. A repository is defined via its URI. This URI can point to a local file or to a webpage.

72.2. p2 plug-ins

`org.eclipse.equinox.p2.core` defines the core functionality of p2. `org.eclipse.equinox.p2.metadata.repository` defines the repository.

72.3. Creating update sites

To export your product, select your product configuration file and select the *export* button on the *Overview* tab.

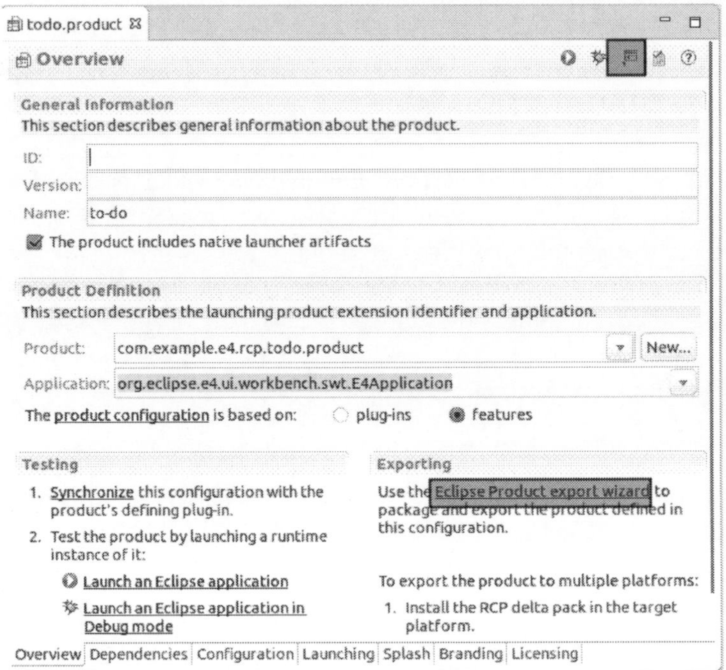

During the export of a product you can select if a *metadata repository* should be created. If you select this, a p2 update site will be created in the export directory. You find this p2 update site in the `repository` folder.

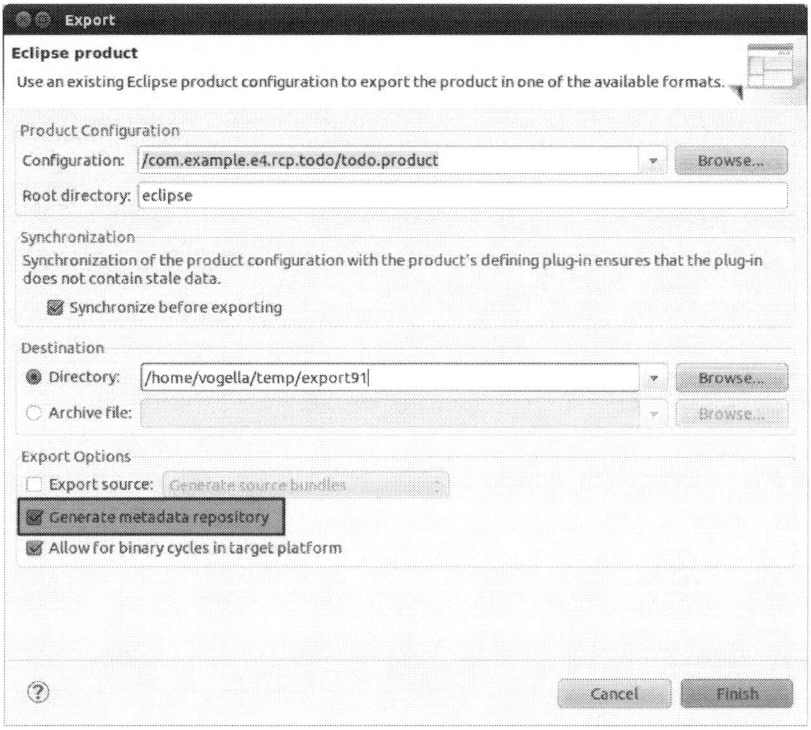

To avoid dependency problems delete the version number from your features in the *Dependency* tab of the product. You can do this via the *Properties* button.

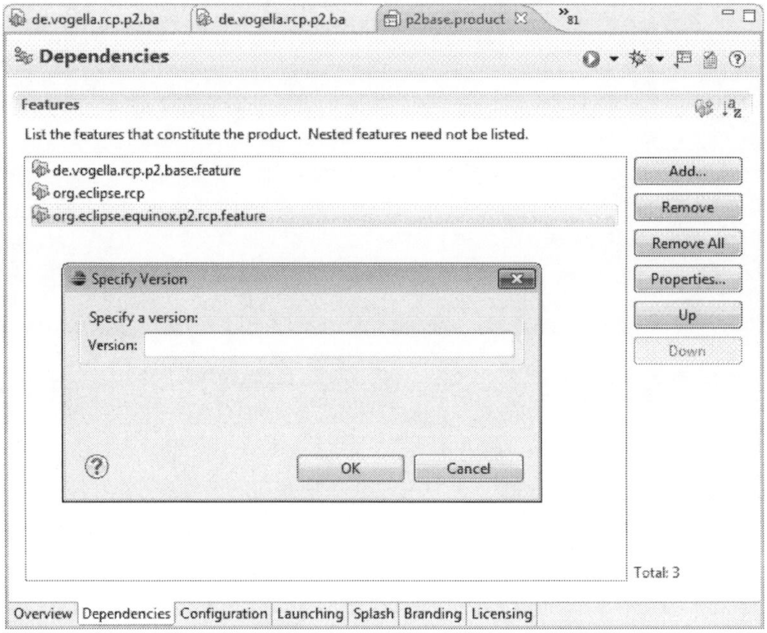

This directory is the update site. You could copy it to a web server so that the user could access it and update his Eclipse application.

p2 also supports file based update sites which can be used for testing. For local testing just copy the application to another folder and configure *p2* to use this update site.

You could configure *p2* at runtime with the new update site but you can also define existing update sites via a `p2.inf` file. The content of the file points to pre-defined locations. They can be file or web based.

p2 can update complete products or individual features.

The *p2* update manager groups features, by default, based on categories. Therefore you usually also create a category for your features via File → New → Other → Category Definition .

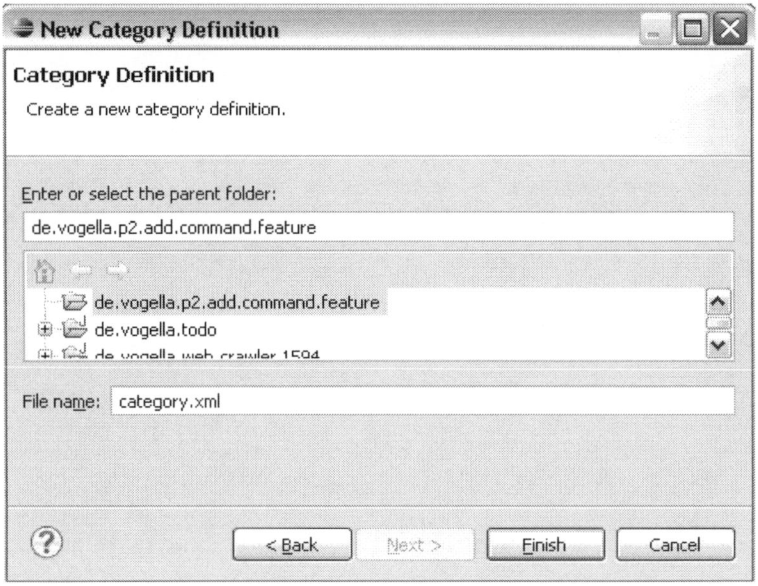

Via the *New Category* button you can create a category. The name you select will be visible as a category in the update manager. Add the related features to this category.

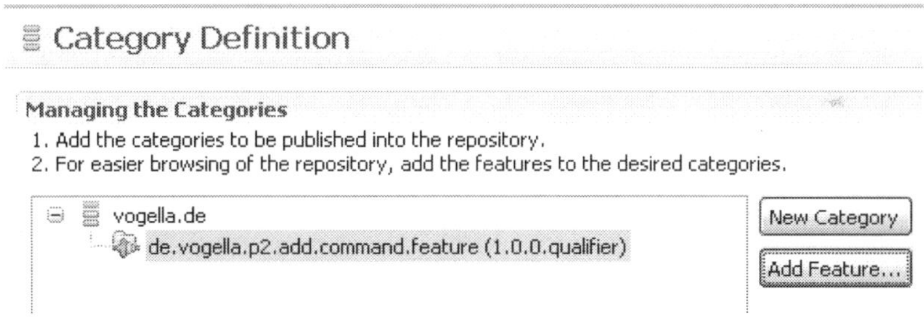

72.4. Eclipse 4 and p2

The default p2 user interface has not yet been transferred to the new Eclipse 4 programming model.

To update your Eclipse 4 application with p2 you use the low-level API of p2.

An example for using the p2 API in an Eclipse application is described in the Eclipse wiki under the following URL: http://wiki.eclipse.org/Equinox/p2/Adding_Self-Update_to_an_RCP_Application

73. Eclipse 4 testing

73.1. Introduction

73.1.1. Unit Testing

A unit test is a piece of code written by a developer that executes a specific functionality in the code under test. Unit tests ensure that code is working as intended and validate that this is still the case after code changes.

73.1.2. Unit Testing with JUnit

JUnit 4.x is a test framework which uses annotations to identify methods that are test methods. JUnit assumes that all test methods can be executed in an arbitrary order. Therefore tests should not depend on other tests.

To write a test with JUnit

- Annotate a method with @org.junit.Test
- Use a method provided by JUnit to check the expected result of the code execution versus the actual result

You can use Eclipse or the `org.junit.runner.JUnitCore` class to run the test.

73.2. Testing Eclipse 4 application

73.2.1. General testing

In general all Java classes in an Eclipse 4 application can be tested similarly to other Java applications. This description highlights the special Eclipse 4 constructs.

73.2.2. Testing user interface components

Eclipse 4 makes testing for user interface components easier compared to Eclipse 3.x. As the components have no hard dependency on the framework, these components can be directly used in a test.

For example take the following *Part*.

```
package com.example.e4.rcp.todo.ui.parts;


import javax.annotation.PostConstruct;
import javax.annotation.PreDestroy;

import org.eclipse.swt.SWT;
import org.eclipse.swt.layout.GridData;
import org.eclipse.swt.layout.GridLayout;
import org.eclipse.swt.widgets.Button;
import org.eclipse.swt.widgets.Composite;
import org.eclipse.swt.widgets.Label;

public class TodoOverviewPart {

 @PostConstruct
 public void createControls(Composite parent){
  parent.setLayout(new GridLayout(2, false));
  Button button = new Button(parent, SWT.PUSH);
  button.setLayoutData(new GridData(SWT.BEGINNING, SWT.CENTER, false,
    false));
  button.setText("Load Data");
  Label label = new Label(parent, SWT.NONE);
  label.setLayoutData(new GridData(SWT.FILL, SWT.CENTER, true,
    false));
  label.setText("Data not available");


 }

 @PreDestroy
 public void dispose(){

 }
}
```

This *Part* can be created via a simple Java Program which has the SWT library included in its classpath.

```
package com.example.e4.rcp.todo.ui.parts;

import org.eclipse.swt.widgets.Display;
import org.eclipse.swt.widgets.Shell;

public class TodoOverviewPartTest {
 public static void main(String... main) {
  Display display = new Display();
  Shell shell = new Shell(display);
  TodoOverviewPart part = new TodoOverviewPart();
  part.createControls(shell);
  shell.open();
  // Create and check the event loop
```

```
    while (!shell.isDisposed()) {
     if (!display.readAndDispatch())
      display.sleep();
    }
    display.dispose();

  }
}
```

The above code can be easily changed to a unit test. Your test class can create the class, provide the required dependencies and run the tests.

73.2.3. Testing Dependency Injection

You can also include the process of dependency injection into the test. Create your own `IEclipseContext` and use the `ContextInjectionFactory.make()` method to create the object which should be tested.

The following code shows an example of how to create your own context and construct the object based on this construct.

```
package testing;


import org.eclipse.e4.core.contexts.ContextInjectionFactory;
import org.eclipse.e4.core.contexts.EclipseContextFactory;
import org.eclipse.e4.core.contexts.IEclipseContext;
import org.eclipse.swt.SWT;
import org.eclipse.swt.widgets.Composite;
import org.eclipse.swt.widgets.Display;
import org.eclipse.swt.widgets.Shell;

public class CreateContextText {
 public static void main(String[] args) {
   IEclipseContext context = EclipseContextFactory.create();
   // Put objects into the context
   context.set("myvalue1", "For testing");
   // More things, for example a LayoutManager
   MyClass test = ContextInjectionFactory.make(MyClass.class, context);
 }
}
```

74. Target Platform

74.1. Developing against the Eclipse IDE

If you develop Eclipse plug-ins, you reuse components of the Eclipse Platform for example *SWT* or *JFace*.

By default these plug-ins are sourced directly from your Eclipse IDE.

This is not an ideal approach, as this makes you dependent on your version of the Eclipse IDE. This can lead to problems, if developers are using different versions of Eclipse. It also makes it difficult to upgrade these plug-ins for everyone at the same time.

If you followed this approach you would also need to install every plug-in required for your product either in your workspace or in your Eclipse IDE.

Another problem with this approach is that you might unintentionally add plug-ins from the Eclipse IDE to your product.

74.2. Defining your Target Platform

Via a *Target Platform* you define the set of plug-ins which are available for development. For example you define which version of the *SWT* and *JFace* plug-in is part of your target platform.

This makes you independent from the Eclipse IDE you are using. Developers with different versions of Eclipse will compile their work against the same set of plug-ins.

A *Target Platform* is defined via a `.target` file. This target file defines the list of plug-ins and features. You typically share this target file between different developers to ensure that everyone is using the same basis for development.

The most effective way of defining your *Target Platform* is to use an (Eclipse p2) update sites. These are of the same type as update sites which you use to install a new set of plug-ins. If the content in the update site defined by your target platform is changed, your local set of plug-ins can also be updated.

It is also possible to define your target platform based on plug-ins in your file system.

74.3. Creating a Target Platform definition

A Target Definition file can be created via File → New → Other → Plug-in Development → Target Definition.

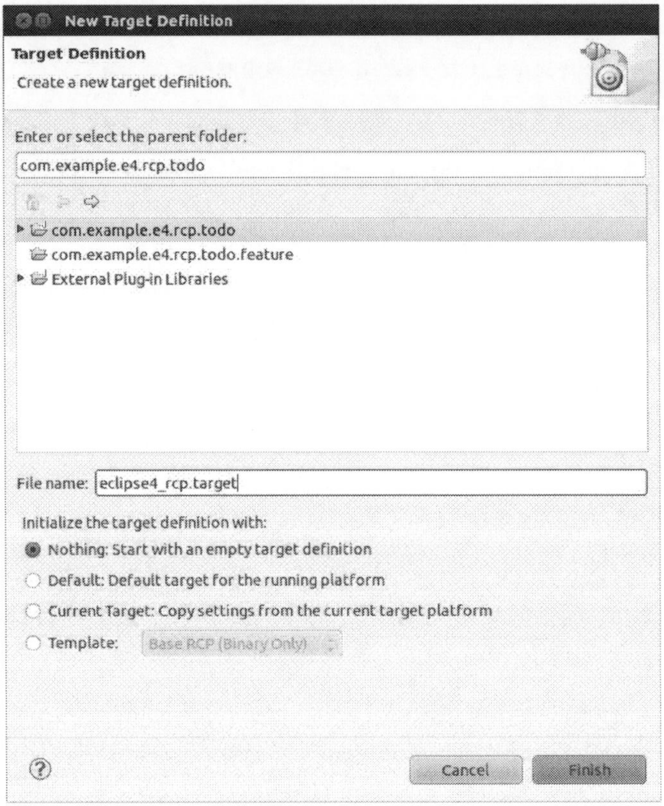

You can add new locations via the *Add* button in the location section. To add an Eclipse p2 update site, select *Software Site* and specify the URL.

After you have defined your Target Definition file, you can set it as the target in your Eclipse IDE via the *Set as Target Platform* button.

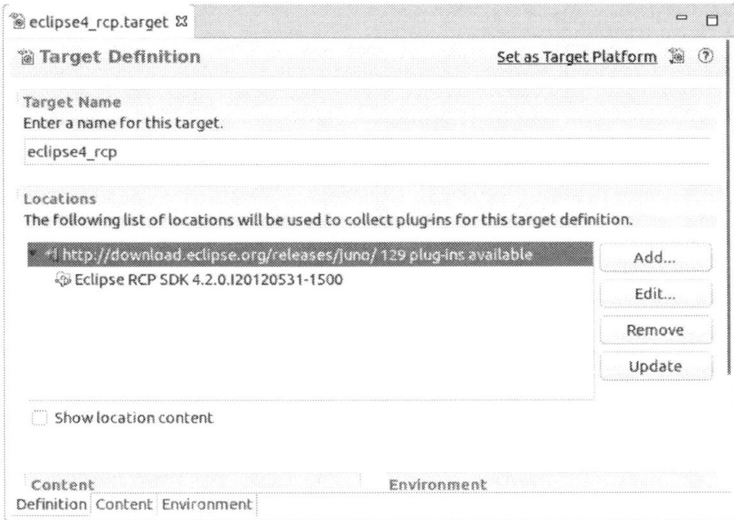

You can switch the target platform in the Eclipse Preferences. Select Window → Preferences → Plug-in Development → Target Platform.

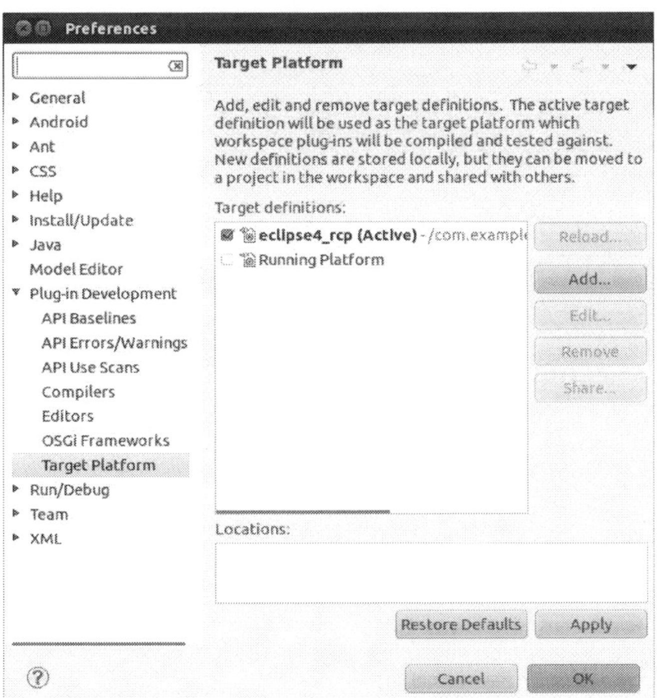

75. Eclipse 3.x applications with the compatibility layer

75.1. Running Eclipse 3.x plug-ins on top of Eclipse 4

Eclipse 4 allows you to run Eclipse 3.x RCP applications and Eclipse 3.x plug-ins. Your Eclipse RCP application should have an existing product configuration file for the migration.

The compatibility layer supports the migration of existing Eclipse 3.x plug-ins and applications to Eclipse 4 and to start evaluating advantages of Eclipse 4, e.g. the application model and CSS based styling.

The compatibility layer converts the relevant extension point information into the application model. In the `org.eclipse.platform` plug-in you find the `LegacyIDE.e4xmi` file which defines the initial window and some *model Addons*.

If Eclipse is started in the compatibility mode, this file is read via the `E4Workbench` class. This class is part of the `org.eclipse.e4.workbench.ui.internal` package. `E4Workbench` will then convert the relevant extension points into elements of the application model.

New programming concepts of Eclipse 4 such as dependency injection for *Views* do not work (out of the box) with the compatibility layer.

75.2. Using features

The easiest way to migrate your Eclipse RCP application to Eclipse 4.2 is to have a feature based product configuration file which includes the standard `org.eclipse.rcp` feature.

In Eclipse 4 this feature has been upgraded to include most of the necessary additional plug-ins for the compatibility mode. If your product is based on this feature you can directly start your Eclipse 3.x product and it will work.

You only need to add two additional features to your product configuration file, the `org.eclipse.emf.ecore` and the `org.eclipse.emf.common` feature.

75.3. Using plug-ins

If you product configuration file is based on plug-ins you have to add the following plug-ins to it:

- org.eclipse.e4.ui.workbench.addons.swt
- org.eclipse.equinox.ds
- org.eclipse.equinox.event
- org.eclipse.equinox.util
- org.eclipse.platform
- org.eclipse.ui.forms
- org.eclipse.ui.intro

After this change you should be able to start your existing application based on Eclipse 4.

75.4. Mixing Eclipse 4 and Eclipse 3.x

Mixing Eclipse 4 and Eclipse 3.x. components is currently not officially supported in the Eclipse 4.2 release.

You can however define your own `LegacyIDE.e4xmi` file and add your model components to this file. Via the *applicationXMI* parameter in your `org.eclipse.core.runtime.products` extension point you point to that file.

For this approach you have to copy the standard `LegacyIDE.e4xmi` file and add your model components to it. This file can be found in the `org.eclipse.ui.workbench` plug-in.

A code example for this approach can be found under the following URL:

```
https://github.com/fredrikattebrant/Simple-4x-RCP-app
```

While this approach seems to work, it is currently not officially supported in the Eclipse 4.2 release. The Eclipse 4 team intend to provide support for such mixed mode hybrid applications in future Eclipse releases.

Part VI. Eclipse 4 Expert Development

Table of Contents

76. Overview

This part of the book contains powerful functionalities which are not necessary required in a typical Eclipse 4 application.

It demonstrates how to define and evaluate your own annotations and your own extensionin points. It also explains the Renderer framework which can be used to replace the user interface toolkit or to work with an extended application model.

Some examples in this part of the book are standalone examples and are not based on the Todo example due to the complexity of the related topics.

77. Eclipse 4 dependency injection and own annotations

77.1. Define and evaluate own annotations

The Eclipse 4 dependency injection mechanism is extensible with your own annotations. You can define your own annotation and define an OSGi service for this annotation which is registered with the Eclipse framework. Eclipse calls your annotation processor if it finds your annotation in a relevant part of the coding.

```
package com.example.e4.rcp.todo.ownannotation;

import java.lang.annotation.Documented;
import java.lang.annotation.ElementType;
import java.lang.annotation.Retention;
import java.lang.annotation.RetentionPolicy;
import java.lang.annotation.Target;

@javax.inject.Qualifier
@Documented
// Target hint not used by Eclipse 4
@Target({ElementType.METHOD, ElementType.PARAMETER})
@Retention(RetentionPolicy.RUNTIME)
public @interface UniqueTodo {

}
```

The definition of your own annotation processor is based on an OSGi service which provides the `ExtendedObjectSupplier` interface from the `org.eclipse.e4.core.di.suppliers` package. Via the *dependency.injection.annotation* property the service defines the annotation for which it is responsible.

```
<?xml version="1.0" encoding="UTF-8"?>
<scr:component xmlns:scr="http://www.osgi.org/xmlns/scr/v1.1.0"
 name="com.example.e4.rcp.todo.ownannotation">
   <implementation
    class="com.example.e4.rcp.todo.ownannotation.[CONTINUE...]
    internal.UniqueTodoObjectSupplier"/>
   <service>
      <provide
       interface="org.eclipse.e4.core.di.[CONTINUE...]
       suppliers.ExtendedObjectSupplier"/>
   </service>
   <property
    name="dependency.injection.annotation"
```

```
    type="String"
    value="com.example.e4.rcp.todo.ownannotation.UniqueTodo"/>
</scr:component>
```

The annotation processor class returns an object. The following code shows an example for an annotation processor which returns an instance of the `Todo` class.

```
package com.example.e4.rcp.todo.ownannotation.internal;

import java.util.Date;

import org.eclipse.e4.core.di.suppliers.ExtendedObjectSupplier;
import org.eclipse.e4.core.di.suppliers.IObjectDescriptor;
import org.eclipse.e4.core.di.suppliers.IRequestor;

import com.example.e4.rcp.todo.model.Todo;


public class UniqueTodoObjectSupplier extends ExtendedObjectSupplier {
@Override
public Object get(IObjectDescriptor descriptor, IRequestor requestor,
      boolean track, boolean group) {
   System.out.println("Own annotation processor");
   // Just for the purpose of this example
   // return a hard-coded Todo
   // You could add checks which makes this Todo unique, e.g.
   // be access the TodoService and reading all existing ID's
   Todo todo = new Todo(15, "Checked", "Checked", false, new Date());
   return todo;
  }
}
```

77.2. Usage

The possible usage of your own annotation and dependency injection is not limited, implementations can create their own annotations to have finer control about the injected values.

A typical approach for using your own annotations would be for the Java Persistence API (JPA). The JPA persistence manager could be injected into the Eclipse 4 application via a new annotation and a corresponding annotation processor.

78. Tutorial: Defining own annotations

78.1. Overview and project creation

The following shows an example for a new annotation.

The annotation processor is just an example implementation. Its name implies that it should make the Todo unique. This logic is not implemented in this example to keep it as short as possible. This example annotation processor will return a Todo with a fixed ID.

Create a new plug-in project called *com.example.e4.rcp.todo.ownannotation* without any dependencies and classes.

Add the `javax.inject`, `org.eclipse.e4.core.di` and `com.example.e4.rcp.todo.model` plug-ins as dependency.

78.2. Define and evaluate annotations

Define the following annotation and export the corresponding package in your `MANIFEST.MF` file.

```
package com.example.e4.rcp.todo.ownannotation;

import java.lang.annotation.Documented;
import java.lang.annotation.ElementType;
import java.lang.annotation.Retention;
import java.lang.annotation.RetentionPolicy;
import java.lang.annotation.Target;

@javax.inject.Qualifier
@Documented
// Target hint not used by Eclipse 4
@Target({ElementType.METHOD, ElementType.PARAMETER})
@Retention(RetentionPolicy.RUNTIME)
public @interface UniqueTodo {

}
```

Create the `com.example.e4.rcp.todo.ownannotation.internal` package and the following class.

```
package com.example.e4.rcp.todo.ownannotation.internal;

import java.util.Date;
```

```
import org.eclipse.e4.core.di.suppliers.ExtendedObjectSupplier;
import org.eclipse.e4.core.di.suppliers.IObjectDescriptor;
import org.eclipse.e4.core.di.suppliers.IRequestor;

import com.example.e4.rcp.todo.model.Todo;


public class UniqueTodoObjectSupplier extends ExtendedObjectSupplier {
@Override
public Object get(IObjectDescriptor descriptor, IRequestor requestor,
      boolean track, boolean group) {
   System.out.println("Own annotation processor");
   // Just for the purpose of this example
   // return a hard-coded Todo
   // You could add checks which makes this Todo unique, e.g.
   // be access the TodoService and reading all existing ID's
   Todo todo = new Todo(15, "Checked", "Checked", false, new Date());
   return todo;
  }
}
```

The service is registered via OSGi declarative services.

```
<?xml version="1.0" encoding="UTF-8"?>
<scr:component xmlns:scr="http://www.osgi.org/xmlns/scr/v1.1.0"
 name="com.example.e4.rcp.todo.ownannotation">
   <implementation
    class="com.example.e4.rcp.todo.ownannotation.[CONTINUE...]
    internal.UniqueTodoObjectSupplier"/>
   <service>
      <provide
       interface="org.eclipse.e4.core.di.[CONTINUE...]
       suppliers.ExtendedObjectSupplier"/>
   </service>
   <property
    name="dependency.injection.annotation"
    type="String"
    value="com.example.e4.rcp.todo.ownannotation.UniqueTodo"/>
</scr:component>
```

Include the new plug-in into your feature. Ensure via the *Start Level* configuration in your product configuration file that this plug-in and the `org.eclipse.equinox.ds` are started before the application plug-in. Also set *Auto-Start* to true. Both settings can be done on the *Configuration* tab of your product configuration file.

79. Creating and evaluating Extension Points

79.1. Eclipse Extensions and Extension Points

Eclipse provides the concept of *extension points* and *extensions* to allow functionality to be contributed to plug-ins by several other plug-ins.

The following table describes the terminology.

Table 79.1. Extensions and Extension Points Table

Term	Description
Plug-in defines Extension Point	If a plug-in defines an *extension points* it allows other plug-ins to add functionality based on the contract defined by the extension point. The defining plug-in is also responsible for evaluating contributions to the defined extension point. Therefore the defining plug-in contains coding to evaluate the extensions.
A plug-in provides an Extension	This plug-in adds a contribution (*extension*) to an existing extension point. Extensions to an extension point are defined in the plug-ins via the `plugin.xml` file. Contributions can be code or data.

79.2. Accessing Extensions

The information about the available extension points and the provided extensions are stored in a class of type `IExtensionRegistry`. The resolution of the extension points and provided extensions happen as a plug-in is in the *RESOLVED* lifecyle status as defined by the OSGi specification.

In Eclipse 4 you can use the dependency injection mechanism to get the `IExtensionRegistry` class.

```
@Inject
public void doSomething(IExtensionRegistry registry){
  // Do someting
  registry.getConfigurationElementsFor("your.extension");
}
```

In Eclipse 3.x you could have queried for a certain extension via the following code.

```
// The following will read all existing extensions
// for the defined ID
Platform.getExtensionRegistry().
 getConfigurationElementsFor("your.extension");
```

79.3. Creating an extension point

A plug-in which defines an extension point must do the following:

- Define the extension point in the `plugin.xml` file
- Write code to load the extensions to this extension point
- Evaluate the contributed extensions and use this information to do something

Extension points are defined via an XML schema file which is referred to in the `plugin.xml` file. This XML schema file defines the details and the contract of the extension point. For example the following shows the relation to the schema file in the `plugin.xml` file.

```
<?xml version="1.0" encoding="UTF-8"?>
<?eclipse version="3.2"?>
<plugin>
 <extension-point id="de.vogella.extensionpoint.greeters"
  name="Greeters"
  schema="schema/de.vogella.extensionpoint.greeters.exsd" />
</plugin>
```

79.4. Extension Factories

If you define your class directly in the extension point you are limited to classes which have a default constructor. To avoid this restriction you can use extension factories to create the object which is then returned. To use a factory implement the interface `IExecutableExtensionFactory` in the class attribute of your extension point definition. The factory receives the configuration elements and can construct the required object.

80. Tutorial: Creating Extension Points

80.1. Overview

In this tutorial we will create two plug-ins. The first one defines an extension point and the second one will contribute extensions.

You can include these plug-ins in your Eclipse application or you could even use them in the Eclipse IDE.

80.2. Create a plug-in which defines the extension

Create a new plug-in project called *de.vogella.extensionpoint.definition*. This example will not make contribution to the UI, select this option in the wizard. Also select "No" for the *Would you like to create a rich client application?* option. The option to create an Activator should be selected.

80.3. Define an extension point

Open the `MANIFEST.MF` file and the *Extension Points* tab. Press the *Add* button.

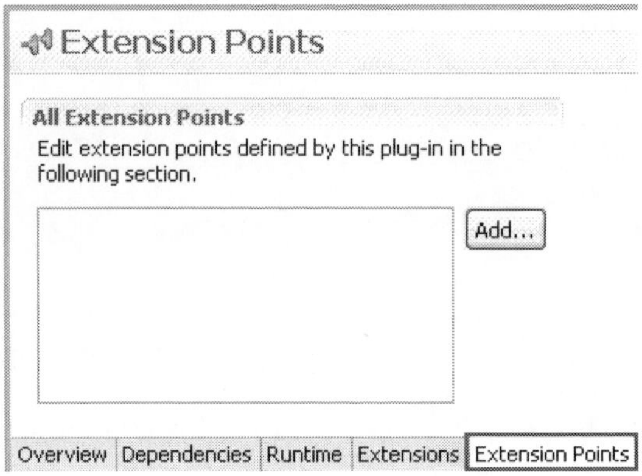

On the following dialog enter "de.vogella.extensionpoint.definition.greeter" as *ID* and "Greeter" as *name*. The *Extension Point Schema* field will be automatically populated based on your input.

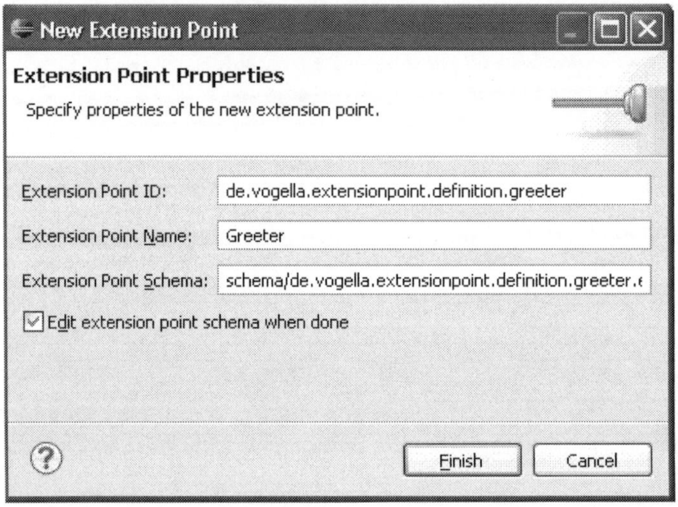

Press *Finish*. The definition of the extension is generated and the schema editor opens. Switch to the *Definition* Tab.

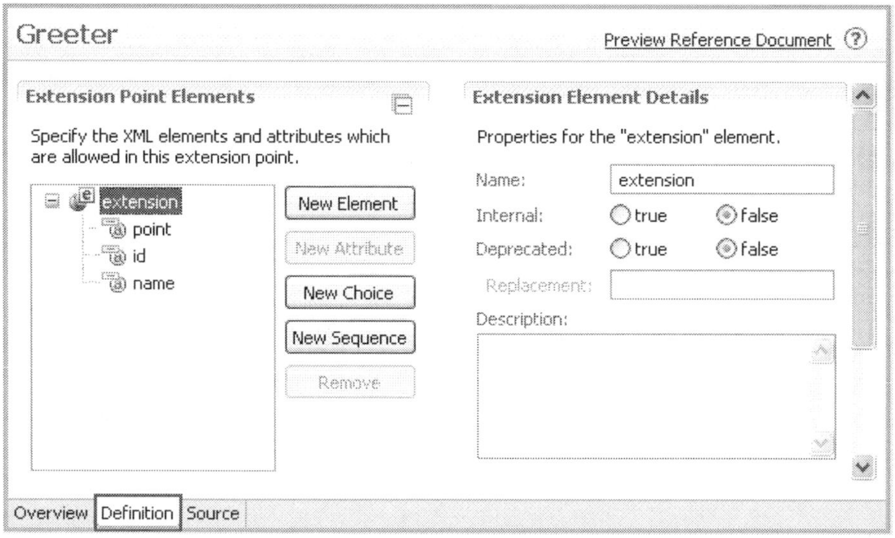

We want to add attributes to the extension point. Click on the *New Element* button. Give the new element the name "client".

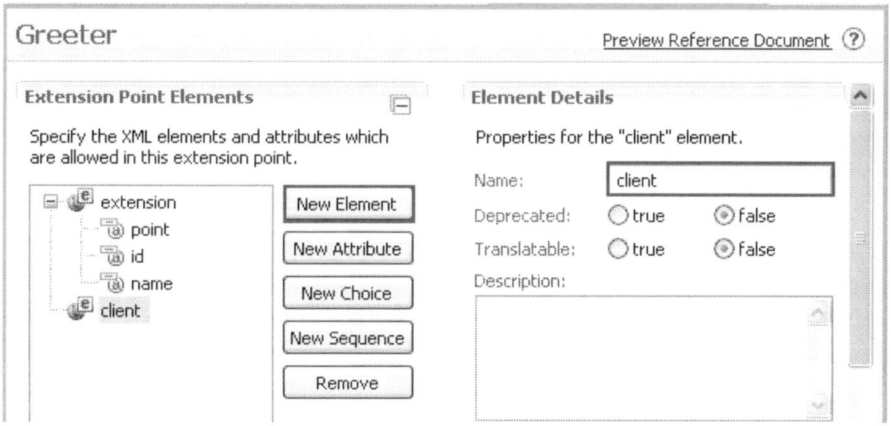

Select the "client" element and press *New Attribute*. Give the new element the name "class" and the type "java". Enter `de.vogella.extensionpoint.definition.IGreeter` as interface name

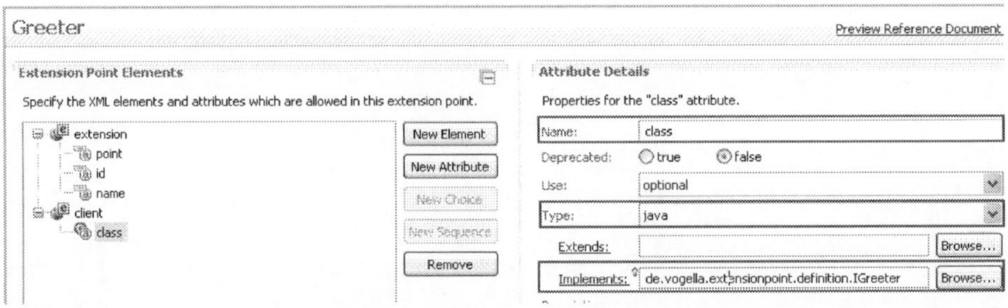

This interface is not yet defined. Press on the hyperlink called *Implements* to create it.

```
package de.vogella.extensionpoint.definition;

public interface IGreeter {
 void greet();
}
```

Go back to your extension point definition and add a choice to the extension point. This defines how often the extension "client" can be provided by contributing plug-ins. We will set no restrictions (unbound).

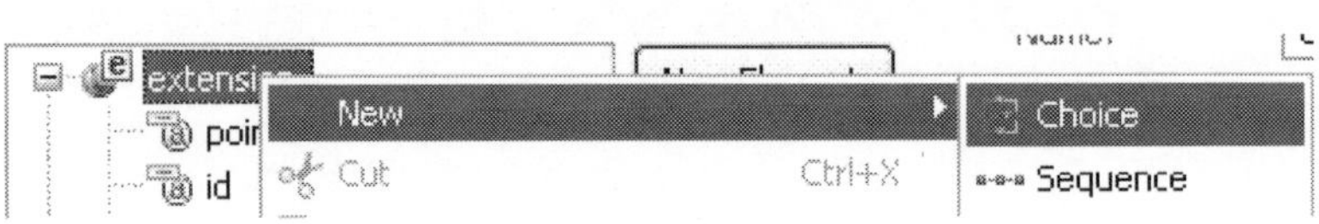

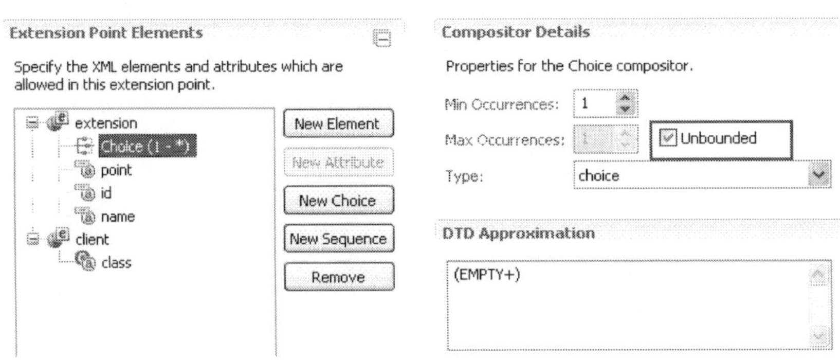

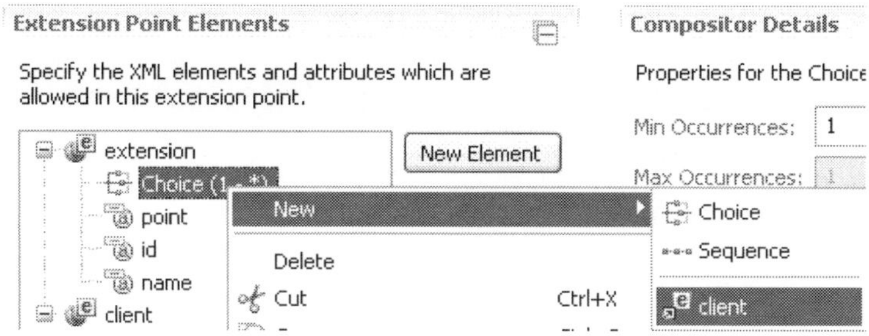

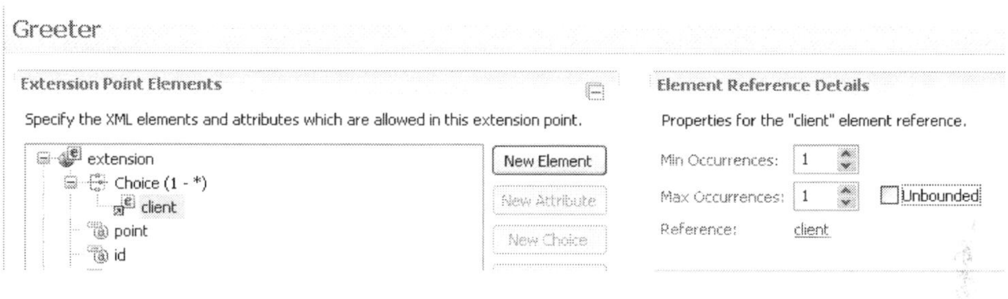

80.4. Export Package

Select the `MANIFEST.MF` file switch to the *Runtime* tab and export the package which contains the `IGreeter` interface.

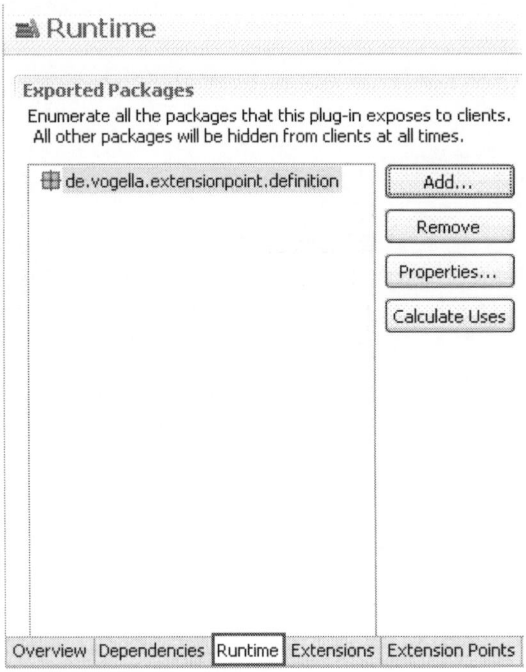

80.5. Evaluating the registered extensions

The plug-in which defines an extension point is typically also responsible for reading and using the provided extensions. It is up to you where in your coding you do this. The following shows the method for the evaluation. In Eclipse 4 the `IExtensionRegistry` can get injected via dependency injection .

We are using the `ISafeRunnable` interface. This interface protects the plug-in which defines the extension point from malfunction extensions. If an extension throws an `Exception`, it will be caught by `ISafeRunnable` and the remaining extensions will still get executed.

```
package de.vogella.extensionpoint.definition.handlers;

import org.eclipse.core.runtime.CoreException;
import org.eclipse.core.runtime.IConfigurationElement;
import org.eclipse.core.runtime.IExtensionRegistry;
import org.eclipse.core.runtime.ISafeRunnable;
import org.eclipse.core.runtime.SafeRunner;
import org.eclipse.e4.core.di.annotations.Execute;

import de.vogella.extensionpoint.definition.IGreeter;

public class EvaluateContributionsHandler {
```

```
private static final String IGREETER_ID =
  "de.vogella.extensionpoint.definition.greeter";
@Execute
public void execute(IExtensionRegistry registry) {
 evaluate(registry);
}

private void evaluate(IExtensionRegistry registry) {
 IConfigurationElement[] config =
   registry.getConfigurationElementsFor(IGREETER_ID);
 try {
  for (IConfigurationElement e : config) {
   System.out.println("Evaluating extension");
   final Object o =
     e.createExecutableExtension("class");
   if (o instanceof IGreeter) {
    executeExtension(o);
   }
  }
 } catch (CoreException ex) {
  System.out.println(ex.getMessage());
 }
}

private void executeExtension(final Object o) {
 ISafeRunnable runnable = new ISafeRunnable() {
  @Override
  public void handleException(Throwable e) {
   System.out.println("Exception in client");
  }

  @Override
  public void run() throws Exception {
   ((IGreeter) o).greet();
  }
 };
 SafeRunner.run(runnable);
}
}
```

Review the `.exsd` schema file and the reference to this file in the `plugin.xml` file.

Run your application. It should write "Starting" to the console. Your extension point is implemented. Other plug-ins can now contribute extensions.

80.6. Providing an extension

Create a new headless plug-in. This plug-in should be called *de.vogella.extensionpoint.contribution*. It should not be an RCP application. Do not use a template to create it.

Select the `MANIFEST.MF` file and the *Dependencies* tab. Add the `de.vogella.extensionpoint.definition` and `org.eclipse.core.runtime` plug-ins as a dependency. Make sure your plug-in has the singleton flag set.

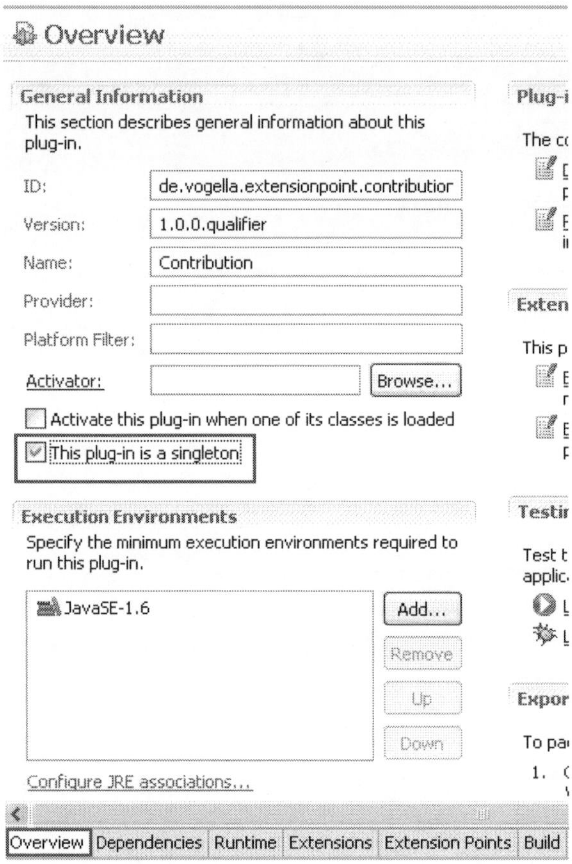

Switch to the *Extensions* tab and select *Add*. Select your own extension point and press the *Finish* button.

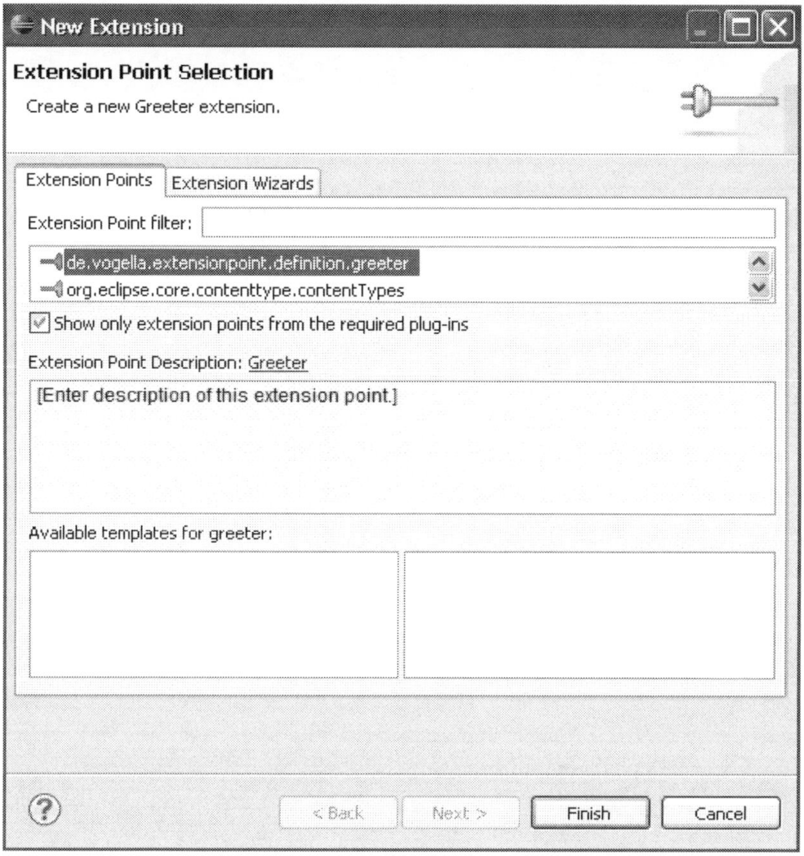

Add a client to your extension point.

Create the `GreeterGerman` class with the following coding.

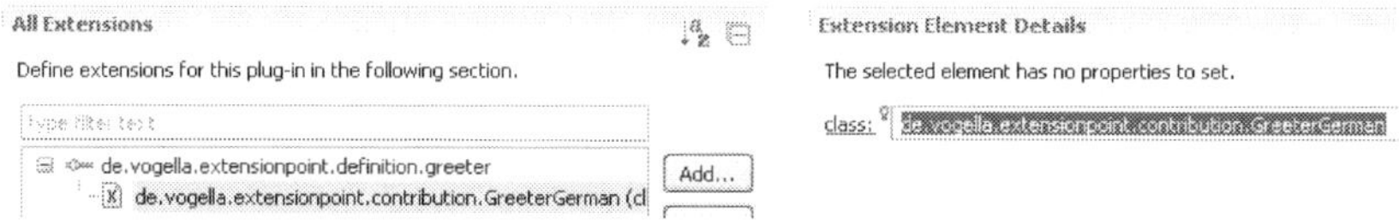


```
package de.vogella.extensionpoint.contribution;

import de.vogella.extensionpoint.definition.IGreeter;
```

```
public class GreeterGerman implements IGreeter {

 @Override
 public void greet() {
  System.out.println("Moin Jungs!");
 }
}
```

80.7. Run the example

Include these plug-ins into your Eclipse application. If you run this application you can trigger the evaluation for the extension points. This should print the text provided by the contributing plug-ins to the console.

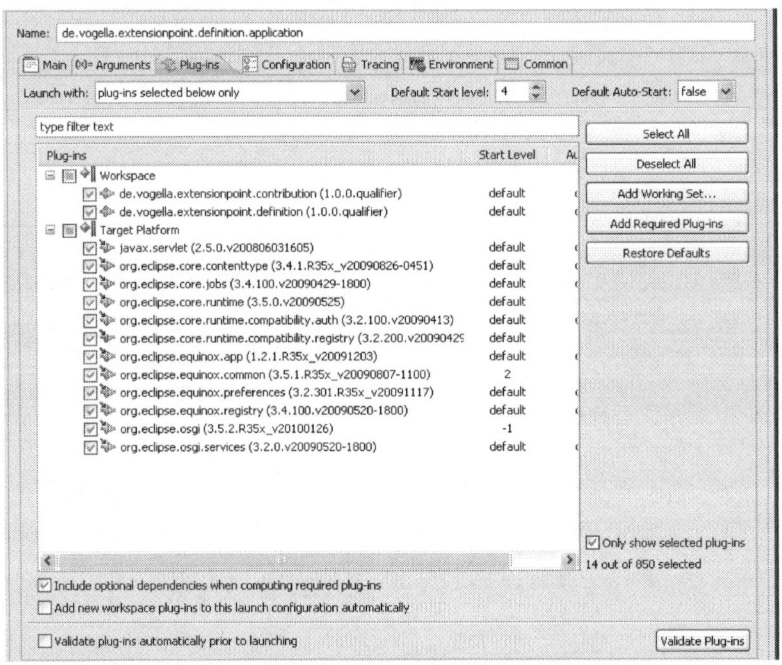


```
osgi> Starting
Evaluating extension
Moin Jungs!
```

81. Renderer framework

81.1. Renderer

The *Rendering Framework* in Eclipse 4 connects the model elements in the Eclipse application model with concrete user interface implementation classes.

A `Renderer` class is therefore responsible for creating user interface objects for certain types of model elements, monitoring their changes and reacting to these changes. Each model element typically has its own renderer object.

Eclipse 4 allows you to exchange the concrete user interface technology via the *Rendering framework* This means that your Eclipse 4 based application could use a different user interface toolkit than SWT. For example you could use JavaFX or Swing for your application.

If you switch your renderer UI toolkit, you also need to re-implement your user interface components. For example a *Part* written in SWT must be re-written in JavaFX to work together with a JavaFX Renderer.

A *Renderer Factory* determines for every model element the renderer. By default Eclipse 4 uses a SWT based *Renderer Factory*. The `org.eclipse.e4.ui.workbench.renderers.swt` plug-in contains this default implementation.

The `WorkbenchRendererFactory` class is the default renderer factory in Eclipse 4. This renderer factory is a big if / else block and returns the correct renderer for each model element.

Classes that implement this interface, implement the `getRenderer()` method. For each model element this method returns an object of type `AbstractPartRenderer`, which is responsible for drawing the model elements and for reacting to changes.

For example, if the model element is an instance of `MPart`, then an instance of the `ContributedPartRenderer` class will be created by this default *Renderer Factory*.

```
// Other if statements above
else if (uiElement instanceof MPart) {
 if (contributedPartRenderer == null) {
  contributedPartRenderer = new ContributedPartRenderer();
```

```
    initRenderer(contributedPartRenderer);
  }
  return contributedPartRenderer;
}
```

81.2. Define Renderer

Eclipse 4 allows you to register a custom implementation of the renderer factory. In this case an `IRendererFactory` implementation from the `org.eclipse.e4.ui.workbench.swt.factories` package is registered with the Eclipse application.

To do this you have to provide the `rendererFactoryUri` property pointing to the new factory class via the `org.eclipse.core.runtime.products` extension point.

Via your own renderer factory you can contribute your own renderer to existing model elements.

81.3. Extend Eclipse application model

You can also extend the application model and define a new renderer for a new model element.

You find a description of this under the following URL: http://www.vogella.com/articles/Eclipse4ExtendModel/article.html

82. Tutorial: Defining a renderer

82.1. Project and classes

The following exercise serves as a simple example for your own renderer. It does not implement a real use case.

Add the `org.eclipse.e4.ui.workbench.renderers.swt` and `org.eclipse.e4.ui.workbench.swt` plug-ins as dependencies to your `com.example.e4.rcp.todo` (short: `todo`) plug-in.

Create in your `todo` plug-in the `com.example.e4.rcp.todo.renderer` package.

Create the following two classes.

```
package com.example.e4.rcp.todo.renderer;

import org.eclipse.e4.ui.model.application.ui.MUIElement;
import org.eclipse.e4.ui.workbench.renderers.swt.SWTPartRenderer;
import org.eclipse.swt.SWT;
import org.eclipse.swt.browser.Browser;
import org.eclipse.swt.layout.GridData;
import org.eclipse.swt.layout.GridLayout;
import org.eclipse.swt.widgets.Composite;

public class BrowserRenderer extends SWTPartRenderer {

 public static final String ID = "de.vogella.javascript.maps.view";

 @Override
 public Object createWidget(MUIElement element, Object parent) {
  final Composite mapComposite =
    new Composite((Composite) parent, SWT.NONE);
  System.out.println(parent.getClass());
  mapComposite.setLayout(new GridLayout(1, false));
  final Browser browser = new Browser(mapComposite, SWT.NONE);
  browser.setUrl("http://www.vogella.com");
  GridData data = new GridData(SWT.FILL, SWT.FILL, true, true);
  browser.setLayoutData(data);
  return mapComposite;
 }

}
```

```
package com.example.e4.rcp.todo.renderer;

import org.eclipse.e4.ui.internal.workbench.swt.AbstractPartRenderer;
```

```
import org.eclipse.e4.ui.model.application.ui.MUIElement;
import org.eclipse.e4.ui.model.application.ui.basic.MPart;
import org.eclipse.e4.ui.workbench.[CONTINUE...]
renderers.swt.ContributedPartRenderer;
import org.eclipse.e4.ui.workbench.[CONTINUE...]
renderers.swt.WorkbenchRendererFactory;

public class MyRendererFactory extends WorkbenchRendererFactory {

 private BrowserRenderer mapRenderer;

 @Override
 public AbstractPartRenderer getRenderer(MUIElement uiElement,
   Object parent) {

  if (uiElement instanceof MPart) {
   if (mapRenderer == null) {
    mapRenderer = new BrowserRenderer();
    super.initRenderer(mapRenderer);
   }
   return mapRenderer;
  }

  return super.getRenderer(uiElement, parent);
 }

}
```

82.2. Register Renderer and start application

Register your renderer in the `plugin.xml` file. Ensure the `bundleclass` points to the right class.

```
<?xml version="1.0" encoding="UTF-8"?>
<?eclipse version="3.4"?>
<plugin>

   <extension
         id="product"
         point="org.eclipse.core.runtime.products">
      <product
        application="org.eclipse.e4.ui.workbench.swt.E4Application"
        name="to-do">
         <property
               name="applicationXMI"
               value="com.example.e4.rcp.todo/Application.e4xmi">
         </property>
         <property
               name="appName"
               value="to-do">
         </property>
      <property
```

```
        name="rendererFactoryUri"
        value="bundleclass://com.example.e4.rcp.todo/[CONTINUE...]
        com.example.e4.rcp.todo.renderer.MyRendererFactory">
      </property>
    </product>
  </extension>

</plugin>
```

If you now start your application, every *Part* will be rendered using the `Browser` widget.

After finishing the test, remove your renderer from the `plugin.xml` file again so that your application works is the same way as before.

Part VII. Best practises and feedback

Table of Contents

83. Best Practices for Eclipse 4 development

83.1. Extending the Eclipse Context

The application can use the Eclipse Context for providing functionality, communication and for changing Eclipse behavior. You have several options to contribute to the context: OSGi services, context functions, context elements, context variables and ModelAddons.

The programming model of Eclipse 4 makes it relatively easy to use OSGi services, compared to Eclipse 3.x. OSGi services are effectively Singletons and do not have access to the Eclipse application context. OSGi services are a good approach for infrastructure services which are Singletons.

Context functions are OSGi services which are typically stored on the application level and have access to the Eclipse application context. If this is required, they can be used instead of pure OSGi services.

Context elements are useful, if values should be stored on certain places in the Eclipse context hierarchy. Also replacing Eclipse platform implementations is a valid use case to use context elements, e.g. to change the default window close handler.

Context functions and *context variables* are useful in situations where the variables need to change, and are different for different levels in the Eclipse context hierarchy.

Model AddOns allow you to contribute Java objects to the application context. The advantages of *Model AddOns* are that they are part of the application model, hence they are very visible components. A *Model AddOn* can register itself to events or contribute again to the Eclipse context.

83.2. Application communication

For user interface scoped communication it is recommended to use *Context variables* or the `EventAdmin` service for communicating the state.

The `EventAdmin` service is a good choice, if there is no scope involved in the communication. The strengths of `EventAdmin` is that arbitrary listeners can listen to events and that the publish / subscribe mechanism is relatively simple.

83.3. Static vs. dynamic application model

If your application model is primarily static, you should define it statically, as this static model provides a good visibility of your application at development time.

If required, add dynamic behavior. These dynamic parts can be evaluated at runtime via the live model editor.

83.4. Component based development

Eclipse and OSGi support component based development.

User interface related and core functionalities should be separated into different plug-ins.

The data model of the application should be kept in its own plug-in. Almost all plug-ins will depend on this plug-in, therefore keep it as small as possible.

83.5. Usage of your own extension points

The programming model of Eclipse 4 has reduced the need for using *Extension points* but Extension points still have valid use cases.

If you have multiple plug-ins which should contribute to a defined API, you can still define and use your own extension points.

83.6. API definition

Eclipse plug-ins explicitly declare their API via their exported packages. Publish only the packages which other plug-ins should use. This way you can later on change your internal API without affecting other plug-ins. Avoid exporting packages just for testing.

83.7. Packages vs. Plug-in dependencies

OSGi allows you to define dependencies via plug-ins or via packages.

Dependencies based on packages express an API dependency as they allow you to exchange the implementing plug-in. Dependencies based on plug-ins imply a dependency on an implementation.

Use package dependencies whenever you intent to exchange the implementing plug-in.

Package dependencies add complexity to the setup as you usually have more packages than plug-ins.

Therefore use plug-in dependencies, if there is only one implementing plug-in and an exchange of this plug-in in the near future is unlikely.

84. Questions and feedback

This chapter explains where you can ask questions, provide feedback and report bugs.

84.1. Eclipse Bugs

Eclipse has a public bug tracker based on *Bugzilla*. *Bugzilla* is an Open Source project.

This bugtracker can be found under https://bugs.eclipse.org/bugs/. Here you can search for existing bugs and review them.

To participate actively in the Eclipse bugtracker you need to create a new account. This can be done by pressing the *Open a New Account* link.

Once you have a user account, you can login to the Eclipse bugtracker. This allows you to comment on existing bugs and report new ones.

84.2. Asking (and answering) questions

Due to the complexity and extensibility of Eclipse you will need additional resources to help you resolve your specific problems. Fortunately the web contains several resources which can help you with your Eclipse problems.

Currently the best places to ask questions are the *Eclipse forums* and *Stack Overflow*.

The *Eclipse forums* can be found under the following URL: http://eclipse.org/forums

Stack Overflow can be found under the following URL: http://stackoverflow.com

The *Eclipse forums* offer several topic specific forums in which you can post and answer questions. To post questions in the Eclipse forums you need a valid user account in the Eclipse bugtracker. The advantage of the Eclipse forums is that, depending on the topic, Eclipse committers are also active there and might directly answer your question.

Stack Overflow also requires a user account and its community is also very active. *Stack Overflow* does not have separate forums for specific questions. In *Stack Overflow* you tag your questions with the relevant keyword, e.g. *Eclipse* and people search for them or subscribe to them.

Both places are excellent places to ask questions. If you ask a question it is in general good advice to be polite and to give a good error description as this motivates people to give you high quality answers.

84.3. Eclipse 4 feedback

The *Eclipse forums* have a forum dedicated to Eclipse 4 questions which can be found under the following URL: http://www.eclipse.org/forums/eclipse.e4

To report bugs and feature requests specific to the Eclipse 4 platform please use the following link and the *UI* component: https://bugs.eclipse.org/bugs/enter_bug.cgi?product=Platform

To report bugs and feature requests specific to the *Eclipse e4 tooling* platform please use the following link and the *UI* component: https://bugs.eclipse.org/bugs/enter_bug.cgi?product=e4

85. Closing words

I hope you enjoyed your learning experience with Eclipse 4.

The Eclipse 4 platform is a major rewrite of the Eclipse code base and makes the programming model of Eclipse very flexible and powerful. Building your application based on this framework enables you to leverage these capabilities and to create powerful native applications.

Eclipse 4 is also under active development. The development team of Eclipse 4 is very interested in receiving your feedback. Please use the Eclipse Forum or the Eclipse bug tracker to provide feedback and bug reports.

I am personally very impressed by the ability of the Eclipse community in redefining the underlying programming model. I believe this ability and the existing ecosystem will ensure that the Eclipse programming model will remain one of the strongest programming models for creating native clients.

Lars Vogel

Part VIII. Appendix

Table of Contents

86. Architectural background of the application model

This section contains some background information about the design goals of the Eclipse 4 application model and has been contributed by Eric Moffat, Eclipse 4 SDK development lead.

86.1. Main areas of the model

Conceptually the model is structured into three areas which are described in the following table.

Table 86.1. Architectural areas of the model

Area	Description
Mix-ins	Abstract interfaces containing the attributes necessary to support their specific roles in some derived concrete types. For example `MContext` contains only the reference to the context, `MContribution` contains the instantiated 'object' and `MUILabel` contains attributes to manage labels and images.
Containment Types	Every concrete container specifies a specific interface as its containment type. It allows the generic to be a specific type and the compiler to generate a compile time error if an attempt is made to add an invalid element to a container. It also means that when creating a domain specific model (or changing the base model) it is relatively easy to loosen the containment rules. For example to allow `MParts` in the `MTrim` area, you would only have to add the `MTrimElement` interface to `MPart`.
Concrete Classes	Elements that the application model itself contains, defined by a combination of various mix-ins and containment types. These are further sub-divided based into packages in the model definition model.

86.2. Advantages of using Mix-ins

Mix-ins allow the Eclipse 4 internal code to manage the *Mix-ins* specifically, regardless of the concrete class they're a part of. For example the `PartRenderingEngine` handles all contexts by checking whether the element being rendered is an `MContext`. It also allows the `findElements()` method of `EModelService` to locate all elements in the model of a specific type; useful for finding all `MDirtyable` elements for saving.

Mix-ins make *Domain Specific Modeling* simpler. The Eclipse 4 team anticipate that more sophisticated clients create domain specific models (and corresponding renderers) so that they could work directly against their own element types.

Having the *Mix-ins* in place makes this much simpler as well as being able to re-use existing code written to manage a particular *Mix-in*.

87. Receipts

This chapters contains a few receipts for typical development tasks and some additional background material.

87.1. Reading resources from plug-ins

You can access files in your plug-in via two different approaches: via the `FileLocator` class or via an Eclipse specific URL. Both approaches require that your plug-in defines a dependency to the `org.eclipse.core.runtime` plug-in.

Both approaches return a URL which can be used to get an `InputStream`.

The following code shows an example with `FileLocator`.

```
Bundle bundle = FrameworkUtil.getBundle(this.getClass());
URL url = FileLocator.find(bundle,
 new Path("path_to_file"), null);
```

The following code shows an example for the usage of the Eclipse specific URL.

```
URL url = null;

try {

  url = new URL("platform:/plugin/"
   + "your_bundle-symbolicname"
 + "path_to_file");

 } catch (MalformedURLException e1) {
   e1.printStackTrace();
}
```

Using the URL to create an `InputStream` and to read the file is demonstrated in the next code example.

```
public String readTextFile(URL url) {
  InputStream inputStream = null;
  String output = "";
   try {
    inputStream = url.openConnection().getInputStream();
    BufferedReader in =
```

```
      new BufferedReader(new InputStreamReader(inputStream));
    String inputLine;

    while ((inputLine = in.readLine()) != null) {
      output += inputLine;
    }
    in.close();

   } catch (IOException e) {
    e.printStackTrace();
  } finally {
    if (inputStream != null) {
      try {
        inputStream.close();
      } catch (IOException e) {
        e.printStackTrace();
      }
    }
  }
  return output;
}
```

87.2. Loading images from a plug-in

The ImageDescriptor class has a static method to create an ImageDescriptor instance directly from a URL. ImageDescriptor is a light-weight representation of an Image. Via the createImage() you can create the Image instance.

```
Bundle bundle = FrameworkUtil.getBundle(this.getClass());
URL url = FileLocator.find(bundle,
 new Path("icons/alt_window_32.gif"), null);

ImageDescriptor imageDescr = ImageDescriptor.createFromURL(url);
imageDescr.createImage();
```

87.3. Specifying the location of the application model file

The file name and location of the application model can be specified in the plugin.xml file. This is done via the applicationXMI property. The path to the file follows the "plug-in id"/"filename" pattern, e.g. test/ApplicationDifferent.e4xmi.

To do this open the plugin.xml file, select the *Extensions* tab and open the org.eclipse.core.runtime.products contribution.

Right click on the *product* entry and select New → Property. Use `applicationXMI` as parameter name and "com.example.e4.rcp.todo/ApplicationNew.e4xmi" as value. This value consists of your plug-in name and the file name of your application model file.

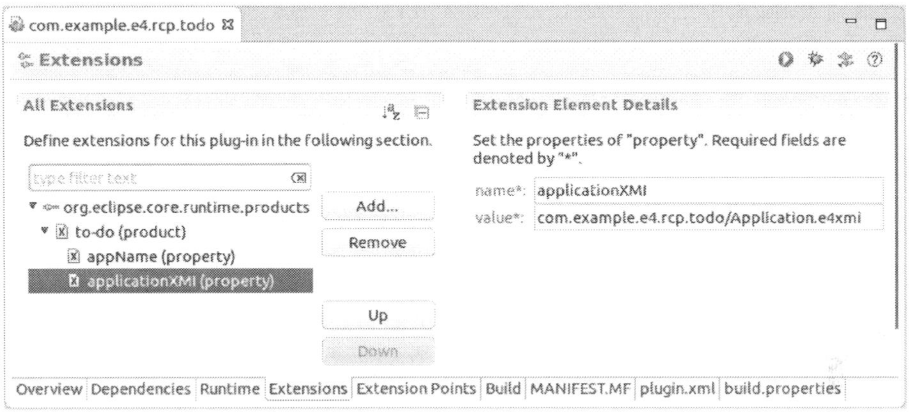

87.4. Getting the command line arguments

The `IApplicationContext` gives access to the command line arguments which were used to start the Eclipse application, e.g. via the run configuration in the *Arguments* tab or via the `.ini` file of your exported product.

```
import java.util.Map;

import org.eclipse.e4.core.di.annotations.Execute;
import org.eclipse.equinox.app.IApplicationContext;

public class GetArgumentsHandler {
 @Execute
 public void execute(IApplicationContext context) {
      // OSGi consumes framework arguments
  String[] args = (String[]) context.
     getArguments().
    get(IApplicationContext.APPLICATION_ARGS);
  for (Object value : args) {
   System.out.println(value);
  }
 }
}
```

87.5. From plug-in to an Eclipse 4 application

87.5.1. Overview

The *Eclipse e4 tooling* project provides a wizard to create a base Eclipse 4 application. It is also possible to convert an Eclipse plug-in project into an Eclipse 4 based application.

This chapter summarizes the necessary steps to serve as a checklist for this conversion process.

Eclipse 4 applications require a product configuration file to start. This product configuration file must define certain dependencies to Eclipse 4 framework classes. The easiest way to do this is the usage of a product configuration file based on *feature*.

The `org.eclipse.e4.rcp` *feature* contains all plug-ins required to run an Eclipse 4 RCP application. It also contains a few optional plug-ins.

Eclipse 4 based applications do not require that SWT is used as the user interface toolkit, but as most Eclipse based applications use SWT this plug-in is also included in the feature to simplify the setup.

Also functionalities for drag and drop and minimizing of user interface components are included.

87.5.2. Conversion process

To convert an Eclipse plug-in into an Eclipse 4 RCP application you have to:

- Create a feature project which includes your application plug-ins
- Create a feature based product configuration file which uses the predefined `E4Application` application
- Add the `org.eclipse.e4.rcp` and your own feature as dependency to your product
- Add the dependencies of `org.eclipse.e4.rcp` to your product
- Create the `Application.e4xmi` application model file

87.5.3. Remove optional plug-ins

`org.eclipse.e4.rcp` includes also some optional plug-ins. You can always create your own feature and leave out or replace plug-ins. For example the `org.eclipse.e4.ui.workbench.addons.swt` plug-in adds the functionality that you can drag and drop and minimize *Parts* in your application. If you do not want that, create your own feature without this one.

87.6. Relevant extension points for Eclipse 4

The following table lists the relevant extension points for Eclipse 4 applications.

Table 87.1. Extension Points relevant for Eclipse 4

Name	Description
org.eclipse.core.runtime.products	Used to define the Eclipse application and the links to the Eclipse 4 configuration file.
org.eclipse.e4.workbench.model	Used to define contributions to the Eclipse application model.
org.eclipse.e4.ui.css.swt.theme	Used to define themes for CSS styling.

88. Reference: Using EGit

The following is a short reference of the EGit team provider to enable you to checkout the example project for this book. This chapter is not intended to give a complete introduction into Git or the usage of EGit.

You find a complete introduction into the usage of EGit under the following URL: EGit Tutorial [http://www.vogella.com/articles/EGit/article.html]

88.1. EGit Installation

Most Eclipse 4.2 packages from Eclipse.org contain EGit in there default configuration. In this case no additional installation is required.

If EGit is missing in your Eclipse installation, you can install it via the Eclipse Update Manager via: Help → Install new Software. EGit can be installed from the following URL: http://download.eclipse.org/egit/updates

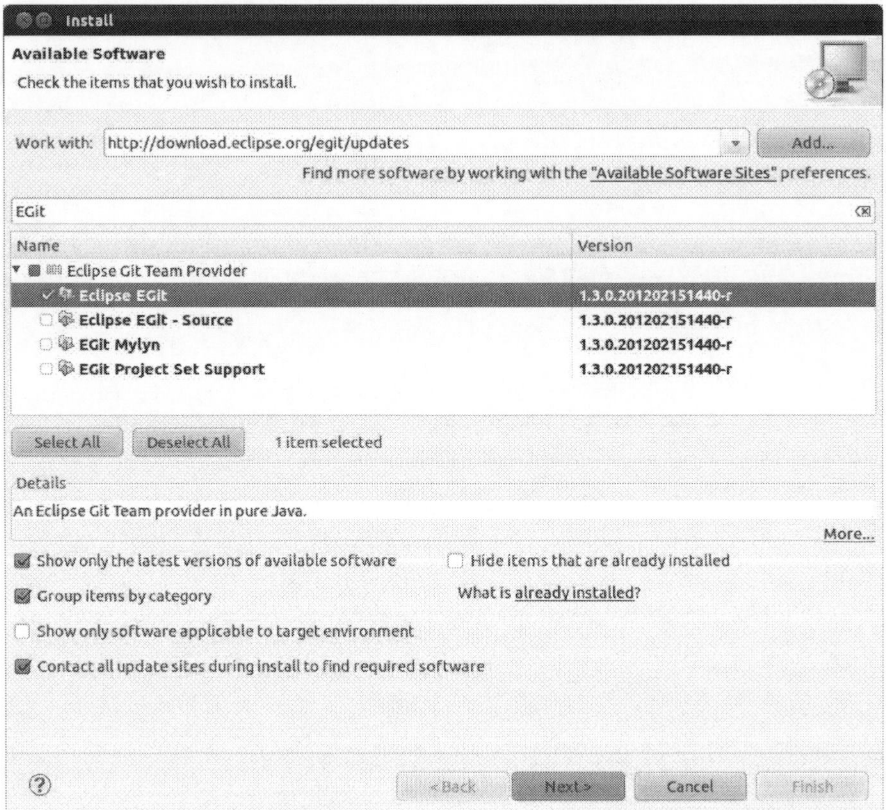

88.2. Clone existing project

EGit allows to clone an existing Git repository.

Select File → Import → Git → Project from Git.

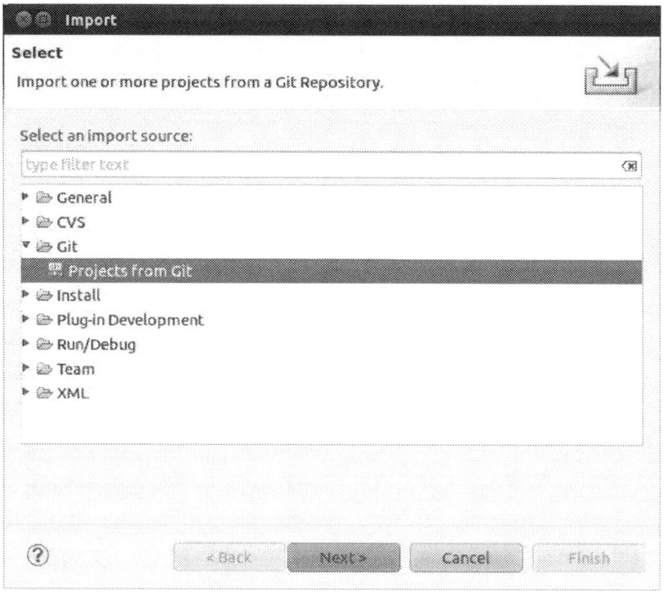

Select *URI* in the next dialog.

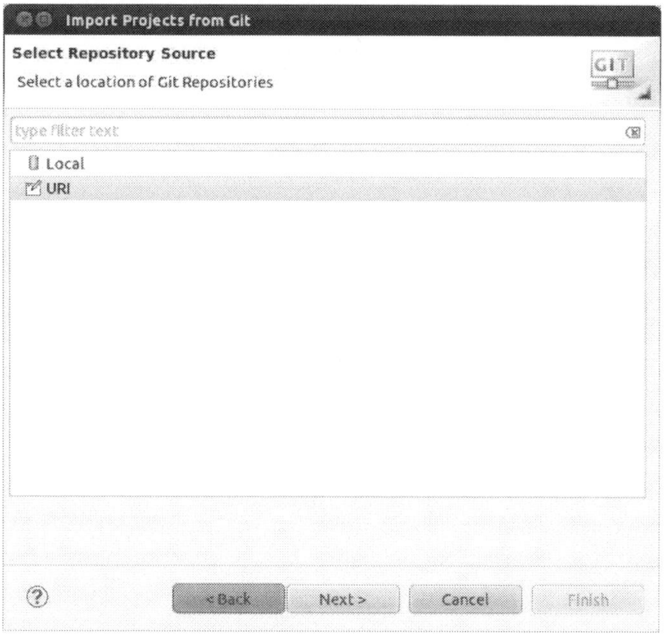

Press clone and enter the URL to your Git repository. Git supports several protocols, e.g. `git://` and `https://`. You only have to paste the URL to the first line of the dialog, the rest will be filled out automatically.

For example the following URI can be used to clone the example projects of the Eclipse 4 application development book: git@github.com:vogella/eclipse4book.git

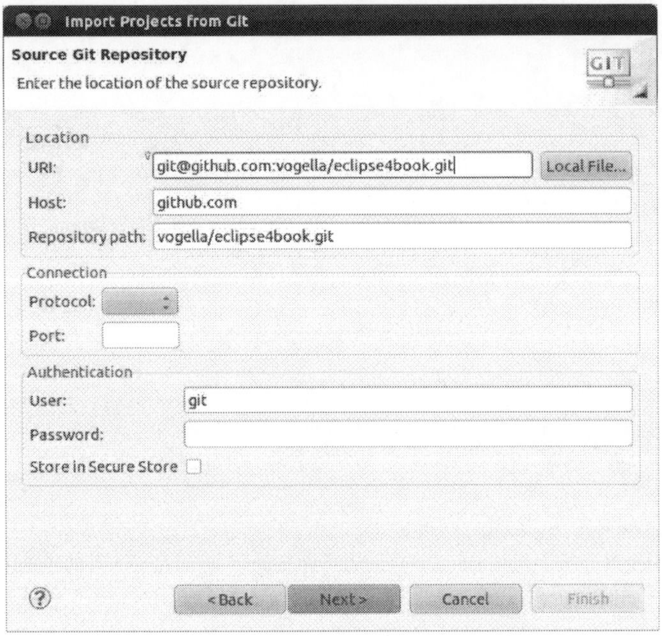

After pressing next the system will allow you to import the existing branches. You should select at least *master* as this is typically the main development branch.

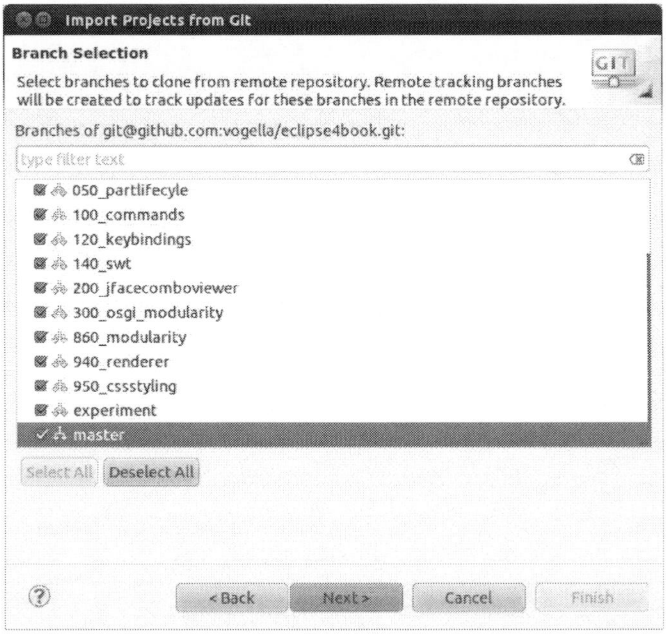

The next dialog allows you to specify where the project should be copied to and which branch should be initially selected.

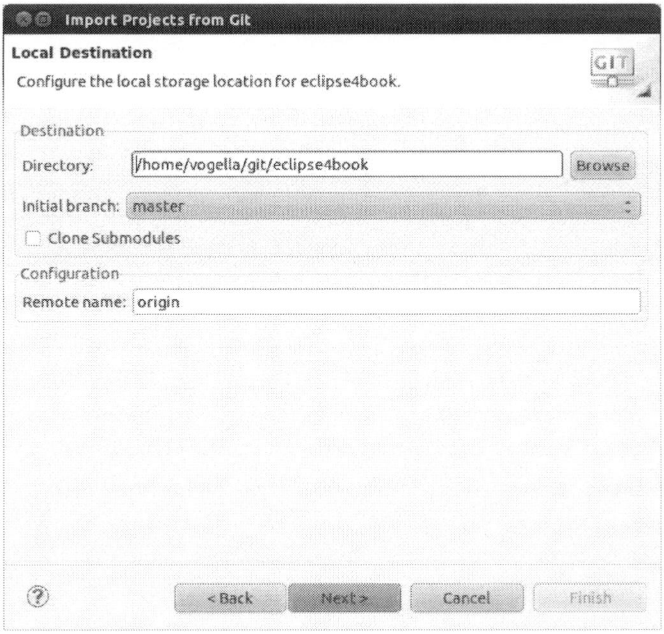

After the Git repository is cloned, *EGit* opens an additional import dialog which allows to import the Eclipse projects from the Git repository.

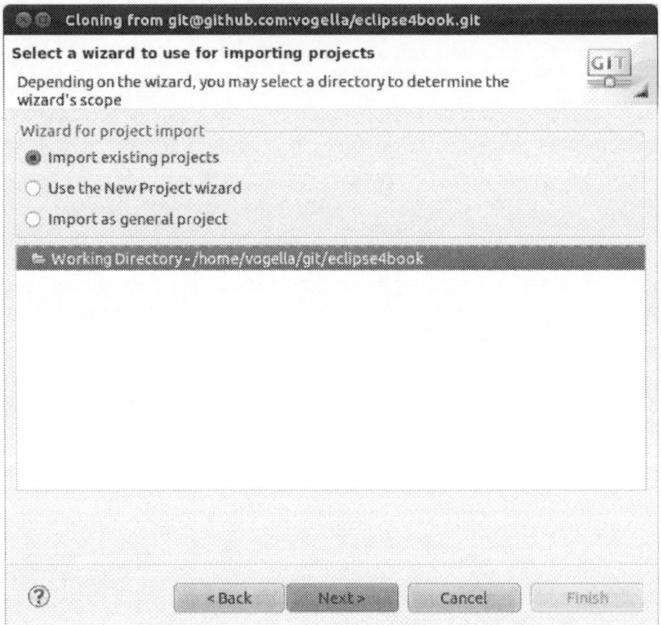

Once this dialog is completed, you have checked out (cloned) the projects into a local Git repository and you can use Git operation on these projects.

88.3. Branching

88.3.1. What are branches?

Git allows you to create *branches*, e.g. independent copies of the source code which can be changed independently from each other. The default branch is called *master*.

Git allows you to create branches very fast and cheaply in terms of resource consumption. Developers are encouraged to use branches frequently.

88.3.2. Switch Branches

Right-click your project and select Team → Branch to create new branches or to switch between existing branches.

89. Eclipse 4 platform development

This chapter describes how to access the latest Eclipse integration build after Eclipse 4.2 and lists the Git repositories for the Eclipse 4 source code. Normally you should not need this access as this book is based on Eclipse 4.2.

89.1. Download and install Eclipse development build

For this book it is recommended to use the Eclipse 4.2 release. The Eclipse e4 project creates regular packages of the next releases. Integration builds of the current source code are triggered weekly. Milestone and release candidate (RC) builds are created based on a predefined time schedule. In general milestone and RC builds are relative stable compared to integration builds.

You find the builds for the next Eclipse release (currently Eclipse 4.3) under the following URL.

`http://download.eclipse.org/eclipse/downloads/`

If you install the latest integration build, currently the corresponding update site for the *Eclipse e4 tooling* project is the following URL.

`http://download.eclipse.org/e4/updates/0.12-I-builds/`

This link might change over the development of Eclipse 4.3. The following URL lists the builds for the *Eclipse e4 tooling* project.

`http://download.eclipse.org/e4/downloads/`

89.2. Getting the Eclipse 4 source code

The Eclipse 4 source code is available via the *Git* version control system. The following list contains the relevant *Git* repositories for Eclipse 4.

```
// Eclipse e4 tooling
git://git.eclipse.org/gitroot/e4/org.eclipse.e4.tools.git

// Eclipse 4 UI
// Some e4 demos, not always working
git://git.eclipse.org/gitroot/e4/org.eclipse.e4.ui.git

// Eclipse 4 platform runtime
git://git.eclipse.org/gitroot/platform/eclipse.platform.runtime.git
```

```
// Eclipse 4 platform UI
git://git.eclipse.org/gitroot/platform/eclipse.platform.ui.git
```

90. Web resources

90.1. Eclipse 4

Eclipse 4 RCP Wiki [http://wiki.eclipse.org/Eclipse4/RCP]

Eclipse 4 Dependency Injection Wiki [http://wiki.eclipse.org/Eclipse4/RCP/Dependency_Injection]

vogella Eclipse Tutorials [http://www.vogella.com/eclipse.html]

Eclipse 4 Build Schedule [http://www.eclipse.org/eclipse/platform-releng/buildSchedule.html]

90.2. Eclipse Bug Tracker and Eclipse Forum

Eclipse Forum [http://eclipse.org/forums] for asking questions and providing feedback.

Eclipse Bug Tracker [https://bugs.eclipse.org/bugs/] for reporting errors or feature requests.

90.3. Eclipse SWT Resources

Understanding Layout in SWT by Wayne Beaton [http://www.eclipse.org/articles/article.php?file=Article-Understanding-Layouts/index.html]

Changing the position of the icon and text in a SWT Tree [http://git.eclipse.org/c/platform/eclipse.platform.swt.git/tree/examples/org.eclipse.swt.snippets/src/org/eclipse/swt/snippets/Snippet230.java]

SWT Snippets (Examples) [http://www.eclipse.org/swt/snippets/]

Eclipse Nebula Project with additional SWT widgets [http://eclipse.org/nebula/]

SWT Graphics [http://www.eclipse.org/articles/Article-SWT-graphics/SWT_graphics.html]

YARI tool suite to debug, spy, spider, inspect and navigate Eclipse based application GUIs (Workbench or RCP). [http://sourceforge.net/apps/trac/yari/]

SWT Development Tools, include Spleak (analyse memory leaks in SWT graphic resources) and SWT Spy plug-in which prints out the info about the SWT widget under the cursor. [http://www.eclipse.org/swt/tools.php]

90.4. JFace Resources

NatTable - Flexible Table / Data Grid [http://eclipse.org/nattable/]

90.5. Eclipse DataBinding Resources

Wiki about the JFace Data Binding [http://wiki.eclipse.org/index.php/JFace_Data_Binding]

WindowBuilder Data Binding Example [https://developers.google.com/java-dev-tools/wbpro/features/swt/data_binding/example]

Using Bean Validation (JSR 303) with JFace Databinding [http://wiki.eclipse.org/index.php?title=JFace_Data_Binding/JSR303BeanJFaceDatabindingValidation]

90.6. CSS Styling

Eclipse Wiki for CSS attributes [http://wiki.eclipse.org/E4/CSS/SWT_Mapping]

90.7. Logging

Blog series about loggin [http://ekkes-corner.blogspot.de/2008/10/logging-in-osgi-enterprise-applications_20.html]

EclipseZone Discussion about Logging [http://www.eclipsezone.com/eclipse/forums/t99588.html]

→ Loading from plugin : 263
→ Context Variables : 268 3gs
→ Eclipse Preferences : 291

→ Eclipse Mix-ins ? ✓

1760896R00230

Printed in Germany
by Amazon Distribution
GmbH, Leipzig